THE PEOPLE'S MONEY

PAOLA SUBACCHI

THE PEOPLE'S MONEY

How China Is Building a Global Currency

Columbia University Press / New York

Columbia University Press
Publishers Since 1893
New York   Chichester, West Sussex
cup.columbia.edu
Copyright © 2017 Columbia University Press

Library of Congress Cataloging-in-Publication Data
Names: Subacchi, Paola, 1962- author.
Title: The people's money : how China is building a global currency / Paola Subacchi.
Description: New York : Columbia University Press, [2017] |
    Includes bibliographical references and index.
Identifiers: LCCN 2016009131 | ISBN 9780231173469 (cloth : alk. paper)
Subjects: LCSH: Foreign exchange—China. | Renminbi. | Finance—China. |
    Monetary policy—China. | China—Commerce.
Classification: LCC HG3978 .S83 2016 | DDC 332.4/50951—dc23
LC record available at https://lccn.loc.gov/2016009131

Columbia University Press books are printed on permanent
and durable acid-free paper.
Printed in the United States of America

c 10 9 8 7 6 5 4 3 2 1

Cover design: Mary Ann Smith
Cover image: © Getty Images

CONTENTS

CONTENTS

7. BUILDING A MARKET FOR THE RENMINBI
117

8. THE RENMINBI MOVES AROUND
137

9. MANAGING IS THE WORD
153

10. THE AGE OF CHINESE MONEY
173

PREFACE

"China, the largest nation in the world, remains both an enigma and a potential factor in world stability."

CHINA: A REASSESSMENT OF THE ECONOMY

W HAT CAN A non-Chinese person add to the debate on China's development? As I was writing this book, I asked myself this very question several times. A Chinese friend of mine— a fine observer of both worlds—offered a reassuring answer. Quoting an old Chinese saying ("The foreign monk is better at reciting the sutras") he claimed that, like a foreign monk, I had the advantage of being more detached than the insiders from the day-to-day discussions and so, perhaps, stood a better chance of grasping the full picture of China' s vision for the renminbi (which means, literally, the "people's money"). And in the spirit of a foreign monk, who brings together the insiders' knowledge and connects all the dots, I started to research and then write *The People's Money*.

Why the renminbi? Because money and finance are the missing bits of China's extraordinary transformation that began almost forty years ago when Deng Xiaoping launched the first economic reforms. China's rise has surprised and fascinated many people around the world. Today its economy is one of the world's largest, competing with the most advanced countries. But it retains many features of a developing economy, from the low income per capita to the limited international use of its currency. To become an economic and financial heavyweight China needs to have a currency that can be used in international trade and finance and that non-Chinese savers and investors want to hold in their portfolio.

What China is doing to transform the renminbi into an international currency and to reform its banking and financial sector is not a linear process. There is so much trial and error, and so many interconnected components, that the whole picture of China's strategy inevitably looks blurred. But there is a picture there—one that the rest of the world must discern to understand China's future. In *The People's Money* I try to assemble this picture by decoding official documents, analysing numbers, bringing in anecdotal evidence and factoring in formal and informal conversations—including the nods and winks from officials who cannot acknowledge explicitly what the grand plan is.

This book presents my current understanding of China's "renminbi strategy" that, if it is successful, should usher in the age of Chinese capital and contribute to building "a moderately prosperous society" by 2020 as spelled out in the country's Thirteenth Five-Year Plan. I have tried to bring together all the policies that have been implemented since 2010 to assess the long-term plans while also offering an overview of China's recent economic history, because to understand current developments it is critical to look at where China comes from. Past developments and current events provide the framework to pin down what is in effect a moving target.

The future of China, and of the renminbi, is of course important for China experts, but this book is not just for them. *The People's Money* tells a story in plain, nonspecialist language and aims to draw in readers interested in economic and financial affairs who feel put off by the excessive specialism in the field. Colleagues who read earlier drafts were surprised not to find any tables or charts. This was a deliberate choice to make the narrative central to the book's structure.

Inevitably *The People's Money* is also a book on the dollar, as it is impossible to talk about the renminbi, and China, without referring to the dollar, and the United States. Deliberately, I tried to steer away from the discussion on whether the rise of the renminbi will turn into a demotion of the dollar. Many books have been written on the future of the dollar, and most of these books have been written by American scholars for the domestic audience. Here I offer different perspective on how the future trajectory of the dollar will be affected by the international development of the renminbi if China succeeds in its long-term financial and monetary reforms.

Throughout the book, if not otherwise indicated, the dollar is the U.S. dollar. I also refer to the Chinese currency as *renminbi*. This is the official name that was introduced when the People's Republic of China was established in 1949. It is also possible to use "yuan," which is the name of a unit of the renminbi currency—like "pound sterling," both the official name of the British currency and "pound that is a denomination of the pound sterling." Originally, the name "yuan" indicated the thaler (or dollar), the silver coin minted in the Spanish empire. Japan's yen and South Korea's won are derived from the same Chinese character. Interestingly, in Chinese the U.S. dollar is "mei yuan," or the "American yuan."

ACKNOWLEDGMENTS

Writing a book often feels like an act of self-inflicted misery. The support, enthusiasm, and friendship of many people helped me contain my misery within tolerable and manageable levels. Even so, I know I was unbearable! Thank you, Stephen and Philip, and Francesco, Martina, and Sabrina (and extensions) for putting up with me.

A bunch of extraordinary women were critical to keep this project on track. Sarah Okoye kept me organized when I was busy with "the book." Leslie Gardner believed in the project from when it was just an idea, arranged the "perfect match" and kept smiling even when everything looked pear-shaped. Bridget Flannery-McCoy was the editor from heaven: intelligent, good-humored and engaged. She helped me turn a boring technical draft into a book that a non-specialist audience may be interested to read.

Julia Leung, former Under Secretary for Financial Services and the Treasury of the Hong Kong SAR Government and then Inaugural Julius Fellow at Chatham House, helped me to see the big picture and to understand the long-term impact of China's renminbi strategy. She was generous with her time in discussing, on a number of occasions, the principal ideas in this book, providing some goalposts at the beginning of the project and sharing her deep knowledge and understanding of China's financial sector.

Yu Yongding was always happy and willing to share with me his thinking and to provide some warnings when my own thinking was too "Hong Kong like." Gao Haihong, Li Jing, and Li Yuanfang not only shared with me many lunches and dinners in Beijing, but also their vast knowledge of China's economy; they supported this project in all possible ways, especially with their friendship. The whole CASS-IWEP team—in particular Liu Dongmin and Xu Qiyuan—provided the physical and intellectual space for numerous workshops to discuss the internationalization of the renminbi.

Special thanks are also owed to Creon Butler, Director of the European and Global Issues Secretariat, Cabinet Office; Mark Boleat, Chairman of the City of London Policy and Resources Committee; and Siddharth Tiwari, Director of Strategy, Policy, and Review Department, IMF. They helped me through numerous conversations and through their participation in a number of conferences and workshops.

Yang Hua, during her post as head of Policy Planning at the Chinese Embassy in London, and George Norris, when he was the First Secretary at the British Embassy in Beijing, helped me reach many experts in China and made some logistical aspects of my China trips less tricky.

Masahiro Kawai invited me to join the Asian Development Bank Institute in Tokyo as a visiting fellow in summer 2013 to learn about the Japanese experience of internationalizing the yen. I am grateful for the numerous conversations and comments on my paper on the yen that provided some of the material I discuss in chapter 6. I also owe special thanks to Giovanni Capannelli, Ganesh Wignaraja, and Hiro Ito.

The library of the Norwegian Nobel Institute in Oslo was a perfect setting for some background work on the economic history of China; it is on one of the open shelves that I found the intriguing report written, in 1975, by the U.S. Congress delegation after an extensive visit to China. I am grateful to Geir Lundestad and Asle Toje for the invitation to spend a few weeks at the Institute as a visiting fellow in 2013.

I would like to mention the visit that Guo Wanda and his colleagues at the China Development Institute (CDI) in Shenzhen organized for me in the summer of 2011. This was my "Marco Polo" moment: Shenzhen is not only where China's extraordinary transformation began but is also one of most vibrant and functional cities in China.

Throughout the research and the drafting I was privileged to have many discussions on the intricacies of China's financial reforms and the internationalization of the renminbi with some of the leading policy-makers in the region. I am grateful to Fang Xinghai, Vice-Chairman, China Securities Regulatory Commission; Xia Bin, counsellor of the State Council; Wu Xiaoling, Vice-Chairman of the Financial and Economic Affairs Committee, National People's Congress; Ma Jun, chief economist, People's Bank of China; Jin Zhongxia, head of the research institute of the People's Bank of China and now Executive Director for China at the IMF; K. C. Chan, Secretary for Financial Services and the Treasury of the Hong Kong SAR Government; Norman Chan, Chief Executive of the Hong Kong Monetary Authority; Mu Huaipeng, Senior Adviser at the Hong Kong Monetary Authority; Kuan Chung-ming, Minister of the National Development Council Republic of China (Taiwan) and Jih-Chu Lee, former Vice Chairperson of the Financial Supervisory Commission, Republic of China and now chair of Bank of Taiwan.

Many officials from the region as well as from international organizations spoke widely and freely to me. Some prefer not to be named, but they know who they are, and are aware of my gratitude.

I had many stimulating, interesting and challenging conversations with many experts and private-sector practitioners who were willing to share ideas and research material with me, and I benefited from comments made to me at many conferences and seminars in the region. All these individuals, in one way or the other, had input on this project. I attempt to list all, but I am sure I will inevitably forget some. A big thank you to Jonathan Batten, Andreas Bauer, James Boughton, Greg Chin, Jerry Cohen, Victor Chu, Di Dongcheng, Kelly Driscoll, Andy Filardo, Alicia Garcia-Herrero, Kate Gibbon, Stephen Green, Thomas Harris, Dong He, Paul Hsu, Paul Jenkins, Gary Liu, John Nugée, Stephen Pickford, Qiao Yide, Changyong Rhee, Andrew Rozanov, Jesús Seade, Henny Sender, Vasuki Shastry, Alfred Schipke, David Vine, Wang Yong, Alan Wheatley, Xu Liu, Jinny Yan, Linda Yueh, Geoffrey Yu, Yinan Zhu.

Paul van den Noord, Danny Quah, Li Jing, and Gao Haihong, all of whom read and made valuable comments on the draft, contributed considerably to improving the final output. Of course they do not bear any responsibility for my mistakes. I am also grateful to three anonymous reviewers for offering a huge deal of constructive criticism.

Jon Turney and Annamaria Visentin "volunteered" to read the whole draft with the eye of a lay reader, and provided the acid test of whether the book can break the barriers of specialism. If our friendship survives this trial, then there is a fair chance for the book of not being too boring.

Obviously this project would not have been possible without the practical support of many individuals. I would like to thank Josephine Chao and Ashley Wu for their help in Taipei and for making every trip across the strait a memorable one. I am grateful to Helena Huang, Matthew Oxenford, and Dominic Williams for their assistance with research. Helena dug out a huge amount of data and was invaluable during the fieldwork in China. A word of thanks for Ben Kolstad who coordinated the production of the book, Sherry Goldbecker, who copyedited it, and Ryan Groendyk at Columbia University Press, and for all my colleagues at Chatham House.

THE PEOPLE'S MONEY

INTRODUCTION

I N JANUARY 2016, China sent shockwaves through the international financial community. The Shanghai Composite Index dropped by 18 percent in the first two weeks of the year, the renminbi had been on a downward trend since late 2014, and for the first time in more than ten years, the economy had begun to show clear signs of slowing down. All this came on the heels of the collapse of the Chinese stock market in June 2015 and the reform, and devaluation, of the exchange rate in August 2015. Furthermore, the country's authorities seemed unable to calm the turbulence, acting erratically and ineffectively "like headless chickens." The introduction of the "circuit breaker" mechanism—a kind of backstop that was devised to automatically suspend trading if stocks fell by 7 percent—ended up generating more panic. The abrupt dismissal of Xiao Gang, chairman of the China Securities Regulatory Commission, with no announcement of a replacement, amplified the sense of uncertainty.

After a spectacular, thirty-year ascent, China is now at a pivotal moment. Its leaders are eager to develop the country as a significant financial power and thus to conclude the process of economic transformation from plan to market that Deng Xiaoping launched in 1978. When President Xi Jinping took the helm of the Chinese Communist Party and the country in late 2012, he changed the course of economic policy, emphasizing the role that the private sector is expected to play in the economy and the attendant need to improve the commercial banking system, develop modern financial markets, and write and enforce commercial laws. The challenge is to reduce state interference—in particular, the tangled web of domestic vested interests that continue to link big banks and state-owned enterprises—and to stop the funneling of resources according to social and political control rather than sound investment strategy. All of this will be necessary for China to achieve the title of economic and political superpower. Embedded deeply within every one of these economic goals and challenges is the vexing question of the renminbi.

Indeed, China now faces the paradox, and limits, of having emerged as a major industrial and trading power without a currency that reflects its standing in the world. Paradoxically for a country that has hugely benefited from opening up to and integrating with the rest of the world, the renminbi is a currency of "restricted globalization." It has limited circulation outside the country, and it cannot be easily exchanged with other currencies or be held in deposit accounts in banks overseas. It is hardly used in international transactions, and non-Chinese individuals and institutions— firms, banks, and governments—rarely hold renminbi in their portfolios. As a result, China largely relies on the dollar to price and sell the goods it produces; it needs dollars to pay for imports, to invest abroad, and to implement its economic diplomacy. It has accumulated a large amount of dollars—approximately $3.2 billion in official reserves[1]—to do all this and has considerable capital available to make foreign acquisitions. However, its power in financial and monetary affairs is limited, and this power needs to be "brokered" through the dollar-dominated international monetary system in order to be fully deployed. Above all, its reserves—the nation's wealth— are vulnerable to changes in the value of the dollar.

As a country becomes more economically integrated at the regional or global level and the size of its economy ranks it among the world's largest economies, the argument for using its own currency in trade and finance becomes more compelling. Currencies are nations' blood, their "genetic" imprint, and their identity, and they epitomize those nations' power and standing in the world. The dollar, for example, characterizes the United

States' identity as a nation, and it is a repository of the country's power and a source of its "exorbitant privilege." China needs an international currency to complete its rise to power, expand its influence in monetary affairs, increase its geopolitical weight, and put it on a par with the United States.

China has reasons beyond the political and diplomatic arguments for wanting and needing to develop the renminbi as a currency that can be used overseas and at the same time to cut its financial and monetary dependence on the dollar. Pricing its trade in renminbi will reduce costs and the exchange rate risks for Chinese enterprises when they engage in overseas trade and financial transactions. Thus, expanding the international use of the renminbi will support the country's business and investments abroad. Above all, by developing the renminbi into an international currency, China can reduce the accumulation of dollars in its reserves and instead use its renminbi surplus to invest and lend abroad—and, if necessary, to finance its debt in its own currency.

Developing the renminbi into an international currency is China's long-term plan, one that should stay in place despite the short-term gyration of the stock market. The template is straightforward: exploit China's role in international trade to promote the use of the renminbi while removing existing restrictions on the movement of renminbi into and out of its domestic market in order to increase the currency's usability outside the country—and therefore its demand overseas. Historical experience shows that a currency's use in international trade should be supported and matched by its use in finance and that allowing more open investment and circulation of that currency is critical to developing its international use.

This is where China is breaking from history. It cannot easily follow this traditional route, given the vestiges of a planned economy that continue to characterize its system—vestiges like the management of the interest rate and the exchange rate, which has fueled the country's growth spurt but also stunted its currency. To allow the renminbi more freedom of movement, China must accelerate institutional reforms and economic rebalancing, and this means that the country can not simply and immediately "open up." To create a liquid and trusted currency that meets the world's demand for safe assets in the way the dollar does today, China needs to do several things:

improve the governance of banks, companies, and institutions; curb corruption; and keep vested interests at bay. Above all, its leaders have to figure out a way to open its financial markets and banking sector while maintaining its unique hybrid, "socialism with Chinese characteristics," where economic planning and state control coexist with markets, foreign investments, private property, and individual initiative.

Better governance and transparency are essential not only to promote greater circulation of the renminbi but also to improve the sense, among non-Chinese holders, that it is a trustworthy currency. Currently, foreigners have limited confidence in China's institutions and political system; even if Beijing ends up lifting all restrictions on foreign engagement with the domestic system, they might still be reluctant to entrust the country with their money.

How can China persuade the rest of the world that the renminbi is a currency worth using and holding, like the dollar, the euro, the British pound, and the Japanese yen? In addition to increasing transparency, openness, and accountability, its authorities need to convince the rest of the world that they will not undermine the currency's external value—that is, the exchange rate—even if domestic circumstances, political as well as economic, call for it. Renminbi holders need to have confidence that no matter where they are and in what circumstances they operate, they will always be able to use the renminbi to exchange it for whatever they need, and that the currency will retain its value.

The whole picture is further complicated by the state of the world economy. In the 1990s and up to 2008, China could get traction from the robust and booming global economy, but when the global financial crisis hit in 2008 and ushered in a period of deep uncertainty, the international environment turned less favorable. The country is now facing the challenge of managing the real economy against the headwinds of lower demand, geopolitical tensions, and its own increasingly unmanageable debt.

That said, Chinese leaders are eager to break up the dollar's hegemony—but not to replace the dollar system with the renminbi system. Rather, they envisage the renminbi as a major currency within a new multicurrency international monetary system that reflects the fact that the world economy is no longer dominated by the United States.

These leaders have their hands full. Will they be able to juggle China's overall transition without undermining social cohesion, political balance, and financial stability? And, central to our discussion, can they meet their goals for the renminbi while retaining a measure of state control? What are the options for China?

I argue that one option is to move forward and accelerate the process of financial reforms. But even if accelerated, reforms within the country's uniquely hybrid economy will take time—and China is in a hurry. So the other option is to develop a system based on managed convertibility—in other words, to encourage the international circulation of renminbis while retaining controls on money moving in and out the country. Many Western experts are skeptical that a currency can be internationalized when significant constraints to its circulation remain in place, but the official rhetoric is that the country can achieve some degree of internationalization of the renminbi while maintaining capital controls.

In this book, I lay out the story of China and its currency over ten chapters. I start by setting the background: in chapter 1, I introduce the concept of international money and frame the subsequent discussion. I explore how capital movements have not only driven the transformation of the world economy in the last twenty years but also created more financial instability and made the global economy more vulnerable to financial crises. I then look at what it takes for a currency to become international money—focusing, in particular, on the development of the dollar. Ultimately, in this chapter, I consider the context of China's extraordinary transformation in the last three decades and how the dollar-driven international monetary system has accelerated this transformation.

In chapters 2 and 3, I delve into the transformation of the Chinese economy since the reforms that Deng Xiaoping introduced in the 1980s and show how both exports and investment have been critical to the country's development. In chapter 3, in particular, I discuss China's system of financial repression, in which the cost of borrowing is kept artificially low. High domestic savings rates and financial repression have kept a lid on the structural imbalances within its domestic financial sector. At the same time, however, they have perpetuated inefficiencies, inhibited reform, and thus constrained the development of the renminbi as an international currency. In these chapters, I address the book's key questions: Why doesn't China have its own international currency rather than depending on the U.S. dollar? And why did its extraordinary development not include the renminbi?

Having set the scene, I then explore China's predicament of being the largest trading nation but not having a currency in which to settle a significant share of this trade (chapter 4). Here I discuss the two key features of China's economic policy—capital controls and a managed peg for the exchange rate—that over the years have resulted not only in the extraordinary transformation of the Chinese economy by keeping exports competitive and powering rapid growth and job creation, but also have resulted in the limited development of the renminbi.

In chapter 5, I look at the costs of operating with a dwarf currency—in particular, the constraints of being an immature creditor (i.e., not being able to lend in renminbi)—and the costs of managing the exchange rate. I conclude the chapter by discussing the difficulties of challenging the dollar system when network externalities and inertia create strong disincentives to change.

The question of how to create an international currency is the focus of my discussion in chapter 6, and here I assess lessons that can be learned from the development of other international currencies—notably, the Japanese yen—in the context of China's renminbi strategy. This strategy is a dynamic process that in a relatively short span of time has evolved from a plan devised to encourage regional use of the renminbi to a more complex, policy-driven framework that aims to turn the renminbi (albeit with limitations) into international money and into an international financial asset by supporting the renminbi in cross-border trade settlement and establishing the renminbi offshore market. Here and in chapter 7, I delve into the measures that the Chinese monetary authorities have put together to overcome the limitations of the renminbi and to build a market for the currency.

In chapter 8, I assess progress on the international use of the renminbi since the launch of the renminbi strategy and look at how the strategy has expanded into many policy areas and sectors and supported the use of the renminbi in the main international financial centers around the world—with the exception of the United States. I also chart China's recent attempt to open up the financial sector through managed convertibility—that is, a system of quotas for capital movements.

In chapter 9, I discuss China's financial reforms and argue that its leaders will need a long time to reform the current system—if they are able to do so at all. Otherwise relaxing controls on capital flows—especially on the outflows—may run against the need to maintain plenty of financial resources for domestic banks. For the time being, therefore, managed convertibility will support the circulation and usability of the renminbi outside China.

I conclude by arguing in chapter 10 that the renminbi has become, in approximately five years, Asia's key regional currency. Furthermore, the renminbi strategy has created the conditions to extend the circulation of the Chinese currency beyond Asia. But more needs to be done, and policies can further push the international use of the renminbi. However, unless reforms are accelerated, the renminbi will continue to be a currency of restricted globalization and it will take many years for it to become a leading international currency. Everything being equal, it will eventually become one of the leading currencies in the new multicurrency international monetary system, eroding the dollar's relative weight. But it will be unlikely to replace the dollar as the dominant international currency because, among other reasons, the world may have shifted away from a single-currency system.

What China is doing is critical for its own development but matters for the world as well. If it succeeds in building a global currency, this will usher in the age of Chinese capital, and our monetary system will be radically transformed from the dollar-dominated system we see today. The government has set this as the direction for the renminbi strategy. But whether it can achieve the goal of transforming the people's money into a currency that all people—Chinese and non-Chinese—are happy to use remains to be seen.

1

MONEY IS THE GAME CHANGER

ONEY IS THE game changer of our time. It circulates around the
globe, facilitating the integration of economies—and countries—
and further integrating our already connected world.[1] Every
day, international currencies worth nearly $2 trillion move across borders.
Roughly 90 percent of these transactions are part of financial flows—that is,
capital directed toward investments rather than the purchase of goods and
services.[2] These international currencies are bought and sold for commercial
and financial reasons, and profits (and losses) result from even tiny changes
in the exchange rates.

Since the 1980s, most countries have relaxed or removed barriers to the
movement of capital. This so-called financial liberalization is the key feature that differentiates the current phase of globalization—the economic
integration of countries that trade with and invest in each other—from
similar episodes that the world has experienced. For instance, in the years
after World War II, the United States and countries in western Europe dismantled many trade restrictions—in 1957, Germany, France, Italy, Belgium,
Luxembourg, and the Netherlands established a customs union and created
the European Economic Community—but they maintained controls on
capital movements.

Increased integration has pushed many countries to completely open their current accounts, which means that money can freely move around to pay for goods and services; many countries have progressively opened their capital accounts as well, meaning that money can freely move around to be invested where opportunities arise. Individuals, companies, and financial institutions can go to international markets to borrow money, raise equity, and diversify their assets, and they can invest in foreign countries to exploit the opportunities offered by rapid economic growth. In relative terms, the growth of investments worldwide has been much more significant than the expansion of world trade. Between 1990 and 2007, just before the global financial crisis, world trade grew nearly fivefold, whereas total international capital flows expanded by a factor of eleven.

Along with financial liberalization, innovation in information technology and the availability of more powerful—and less expensive—computers have allowed money to circulate more quickly. It is now possible to move large amounts of money across international borders at the touch of a button. The use of computers in finance has increased the bandwidth between markets and has made it possible to automate the high-frequency trading of international currencies through a system that responds far more quickly than any human can. As a result, the global foreign exchange market has expanded rapidly in the last two decades, as evidenced by the daily market turnover. Since April 1989 (when statistics on them were first collected), foreign exchange transactions have grown almost eightfold.[3]

Financial globalization has been transformational for two reasons. First, as money moves around and fuels economic activity, it generates more money, and the world becomes richer. In his best-selling book *Capital in the Twenty-First Century*, the French economist Thomas Piketty observed that between 1987 and 2013 the average income per adult worldwide grew at an annual rate of 1.4 percent above inflation. This growth was stronger, and particularly significant, in the developing countries. Using an indicator more widely available than income per adult, we see that the average annual income per capita grew by 115 percent (in real terms in 2010 U.S. dollars) in emerging-market economies between 1990 and 2014—from approximately $2,265 to $4,870.[4] In South Korea, for example, the average annual income per capita increased from approximately $3,000 in 1987 to approximately $25,000 in 2014; in Malaysia, it went from just below $2,000 in 1987 to almost $10,000 in 2014.[5] The poorest countries also saw their income per capita grow significantly—even if many people still fell below the international poverty line, living on less than $1.90 a day. Take Ghana, for instance: the average annual income per capita went from less than $400 in 1987 to about $1,600 in 2014, but approximately one-quarter of the population still lived below the international poverty line.[6]

Many people have seen their living standard improve, and some have become very rich. Between 1987 and 2013, the average wealth of each adult in the world grew by an annual average of 2.1 percent in real terms. However, the richest individuals worldwide saw their wealth increase at three times this rate.[7] The number of billionaires has also gone up. Today there are more than 1,800 billionaires in the world, with a combined wealth of almost $7 trillion.[8] This is larger, in nominal terms, than Japan's economy. Many of these super-rich individuals are in developing countries, with China, India, and Russia leading the pack (with 251, 84, and 77 billionaires, respectively). The United States, however, tops the list with 540 individuals.

It is not just individuals that have become richer—the wealth of nations has expanded, too. Countries that play a key role in the global manufacturing chain (such as China) or in the energy supply chain (such as Saudi Arabia and other oil-producing countries) have accumulated a large amount of dollars and financial resources. In the aggregate, the financial wealth in the hands of nations is now more than $10 trillion (a sevenfold expansion since 1995, when it was just $1.4 trillion) and is held in central banks' foreign exchange reserves and in sovereign wealth funds. Reserves are normally used to manage and stabilize the exchange rate (more on this point in chapter 5) and can be deployed in case of a currency crisis. Sovereign wealth funds— investment funds owned by sovereign states—address the long-term development needs of countries that depend on natural resources: they ensure that the "wealth of nations" remains intact for the benefit of future generations.[9]

The second reason financial globalization has been so transformational is directly related to the first: more money means cheaper money. Later in this chapter, I will look at the effect of cheap and easily available money—how it has glued the world economy together but also how it has led to imbalances and misallocations of financial resources that make the global economy more vulnerable to financial crises. However, in order to understand both the opportunities and the dangers that cheap money creates as it moves around the world, we first need to understand what it takes for money to move around the world at all.

WHICH MONEY FOR INTERNATIONAL TRADE AND FINANCE?

There are many different types of money in the world economy, from national currencies (like the dollar) to supranational ones (like the euro)—and even virtual crypto-currencies (like the bitcoin). Being issued by a sovereign state and backed by that state's central bank is the key feature of a currency—and what differentiates "real" money from, for instance, gift cards and airline miles. In this sense, crypto-currencies are not conventional money. The bitcoin, for example, is not issued by any government, and its supply does not depend on any central bank decision but rather is mathematically predetermined.[10]

Domestic firms, multinational companies, governments, international organizations, individuals, and even criminals need money to pay for international exchanges of goods and services. There are about 180 official currencies that are issued by sovereign states or by groups of sovereign states, but not all these currencies qualify for international use. To be used internationally, a currency must, at the very least, be internationally acceptable as a means of exchange—that is, it must be accepted for transactions in goods and services in and between foreign countries.

Another key feature of international money is that it is liquid, meaning that there is enough of it to meet demand at any given time. The world economy functions best when there is plenty of international liquidity, which ensures that international transactions—for example, the import/export of goods and services—can be easily and rapidly settled.

Furthermore, international players need money that they can set aside until they need it, knowing that, rain or shine, it will maintain its value. Storing value is an important function of money; it allows individuals, households, businesses, and even governments to save and invest. They don't need to consume today in order to maximize the amount of goods and services they can get for their money because they will be able to buy approximately the same amount with that savings in the future. This allows individuals, firms, and nations to save in order to consume or invest at a later stage. Countries, for instance, may save in anticipation of a later increase in public spending—for example, to cope with an aging population. Individuals do something similar when they save to ensure an income stream when they retire from work. Savings also help in withstanding unexpected events or shocks. If a country's exports suddenly drop, it can use savings to pay for essential imports such as food and energy. Countries also need enough reserves to cope with a sudden dearth of liquidity, as happened in the United States after the collapse of Lehman Brothers in the fall of 2008. In all these cases, funds are held in currencies that are trusted to keep their value.

Finally, because money is also used by the official sector, the currencies that are most viable for international use are those that can act as a benchmark for foreign exchange reference rates—for example, all other currencies are quoted against the U.S. dollar or the euro—and as a means of intervention in foreign exchange markets. These leading international currencies not only provide stability and liquidity to the international monetary system but also can offer an anchor to other, weaker currencies so they can achieve stability by proxy.

Today international money is fiat money: governments declare it legal tender within their jurisdictions. It is based on credit, and its value is unrelated to the value of any physical good—for instance, gold or silver. The credibility of and trust in the policies and the institutions of the country that issues an international currency are therefore critical.[11] Foreign holders of international currencies must trust the issuing governments not to pursue policies that can undermine the value of that currency (e.g., keeping interest rates low to support domestic growth can weaken the currency) or its stability. If the currency becomes unstable, with wide and protracted fluctuations, then individuals, businesses, foreign central banks, and governments may lose confidence and switch to other, more stable assets. A country that issues an international currency therefore needs to instill and maintain confidence in the value of that currency. This value can be ascertained by looking at the long-term trend in the currency's exchange rate variability (which indicates how stable its value is) and at the country's long-term inflation rate and its position as an international net creditor. Also, confidence in the general political stability of the issuing country is essential for nonresidents to hold that country's currency.

Given all this, what currencies have become international money, and why? Many different factors underpin a currency's international use. The size of the issuing country's economy and its share of world trade, market development, preferences, and habits are the most crucial. The main international currencies—the U.S. dollar, the euro, the Japanese yen, and the British pound—are issued by countries whose economies and external sectors are among the world's largest.

These currencies all meet the requirements discussed above. There is no (or very little) restriction on their cross-border use and circulation. They can be acquired and exchanged everywhere in the world. Take the British pound, for instance. People who are not resident in Britain can buy pounds for different purposes, from trade to tourism, and can easily hold them in sterling-denominated bank deposits in their countries. (This has not always been the case: in the post–World War II years, Britain imposed stringent capital controls on the amount of pounds that could be moved into and out of the country to be traded in international markets. We'll explore some of the reasons for controls like these when it comes to China in the ensuing chapters.)

In addition, these countries all boast a liquid and diversified financial sector, a well-respected legal framework for contract enforcement, and stable, predictable policies. The financial sector is key in developing and supporting an international currency, as international investors need to have access to a wide range of financial instruments denominated in that currency that are tradable in different markets. They also need well-developed secondary markets with a wide variety of financial instruments on offer, available liquidity, and limited constraints to capital movement.

An international currency is not just a vehicle for financial intermediation. It also allows the issuing country to play the role of world banker—that is, to transform short-term liquid deposits into longer-term loans and investments, all denominated in its currency.[12] This transformation extends the duration of investments and provides funding for long-term projects; at the same time, by linking the supply of and demand for financial resources, it helps economic growth. But it is also potentially destabilizing for the domestic economies involved as well as for the world economy if the mismatch between short-term liabilities and long-term assets becomes irreconcilable—as we learned from the sub-prime mortgage market in the United States, where the 2008 global financial crisis originated. In that case, the collapse of the property market and the default of borrowers with poor credit ratings—indeed, sub-prime borrowers—triggered the collapse of the banking system and fueled a global financial crisis. How? Bank deposits were transformed into mortgage loans to sub-prime borrowers. Then these sub-prime mortgages were repackaged in financial products and sold to other banks, insurance companies, and assorted financial institutions. When the property market in the United States dropped and the guarantees/collaterals of all those loans lost significant portions of their value, the value of those financial products and of the banks that had them in their portfolios collapsed.

RESERVE CURRENCIES

A currency has truly gained international standing if it becomes a reserve currency—so named because central banks feel the currency is liquid and stable enough to hold in their reserves. With one notable exception, the share of a reserve currency in the world's official reserves roughly reflects the size of the economy of the issuing country and closely reflects the use of that currency in trade. (The exception, of course, is China—a puzzle we'll get to very soon.) The pound, for example, accounts for approximately 5 percent of total official foreign exchange reserves, and the size of the United Kingdom's economy is a bit less than 4 percent of the world economy. The economy of Switzerland is even smaller (less than 1 percent of the world economy), and the Swiss franc has a 0.3 percent share of official reserves.[13] Part of the reason the pound and the franc are reserve currencies is historical—before World War II, the pound was the leading international currency—and part is financial—both the United Kingdom and Switzerland are home to some of the biggest and most dynamic international financial centers.

Because of Switzerland's institutional framework and its neutral position in foreign policy, its franc also plays the role of a safe haven in times of crises. Safe-haven currencies are viewed as particularly reliable because of the sound economic policies, the strong institutional framework, and the political (and geopolitical) stability of the countries that issue them. Savers and investors turn to and hoard safe-haven currencies when financial instability or geopolitical risks are high.

But this comes with a cost. When demand strengthens, so does the exchange rate, and a currency that is too strong can be detrimental to the domestic economy. For example, between the onset of the financial crisis in September 2008 and September 2011, the value of the Swiss franc increased nearly 50 percent compared to the euro, as investors flocked to it as a haven from economic uncertainty. On September 6, 2011, the Swiss monetary authorities declared that "the current massive overvaluation of the Swiss franc poses an acute threat to the Swiss economy and carries the risk of a deflationary development."[14] Their solution was to cap the value of their currency and set a minimum exchange rate of 1.20 francs to the euro, and they stated that they were "prepared to buy foreign currency in unlimited quantities" to "enforce this minimum rate." In the end, this strategy proved too difficult to maintain, and on January 15, 2015, in the wake of the European Central Bank's turn to quantitative easing (QE is an unconventional monetary policy measure in which the central bank buys financial assets on the market in order to increase their price and so lower the yield), the Swiss monetary authorities let the franc float again. This was unexpected. Even Christine Lagarde, managing director of the International Monetary Fund (IMF), said she found the move "a bit surprising"[15]—especially because the Swiss National Bank had reiterated its commitment to the policy of anchoring the franc to the euro only a few weeks earlier and had introduced negative bank deposit rates to support the currency ceiling. Although the abrupt move certainly undermined the credibility that the Swiss central bank had established over the years, the franc soared by 30 percent in early trading after the announcement.

In recent years, the definition of reserve currency has become more nuanced, with a de facto distinction between currencies that are held in central banks' reserves and *key* reserve currencies that are also part of the IMF's basket of Special Drawing Rights (SDRs).[16] Inclusion in the SDR basket is a way to draw a line between the major reserve currencies and other international currencies that are used less extensively and are held in reserves on the margin. It is, above all, the implicit recognition that a currency is a full member of the international monetary system. The dollar, the euro, the pound, the Japanese yen, and, since December 2015, the Chinese renminbi are the only currencies included in the SDR basket—and the renminbi, as I discuss throughout the book, is different from the other currencies in the basket. These are the currencies of the largest economies (in the case of the United States, China, Japan, and the euro area) or of economies that are systemically important (in the case of Britain)—meaning that their policies may have systemic impact on other countries—because of the size of their financial sector. Dominant among those currencies in the SDR basket is the dollar, with a 41.73 percent share, followed by the euro at 30.93 percent. The renminbi holds 10.92 percent, whereas the yen and the pound have 8.33 and 8.09 percent, respectively.[17]

IN THE DOLLAR WE TRUST

The dollar is the leading international currency. It is the foremost key reserve currency (with an approximate 65 percent share of official reserves[18]), and it is used to price and invoice most international trade and to settle most cross-border sales. More than any other currency, the dollar glues the world economy together.[19]

The dominance of the dollar goes back a long way. In 1943, American negotiators who were preparing to discuss postwar recovery reckoned that the dollar would "probably become the cornerstone of the postwar structure of stable currencies."[20] Indeed, at the conference in Bretton Woods the following year, the dollar became the standard for the international monetary system. Countries that participated in the conference agreed to peg their currencies to the dollar and to maintain the exchange rates within a 1 percent band—that is, their currencies could not appreciate or depreciate against the greenback by more than 1 percent. The dollar provided liquidity to a system ultimately underpinned by the gold reserves of the United States, which at the time amounted to three-quarters of all gold stored in central banks around the world. Within this system, the dollar, at least in theory, was convertible into gold at the rate of $35 an ounce.

At Bretton Woods, the dollar was put at the heart of a new multilateral legal framework for monetary and financial relations. This framework was underpinned by two institutions also created at Bretton Woods: the IMF and the International Bank for Reconstruction and Development (now part of the World Bank). The IMF, in particular, was established to monitor the fixed-exchange-rate arrangements between countries (although adjustments were allowed in case of "fundamental disequilibrium") and to extend balance-of-payments assistance (i.e., loans) to countries at risk.[21]

However, the Bretton Woods system presented an unresolved contradiction between the goal of maintaining the value of the key reserve currency and that of ensuring liquidity to the world economy. To provide the necessary liquidity to the international payment system, the country that issues the key reserve currency eventually ends up running a current-account deficit— reflecting the amount that a country borrows to finance consumption and investments that exceed domestic savings. Persistent current-account deficits eventually undermine confidence and trust in the currency because foreign holders expect a depreciation of that currency in order to narrow the deficit.[22] In 1960, the Belgian economist Robert Triffin expounded this dilemma, which has been known ever since as the Triffin dilemma.

As confidence in the key reserve currency begins to erode, other countries need to reduce their surpluses in the current account, let their currencies appreciate, or switch to other reserve assets. But within the Bretton Woods system, switching to other reserve assets was not an option because all other currencies were anchored to the dollar. Therefore, if other countries were not prepared to reduce their current-account surplus or allow the appreciation of their currencies, then the United States' current-account deficit would continue to grow, reducing confidence further. In the late 1960s, the United States maintained that its allies could do more to reduce their surpluses by inflating or revaluing their currencies. The Europeans and Japanese, on the other hand, argued that it was the responsibility of the United States to make the first move and reduce its large deficit—which the United States was financing by issuing dollars. They had one major lever that they could use to curb the United States' policy autonomy, which was to demand the conversion of accumulated dollar balances into gold. But this amounted to a "nuclear option," given the huge damage it would have done to the diplomatic relations between the United States and its Western allies. This strategy would have also caused considerable capital loss—there were more dollars than gold, so it would have been impossible to convert all dollar holdings by central banks into gold. This made most governments reluctant to demand the conversion of the dollars they held.[23] Eventually, in August 1971 the United States unilaterally decided to suspend the convertibility of the dollar and to let it find its own level in the currency market. The Europeans and the Japanese were left with no other option but to accept that the Bretton Woods system had come to an end.

Nonetheless, the dollar remains the currency of choice for individuals, businesses, and nations despite some challenges to its dominance (most notably, from the euro). Although the world has transformed since the end of the Cold War, the international monetary system has not intrinsically changed, and the dollar still plays the dominant role. All in all, the size of the U.S. economy, its liquid and well-diversified financial markets, its solid public institutions, and its effective legal system have made the dollar an attractive currency to non-U.S. residents who look for a stable and secure shelter from financial shocks and geopolitical risks. Habits, network externalities, and inertia also explain a great deal of the dollar's success; the extensive use of the greenback internationally has prevented other currencies from developing sufficient networks to challenge its dominance.

Since the dismissal of the Bretton Woods system, non-American holders of dollars have trusted the U.S. monetary authorities to promptly meet the demand for liquidity without undermining currency value. Because of its role as the key international currency, the greenback needs to be available in ample supply—and in an amount greater than that of any other international currency. As a result, the intents and actions of the U.S. government and the Federal Reserve are scrutinized much more than those of any other government or central bank that issues reserve currencies.

In principle, loss of confidence and trust could trigger a massive capital flight if foreign investors decide that their best option is to divest themselves of dollar assets—in short, to take the money and run. Uncontrollable capital outflows and speculative attacks can endanger the stability of the dominant international currency—and eventually of the country that issues it. For example, when Great Britain abandoned the gold standard in 1931—followed by the United States and other countries—investors started moving their money elsewhere, fearing a collapse of sterling. Governments further reacted by introducing restrictions on trade and foreign exchange operations, and this marked the collapse of the international economic and trading system.

In practice, however, foreigners have maintained confidence in the dollar through its various ups and downs. The demand for dollars strongly increased in the years before the financial crisis. For example, the implied demand for dollars as a share of the U.S. gross domestic product (GDP) expanded more than the U.S. economy did between 1990, when it was 10 percent, and 2008, when it had grown to 20 percent.[24] This demand did not significantly drop after 2008; despite the collapse of the banking and financial sector in the United States, the dollar became the safe-haven currency that many foreign investors wanted to hold. In 2011, the demand for dollars was over 23 percent of the U.S. GDP, and it was approximately 17 percent some five years later.[25] Ultimately, in fact, there is no alternative—yet—to the dollar, and this explains why non-U.S. individuals and organizations have stuck to the greenback regardless of U.S. domestic policies and their short-term impact on the currency.

WHEN MONEY IS CHEAP

Financial liberalization has made it easier for individuals, firms, and governments to move money around the world—to pay for goods and services, to invest in high-growth economies and industries, and to borrow at the most favorable rates. When borrowing conditions ease, money becomes more easily available, and that causes the costs of borrowing (i.e., interest rates) to drop, so money also becomes cheaper. This is what we saw during the economic expansion of the late 1990s and early 2000s, a period that became known as the Great Moderation. With cheap goods from developing countries and low oil prices, consumer price inflation dipped to historical lows in both the United States and Europe. Subdued inflationary pressures, in turn, offered central banks that have price stability as their key mandate a rational argument to support a prolonged accommodative stance in monetary policy—that is, to lower interest rates and thus the cost of borrowing.

Cheap money can be great for oiling the wheels of the global economy, but it carries significant risks. First, it encourages excessive credit growth and thus unsustainable consumption and investment. In the years before the global financial crisis, credit was readily available (especially in the United States), and many people fell victim to the illusion of being able to consume more than they could afford. Spain, likewise, saw excessive credit growth that fueled a property market bubble and drove domestic demand, which, in turn, generated a significant current-account deficit. In 2007, this deficit was equal to 10 percent of Spain's GDP—twice the deficit-to-GDP ratio of the United States, which, as I'll discuss in the next section, was deemed too imbalanced.

Another problem with cheap money is that low interest rates tend to encourage investors to "search for yield" and to foster a willingness to run more risks, as risky investments yield higher returns. Excessive exposure to risky and low-quality assets can lead to volatility, financial instability, and—as was the case in 2008—episodes of crisis. The booming residential mortgage market in the United States, generated by easily available credit, in turn fueled a booming residential housing market and strong private consumption growth. Spiraling indebtedness was deemed sustainable because of the unrealistic expectations of many people (and banks) that the housing market would continue to expand: they believed that as long as demand was strong—and house prices were increasing—the underlying debt could eventually be repaid and the risk was therefore low. Money continued to flow in, the cost of borrowing remained low, and the number of sub-prime mortgages grew.

In the years leading up to the crisis, cheap money created financial anomalies that could not be ignored. In February 2005, Fed Chairman Alan Greenspan drew attention to a "conundrum" in the world bond market: long-term interest rates had declined despite an increase in short-term rates.[26] Long-term investments usually have higher yields than short-term investments, to reflect the longer duration and thus potentially more risk for investors. "This development," explained Greenspan, "contrasts with most experience, which suggests that, other things being equal, increasing short-term interest rates are normally accompanied by a rise in longer-term yields."[27] He found it inexplicable that investors were prepared to lend money in the longer term at lower rates than in the short term. Did this mean that institutional investors would continue to lend to the United States despite increasing indebtedness? It seemed hard to believe because in those years the country was running a large twin deficit: in the current account (as imports significantly exceeded exports) and in the budget account (as the public sector consumed significantly more than the taxes it collected). Credit tends to dry up when both deficits are growing, as creditors grow doubtful of the debtor's ability to eventually repay the debt.

Ben Bernanke, who replaced Greenspan as head of the Fed a few weeks later, came up with a hypothesis to explain the conundrum—the "global saving glut" hypothesis. Bernanke maintained that the excess of savings over investment by so-called saving glut countries—developing countries and, in particular, the manufacturing economies of Asia and the oil exporters—had led to the global fall in real interest rates and to increased credit availability. It was a case of excess supply over demand. The significant increase in the supply of savings globally could therefore account for the "relatively low level of long-term interest rates."[28]

As we know now, the saving glut hypothesis was just one facet of a much more complex dynamic—but it was an argument that suited many people who did not want to see the end of cheap money. During the final years of his chairmanship, Greenspan had made a point of not intervening to burst the bubble because he thought that the role of central banks was not to curb exuberance, not knowing how the markets would react, but to provide support and "clear up the mess" after the bubble has burst.[29] He therefore challenged the conventional view that the role of central bankers was to break up the party and take away the punch bowl.[30] And even if he had wanted to, it would have been a difficult task: when money is cheap and many are gaining, it is difficult to change policy course. "As long as the music is playing, you've got to get up and dance," said Chuck Prince, a former chief executive of Citigroup in an interview with the *Financial Times* in 2007.[31]

In 2008, the music stopped. The global financial crisis forced the United States to cut the level of its debt. Demand for imports went down, and the trade deficit narrowed. During the postcrisis slump, monetary policies became even more accommodative, with unconventional measures such as QE devised to support growth. In the years after the crisis, interest rates were near zero in developed countries; central banks in the United States and Britain—followed, some years later, by the Bank of Japan and the European Central Bank—had to embrace QE in order to maintain liquidity in their economies. Many investors were pushed to search for yield in the more rewarding but also more risky emerging markets, and the resulting strong capital inflows drove currency appreciation in a number of developing countries. In the fall of 2010, Brazil's finance minister Guido Mantega complained that the Fed's monetary policy had forced a number of countries to lower their exchange rates in order to keep their exports competitive. "We're in the midst of an international currency war, a general weakening of currency," he said in an interview with the *Financial Times*. "This threatens us because it takes away our competitiveness."[32]

Capital flows reversed in 2013 when Bernanke signaled a possible end of QE. Investors began to question the strength and credibility of some fast-growing emerging-market economies and became more selective. This revealed imbalances, especially in countries where cheap money had fueled excessive debt. India, Brazil, Indonesia, South Africa, and Turkey were singled out as the "fragile five" for their inability to withstand capital outflows (foreign money leaving the country and moving somewhere else). When Bernanke revealed the planned "tapering" of the Fed policy in the spring of 2013, money did, in fact, flow out of these markets, causing havoc. This "taper tantrum," as it has come to be known, was a powerful illustration of just how integrated the world economy had become, with emerging-market economies and developing countries bearing the brunt of the policies implemented by developed countries. As Raghuram Rajan, the governor of the Reserve Bank of India, put it in an interview with Bloomberg India TV: "International monetary cooperation has broken down." He added: "Industrial countries have to play a part in restoring that [cooperation], and they can't at this point wash their hands off and say, we'll do what we need to and you do the adjustment."[33]

The 2013 taper tantrum provided a preview of the more severe episode of financial and monetary instability that broke out in January 2016. In the first two weeks of the year, the Shanghai Composite Index fell 18 percent, coming very close to the trough of the stock market crash in the summer of 2015; the value of the renminbi was also driven downward by news about the slower-than-expected growth of China's economy. Unlike in 2013, in 2008, and even in 1997—when the Asian financial crisis devastated many economies in the region but left China unscathed—China was at the center of this financial instability. The process of developing the renminbi as an international currency, which I will discuss in the rest of the book, has made China much more open to financial globalization than was the case in 1997, and it is now easier for money to move into and out of the country. But China's banking and financial system is not strong enough to absorb domestic shocks, allowing them to bounce through the global economy.

DOLLARS AT THE HEART OF CHINA'S TRANSFORMATION

Financial globalization, with the dollar at its heart, has provided the context for the development of China (and Asia) throughout the 1990s and the 2000s. Cheap money—really, cheap dollars—fueled the demand for the goods that China and other Asian countries were producing. The result was spectacularly intense economic activity that led to strong economic growth (in China especially, but also in the rest of Asia). However, China's model of development also provided a fertile ground for significant financial imbalances. For about a decade, until the global financial crisis of 2008, the rest of the world witnessed the abnormal and potentially unsustainable situation in which China's excessive saving supported the United States' excessive consumption. And while people in the United States borrowed (largely from China) and spent, global demand remained high, and the global economy continued to expand.

When the U.S. trade deficit with China peaked in 2006 and 2007 on the back of strong demand, it was more than $800 billion, or 5.8 percent of U.S. GDP.[34] In order to finance its trade deficit, the United States had to run a current-account deficit, which, as noted earlier, is the amount that a country borrows from abroad to finance consumption and investments that exceed domestic savings.[35] In 2007, for the third year in a row the United States ran a current-account deficit of over $700 billion, equivalent to approximately 5 percent of the country's GDP.

The mirror image of the United States' current-account deficit was China's surplus. In 2007, China's current-account surplus peaked at just more than 10 percent of the country's GDP.[36] The synchronized expansion of the deficit and the surplus of these two countries is a fitting illustration of the paradox that the world economy was experiencing in the years before the global financial crisis: the world's largest economy, the United States, was running a current-account deficit that was financed to a substantial extent by emerging-market countries—China, in particular.[37]

In some ways, these two countries are natural complements to each other. China's model of growth since the 1980s has revolved around exports, foreign investment, and the accumulation of foreign exchange. Over the same period, the United States has focused on domestic demand—in particular, private consumption—to drive growth. In both countries, policy makers use their policy instruments to ensure full employment of resources—especially the labor force. During this time, savings significantly increased in China, and indebtedness significantly expanded in the United States. The numbers are noteworthy: in China, aggregate savings were just over 50 percent of GDP, whereas in the United States they were approximately 17 percent of GDP.

In the years before the global financial crisis, savings in China and borrowing in the United States managed to keep global demand high, and this largely contributed to the expansion of the world economy. But to keep the balance between China and the United States—and between surplus and deficit countries—the exchange rate in China had to stay low enough to keep exports cheap, and the interest rates in the United States had to stay low enough to spur consumption and employment. In other words, the mirror image of China's low real exchange rates was low U.S. domestic interest rates—the so-called Greenspan put. This was possible thanks to strong demand for U.S. financial assets from China and other surplus countries—Bernanke's saving glut.

To some extent, the policy outcomes in the two countries were jointly determined. As long as China continued to manage the exchange rate and as long as the United States could use low interest rates (i.e., cheap money) to maintain growth, the system held together. In addition, from 2003 through 2008, the final years of the Great Moderation, there was no pressure to correct the deficit/surplus mismatch. Both the United States and China were able to meet their targets for GDP growth and full employment of resources, and the rest of the world was experiencing strong growth (although some countries, including Spain and Ireland, were also building trade and financial imbalances). There was no incentive to correct this system, and few experts or policy makers saw these imbalances as a problem.[38] It was seen simply as a reflection of a loan from East Asia to the United States.[39]

The situation drastically changed with the onset of the global financial crisis. The dollar weakened, and interest rates dropped even further from the already low levels of the precrisis years. As they have remained very low, the world has continued to be flooded with cheap money. Furthermore, as the Fed—as well as the Bank of England and the European Central Bank—has cut interest rates to near zero (and negative interest rates introduced very recently) and embraced QE, money has continued to move around the world in the search for yield, especially to the developing countries. Whereas developed countries, until very recently, have been saddled with low confidence, high unemployment, and low demand, the economies of developing countries have been expanding dynamically in the postcrisis years. (But since 2015 this dynamic seems to have run into difficulties.)

For many years, dollars have oiled the wheels of the international money machine,[40] fueling the demand for goods that China and other developing countries have become more and more adept at producing. In the next chapter, I'll discuss how China has managed to exploit the dollar-based system and the availability of cheap capital to its own advantage. This has resulted in the country's overall transformation and strong economic expansion. But the limits of China's system—a currency with restricted international circulation, a repressed banking sector that misallocates financial resources, and limited public provisions for health care and retirement (chapter 3)—have constrained the development of the domestic banking and financial sector and have cemented the role of the renminbi as a currency with limited international use.

2

CHINA'S EXTRAORDINARY BUT STILL UNFINISHED TRANSFORMATION

C HEAP AND EASILY available money provides the context for China's transformation, and this transformation is the extraordinary story of our time. As the world was getting richer and money was moving around, China, having embraced economic reforms, was preparing to become more integrated into the world economy and thus to harness the openness of the rest of the world. In fact, throughout the late 1990s and early 2000s—roughly between the Asian financial crisis and the global financial crisis—cheap money spurred consumer demand, which, in turn, drove the growth of Chinese exports and channeled investment into China. The country's economy expanded at a remarkable pace, and by the first decade of the new century, it had regained the position within the world economy that it had lost almost one hundred years earlier.

Indeed, at the beginning of the twentieth century, China boasted one of the largest economies in the world, with a 9 percent share of global gross domestic product (GDP) in 1913.[1] Two world wars, a major war with Japan, and a long civil war wreaked havoc on the economy. When the People's Republic of China was established in 1949, the whole country was in tatters. Although it was still a significant exporter, if not a major one (ranking thirtieth in the world) in the 1950s, all this began to change when Mao Zedong launched the first Five-Year Plan in 1953.[2] The Maoist doctrine of self-sufficiency, implemented during the Cultural Revolution (1966 to 1976), left China largely isolated from the rest of the world. Its international trade dwindled, as what imports there were (such as commodities and semimanufactured goods) went to feed the country's autarchic industry and exports slowed to a trickle. In 1977, the sum of China's imports and exports was less than $15 billion, and its share of world trade was a mere 0.6 percent. The country's economy was decimated, and its share of global GDP had shrunk to just over 2 percent.[3]

China was even more isolated from international capital markets. With the exception of short-term trade credits, it did not borrow in international commercial markets or from international financial institutions such as the World Bank. It did not receive foreign aid from bilateral agencies. It did not receive foreign direct investment and did not invest abroad.[4] When the Communist Party took power in 1948, China issued a unified currency—the renminbi—to replace the variety of regional currencies that had been in use until then.[5] To make imports cheaper, the central government fixed the renminbi's exchange rate at an artificially high level. The result was a highly overvalued currency and a dual currency market where the official rate was much higher than the unofficial one.

With China nearly impenetrable by the non-Chinese, it was difficult for foreign experts to predict how the country would develop over the long term. In a 1975 report on its economic conditions based on an extensive visit, a group of American experts agreed that the country could advance significantly because of its ability to expand industrial capacity and output. But they maintained that it would not move into the group of leading economies. "Even if the People's Republic succeeds, and it almost surely will, in further outdistancing most other large LDCs [less developed countries] by the year 2000, it can hardly make up the enormous gap between itself and the countries in the front ranks. . . . Peking will need much more time to achieve industrial parity."[6] And a couple of decades later, in 1999, the *Economist* argued that China's economic growth and modernization could not be sustained unless gradualism in reforms was replaced by "shock therapy."[7]

China proved them wrong. In 2010, it dwarfed Japan as the world's second-largest economy, and it is now on the verge of overtaking the United States (by some measures, it has already done so). Over the last thirty years, a confluence of internal and external factors, sustained economic reforms, and a policy of openness have spurred economic growth on an unprecedented scale. The country's large population has provided cheap labor, helping it to harness the benefits of the expansion of the world economy. Artificially low interest rates have enabled its state-owned enterprises to borrow cheaply. (State-owned enterprises are those with a sole or majority state owner.) Adjustments to the exchange rate have kept its exports competitive. Foreign direct investment, encouraged since the onset of economic reforms in the 1980s, has brought in skills, technology, international best practice, and exposure to external markets—and, of course, capital. Between 1978 and 2015, China's real GDP grew about thirtyfold to almost $11 trillion. This makes up 15 percent of world GDP.[8] Annual income per capita increased from about $300 in the early 1980s to approximately $8,500 today (in nominal terms).

It's hard to overstate how unexpected and unusual China's transformation was, in both its speed and its scale. In the past, a country's development—the shift from low-value to higher-value industries, the increase in income per head, and the improvement in overall living standards—always took at least two generations; China achieved it in less than one. It has come as a surprise even to the Chinese themselves (Deng Xiaoping had more modest expectations, reiterating that "if we can make China a moderately developed country within a hundred years from the founding of the People's Republic, that will be an extraordinary achievement"[9]). I often ask Chinese officials whether they could have predicted such a successful outcome thirty years ago, and the answer is always no. Once I posed the same question to a former Japanese deputy finance minister who was a careful observer of China. Without hesitation, he answered: "Not in my lifetime." Against this prediction, the country became the great success story of our time.

One real puzzle, however, is that the country's currency has not kept up with its extraordinary development. Although China is now a superweight in the world economy, the renminbi has limited circulation outside its borders and limited liquidity. Most of China's exports (about $2.7 trillion a year[10]) and imports (about $2.3 trillion a year[11]) are invoiced in dollars, and dollars are exchanged to pay for them. This is the case for goods that the country trades not only with the United States but also with most of its trade partners. China is a global power with a "dwarf" currency.

How has China managed to grow so quickly, and why has its currency not kept up? In this chapter, I will take a closer look at the country's extraordinary transformation, exploring where it has come from and what it has managed to achieve. I will argue that this has been possible because of the parallel opening of the world economy and the country's ability to become part of the expanding global markets where the dollar is the dominant currency. China has a unique development model and is in the middle of an ongoing transformation from a system based on economic planning to a more market-oriented economy—"market socialism" in Deng's words.[12] Trade and investment are the forces that have been driving the country's development. In the following chapter, then, I will look at how the dollar system and financial repression have facilitated this development—and how they are now starting to hold the country back. The downsides of having a dwarf currency are beginning to show.

TRADE: ONE OF THE DRIVERS OF CHINA'S SUCCESS

In the late 1970s, China started to embrace a strategy of trade liberalization and to reverse years of isolation, autarky, and self-sufficiency. Some signs that it wished to open to the rest of the world were already evident in the early 1970s, with President Nixon's famous visit and the rapprochement with the United States. But it was when Deng Xiaoping came to power after the Cultural Revolution that the conditions for the rapid growth of China's foreign trade were set.[13]

In the early 1980s, Deng announced the opening of special economic zones, and in 1988, Premier Zhao Ziyang unveiled a coastal development strategy. What followed was a combination of strategy and luck, as China's successful opening up and its exploitation of international trade overlapped with the extraordinary integration and expansion of the world economy that followed the end of the Cold War in the early 1990s. The Chinese authorities eagerly exploited this opportunity, pushing the state-owned firms (more on these in chapter 3) to meet the demand for cheap consumer goods and intermediate goods. The country's coastal provinces became one big export platform. As demand grew, so did exports, helping the growth of China's economy. Dollars—the currency used to settle all these transactions—began to flow in. In 2001, the country formally entered the world economy and became a member of the World Trade Organization (WTO). Joining the WTO gave a further boost to China's exports.

Emboldened by China's new global position and greater market access— and also needing to come into compliance with WTO standards—Premier Zhu Rongji began pushing reforms through—in particular, the downsizing of the state bureaucracy.[14] Tariffs were significantly reduced, and the authorities agreed to eliminate trade licenses, which had previously restricted cross-border business to only a few favored firms.[15] The authorities also agreed to adopt international standards for intellectual property rights protection and for the treatment of foreign businesses operating in the domestic economy. To this day, problems remain in the implementation of the WTO rules, especially with regard to intellectual property rights protection and the treatment of foreign companies. Nonetheless, China has made significant progress in reducing tariffs. The average bound tariff rate—the most-favored-nation tariff rate that is part of a country's commitments to other WTO members—is now 9.2 percent, compared to 34.4 percent in India and 30.7 percent in Brazil.

The effects of this transformation are all around us. Having turned into one of the largest exporters and manufacturers, China is now the main trade partner for both the United States and Europe. In 2014, it traded approximately $5 trillion worth of goods and services, comprising over 10 percent of world trade.[16] Compare these numbers with China's contribution to world trade in 1990: $115 billion dollars, or less than 2 percent.[17] Trade is now an important engine of China's economic growth. The sum of its exports and imports of goods and services amounts to around 47 percent of its GDP; in 1978, this share was less than 10 percent. For Japan, India, and Brazil, for instance, trade accounts for approximately 25–30 percent of their GDP.[18]

Just as Great Britain was from 1850 to 1900, the United States was from 1900 to 1960, and Japan was from 1960 to 1990, China is now the world's largest producer of ordinary consumer goods (accounting for about one-third of the world's total production), such as home electrical appliances, toys, bicycles and motorcycles, footwear and textiles, computers, cameras, mobile phones, watches, machine tools, and even Christmas ornaments. It is the leading trade partner for 124 countries.[19] Seventy companies on the Fortune Global 500 list are Chinese (up from only eleven in 2002).[20] The country's firms have become world leaders in a number of sectors. In electronics, for instance, they account for approximately 75 percent of the global output of smart phones and more than 85 percent of that of personal computers. "Made in China" goods, especially those at the lowest rank of the consumer goods market, have come to epitomize the transformation of the world economy at the turn of the last century and at the beginning of the new one.

Although only 15 percent of China's total exports these days come from labor-intensive sectors such as textiles and footwear, cheap labor remains at the heart of the country's economic success. For instance, with wages and other labor costs of approximately $4.46 per hour, its car industry has an advantage over car producers in countries where labor costs are much higher. In developed countries, labor costs per hour in the car industry range from $35 in the United States to $45 in Japan to almost $60 in Germany and France. Even an emerging-market economy such as Mexico faces higher costs, at $6.48 per hour.[21] As a result, China now has the world's largest auto industry, with almost 25 million vehicles produced in 2015—a huge increase since 2000, when a mere 2 million were produced.[22] It is now well ahead of its competitors in terms of production volume. In 2015, a bit more than 12 million cars were produced in the United States, just over 9 million in Japan, less than 6 million in Germany, and approximately 5 million in South Korea.[23]

Much of China's advanced production involves export processing, and as a consequence, semifinished or finished components from other countries make up a significant share of imports.[24] For example, Apple outsources the production of iPads and iPhones to Foxconn, a company headquartered in

Taiwan that has thirteen factories in mainland China, the largest of which is based in Shenzhen. The firm imports device components, assembles them into finished products, and ships them out to markets in North America and Europe.

It is, however, China's imports of energy and commodities that, above all, give a sense of the country's industrial transformation. It is now the world's largest total energy consumer, accounting for nearly half of the world's growth in energy consumption over the previous decade.[25] Its oil imports are the fastest growing in the world (a stark contrast to the 1980s, when it used to export oil), and it consumes approximately 12 million barrels per day—more than any other country outside the Organization for Economic Cooperation and Development but behind the United States, which consumes almost 20 million barrels per day.[26] Demand for commodities is driven by heavy industry's need for gasoline, electricity, iron ore, copper, and other natural resources. In 2014, China produced 823 million metric tons of steel, compared to 128.5 million metric tons in 2000. Japan came in a distant second with 111 million metric tons of steel output, followed by the United States with 88 million metric tons and South Korea with 72 million metric tons.[27]

Despite the immense growth in manufacturing, this sector employs only about 30 percent of China's total labor force; approximately 35 percent of China's working population is still employed in agriculture (the service sector accounts for the other 36 percent).[28] The proportion of agricultural employment is very large and suggests that, despite its huge effort to modernize, the country still has a long way to go to overturn and upgrade its economy. This is how economies develop and modernize: they expand the relative weight of manufacturing and services—the secondary and tertiary sectors—as they reduce that of the primary sector (mainly agriculture and fishing but also mining and extraction). As China continues along its path of development, the share of employment in agriculture will drop, and the shares in manufacturing and services will go up (the increase of the latter is likely to be stronger than that of the former). In the United States, only 1 percent of the labor force is employed in agriculture. The service sector, on the other hand, absorbs most American workers (almost 80 percent), whereas manufacturing employs less than 20 percent. This distribution is common to most advanced countries, where technological innovations and organizational improvements have significantly reduced the number of people employed in agriculture relative to other sectors—in particular, services.

One of the major consequences of this shift away from agriculture has been the urbanization of the country. Industry and services tend to be concentrated in urban settlements; thus, people continue to move from the countryside to cities. Like Europe at the time of the Industrial Revolution, China now hosts some of the largest and fastest-growing cities in the world. Take Shenzhen. According to the official census, it is a huge city of 10 million people—the locals double that figure to account for immigrants that are not officially registered—and China's sixth-largest city; it is much bigger than any large city in Europe or North America (London and New York have approximately 8 million inhabitants each). Many of these cities have grown so fast that they have outpaced global awareness: as I was driving through Shenzhen during one recent visit, I could not avoid wondering how many people in Europe or the United States have ever heard of it—or of the neighboring, equally giant cities of Guangzhou and Dongguan.

Nowadays more than 50 percent of China's population lives in cities, a huge increase from only 20 percent in the early 1980s. Hundreds of millions of people have moved to urban centers to work in manufacturing and services, and with China's continued urban expansion, these large cities will become even larger. Albeit different in relative size, such urban development can be compared only with the growth of London and Manchester at the time of Britain's Industrial Revolution in the nineteenth century.

FOREIGN DIRECT INVESTMENT: THE OTHER FORCE BEHIND CHINA'S ECONOMIC TRANSFORMATION

At the beginning of the process of economic liberalization and the shift from plan to market, the Chinese authorities realized how important foreign investment was for the country's development. It brings in not only capital but also skills, knowledge, and innovation. These factors, even more than capital itself, have been critical for the country's economic growth. As Deng Xiaoping explained in 1992 during the "Southern Tour" (or "Southern Sojourn," the extensive visit to China's southern provinces that he undertook in his retirement to build public support for Jiang Zemin's reforms): "At the current stage, foreign-funded enterprises in China are allowed to make some money in accordance with existing laws and policies. But the government levies taxes on those enterprises, workers get wages from them, and we learn technology and managerial skills. In addition, we get information from them that will help us to open more markets."[29]

During China's transformation, capital was, in fact, the least important consideration; the country's export-heavy strategy meant there was always a surplus in the trade balance (in other words, it always produced more than it could consume), and the individual savings rate was high. What it needed (and to some extent still needs) was knowledge, technology, and skills. The authorities therefore started to encourage foreign companies that were eager to participate in China's expanding domestic market to invest in the country. The opening of the country to foreign capital began in 1979–1980, with the implementation of the joint venture law and the establishment of the special economic zones.

And, indeed, with a system in place to ensure that there were plenty of dollars to drive the country's development, dollars began to pour in. Foreign direct investment has increased almost without interruption since the early 1980s—and this despite increasing awareness abroad of corruption and weak governance. Throughout that decade, China received an average of $1.8 billion a year in foreign direct investment. These sums soon surpassed the amount China was borrowing from the World Bank, making foreign direct investment a far more important source of foreign capital.[30]

China receives more foreign direct investment than any other developing country (and, of all recipients, is behind only the European Union and the United States).[31] A cumulative total of more than $2 trillion flowed into the country between 1990 and 2010. These days it gets an average of $128 billion a year in foreign direct investment.[32]

In the early 1990s, as part of the bevy of reforms to prepare for and support China's application for membership in the WTO, the government started lifting restrictions on foreign investment in sectors such as retailing. As a result, major multinational companies (Nike, Benetton, Giordano, and Baskin-Robbins, just to name a few) began production operations in Beijing, Shanghai, and Shenzhen and also opened shops in the country's main cities, attracted by the large domestic consumer market. Investing in China became a key element of the business strategy of most multinational companies.

The increase in foreign direct investment has also helped China's manufacturing sector get more integrated into regional and global supply chains. Multinational companies headquartered in Europe and the United States have invested in greenfield plants and opened production facilities and factories; for example, both Germany's Mercedes-Benz and Britain's Jaguar Land Rover have factories in China. The country is now part of the global business system of a large fraction of U.S. and European multinational companies across different sectors—including Apple, Coca-Cola (with 41 bottling plants and almost 50,000 employees in China), Volkswagen, Bosch, and Adidas, to mention just a few. Firms with foreign stakeholders account for approximately 28 percent of China's overall value-added industrial output.[33]

Foreign multinational firms have made critically important contributions to China's transformation across industries. The interaction with and exposure to leading-edge technologies—and the need to comply with international quality standards and good practice—have contributed to the country's productivity growth and modernization. These benefits extend beyond the production of goods and services to include, increasingly, far more advanced operations, such as research, design, and innovation. In other words, foreign capital has not only supported China's development but also better equipped domestic firms to compete in international markets.

With more foreign companies operating in China, joint ventures between Chinese and foreign firms also sprang up. The outcome of these partnerships, and of the large amount of foreign capital inflows, is reflected in the strong growth of exports of foreign-invested firms. The share of these exports within China's total exports increased from a mere 1 percent in the mid-1980s to nearly 50 percent in recent years.[34] These partnerships are particularly relevant in the high-tech and high-value consumer product sectors that produce, for example, DVD players, LED and plasma TV screens, high-end electronics, and microwave ovens. By the mid-2000s, Chinese firms with foreign stakeholders accounted for almost 90 percent of exports in these sectors. Partnerships and joint ventures with foreign companies have also been critical to the development of the country's large automobile sector. For instance, in 2014, Jaguar Land Rover, in cooperation with China's Chery Automobile Company, launched a $1.1 billion project and opened the first production center in China. Mercedes-Benz, in a joint venture with Beijing Benz Automotive Ltd., has been manufacturing cars in the country since 2004. Joint ventures with Chinese firms have also helped foreign companies expand into the growing domestic market. Such joint ventures, for example, account for approximately 30 percent of total auto sales for Volkswagen and General Motors.[35]

But investment no longer flows just one way. Chinese companies have also become active abroad and have started acquiring stakes in companies around the world. The turning point came in 2005, when Nanjing Automobile Group acquired MG Rover, a British car company with a well-established brand. This acquisition showed definitively that China could be an equal partner in global markets.

CHINA GOES OUT

Chinese investment abroad started on a small scale soon after Deng Xiaoping came to power in 1978. Already in his seventies when he took charge, Deng embarked on a series of official trips abroad. In November 1978, he visited Singapore and "glimpsed a vision of China's possible future,"[36] and a few months later he went to the United States—the first Chinese leader to visit since 1949.[37] Both trips made a huge impression on him and perhaps evoked earlier memories—he had spent several years in France as a student.[38]

According to the official Chinese narrative, these trips provided the inspiration for and marked the beginning of China's "go out" strategy. "From then on," China's government literature says, "China said 'good-bye' to isolation and stepped onto the path of 'opening to the world' and 'opening to the future.'"[39]

In China, *opening up* is a popular term for pursuing reforms, learning from good practice, modernizing the country, and engaging with the rest of the world while developing—in the words of current leader Xi Jinping— "socialism with Chinese characteristics."[40] Opening up extended to firms, which were encouraged to invest abroad (even if, in the early days of the reforms, they still needed direct approval from the State Council to operate overseas). The State Council designated 120 state-owned enterprises as "national champions" that would lead the internationalization of Chinese enterprises and provided them with high-level political support and financial subsidies in order to achieve this.[41]

In 1997, President Jiang Zemin unveiled a new phase of the country's opening up in a speech to the Fifteenth Congress of the Chinese Communist Party, in which he advocated the active participation of Chinese companies in foreign markets and foreign countries. "Implementation of the strategy of 'going out' is an important measure taken in the new stage of opening up," said Jiang. "We should encourage and help relatively competitive enterprises with various forms of ownership to invest abroad in order to increase exports of goods and labor services and bring about a number of strong multinational enterprises and brand names."[42]

China's "going out" (or "going global," as it is also called) is a multifaceted policy initiative that was devised to encourage its commercial firms to establish partnerships with foreign companies, to acquire stakes— usually minority stakes—in companies abroad, or to bid for contracts (mostly for large infrastructure projects).[43] This initiative combines commercial and diplomatic goals and is consistent with the four motivations usually cited in the economic literature as driving companies to invest abroad: access to valuable commodities or energy; interest in more efficient, lower-cost processes; expansion into new markets; and acquisition of new assets.[44]

First of all, the authorities aimed to facilitate Chinese companies' access to oil, energy, and commodities and to satisfy the country's growing demand for primary resources. Most investments of this type were in resource-rich developing countries. Altogether, in the years between 2011 and 2014, Chinese oil companies spent approximately $73 billion to purchase oil and gas assets in the Middle East, Canada, and Latin America, and to invest in exploration operations[45] and more than $90 billion to secure bilateral oil-for-loans deals with several countries (including Russia, Brazil, Venezuela, Kazakhstan, Ecuador, and Turkmenistan). China National Offshore Oil Corporation has been particularly busy since 2001, making acquisitions in countries such as Angola, Brazil, Equatorial Guinea, Indonesia, Kenya, Burma/Myanmar, Nigeria, and Uganda. In 2011, it acquired Canadian oil sands producer Opti Canada for $2.1 billion after the latter filed for bankruptcy protection.[46]

Going out was also a way to introduce market-driven practices and help the money-losing state-owned conglomerates turn into modern and efficient enterprises. As Jiang pointed out in his speech to the Fifteenth Congress: "We should form large internationally competitive companies and enterprise groups through market forces and policy guidance."[47] For the authorities, going global and pushing state-owned enterprises into international markets in order to make them more competitive were part of the overall reform of the state-owned companies (more on this in the next chapter).

In 2004, there was a clear shift toward the third motivation—access to overseas markets—especially in the engineering and construction sector. The going out policy guided expansion into new markets and established an international presence for many Chinese firms. In some cases (as with oil companies), overseas investments were driven by the need both to acquire resources and to expand into new markets. In recent years, companies have focused more on the fourth motivation, using their financial resources to merge with or to acquire significant stakes in overseas companies in order to upgrade their nonfinancial assets (such as technology, brand, and market share). For example, in 2010, Zhejiang Geely Holding Group, an automotive manufacturing company headquartered in Hangzhou, bought the

Swedish company Volvo Cars for $1.5 billion. Through this acquisition, Geely acquired Volvo Car's well-established international brand, technology, and global distribution network—as well as its serious financial troubles. In the three years before the acquisition, the company had lost an average of $1.8 billion per year before taxes, and net sales had declined by almost 20 percent.[48]

China also has a fifth, somewhat unique motivation for investing abroad: to acquire friends and commercial advantages around the world through financial diplomacy. Its state-owned enterprises tend to be more sensitive to national strategic priorities than to pure corporate priorities.[49] This makes them more willing than private firms to direct their investments toward foreign countries that do not have a strong record of public institutions, good governance, and positive sovereign ratings. For instance, in 2014, China signed a $2 billion deal with Zimbabwe for the construction of a coal mine, power station, and dam, secured against Zimbabwe's future mining tax revenues. Similarly, Chinese-backed loans to Russian companies are estimated to total $30 billion, many of them secured by oil shipments to China.

Such a preference is counterintuitive and conflicts with the established theory that in foreign direct investment a high level of political risk correlates with a low level of attractiveness. Investing in countries with poor economic and political governance is a risky strategy, as it exposes China—like any other investor—to the possibility of substantial losses, especially at times (like now) when low oil and commodities prices increase the risk of default for some oil-producing countries. Venezuela, for example, with 95 percent of its exports in oil, has been through significant hardship since 2014, and GDP has been down by almost 6 percent since the beginning of 2015, whereas inflation is more than 100 percent. Therefore, during President Xi Jinping's visit in January 2015, China agreed to invest $20 billion to help the country—on the top of $50 billion in credit it had extended since 2007.[50]

Propelled by these five interrelated motivations, China began to expand its presence overseas after joining the WTO in 2001. Membership in the WTO provided the context and the regulatory framework, and even the legitimacy, for its "going out" strategy. This, coupled with the simultaneous easing of foreign exchange controls and more active assistance for firms with overseas expansion plans, spurred a strong surge in the country's outward foreign direct investment, which grew from $47 billion in 2001 to $110 billion in 2008[51]—still, however, considerably less than the overall stock of inward direct investment (almost $400 billion that same year).[52] The 2008–2009 global financial crisis slowed things down, but China's overseas direct investment rebounded by 2010—notably, that directed toward developed countries where the crisis had created interesting investment opportunities and had weakened the political barriers preventing foreigners (especially Chinese) from "buying chunks of the country."[53] Strong foreign direct investment is poised to continue: the Thirteenth Five-Year Plan, for the period 2016 to 2020, like the previous plan, encourages Chinese enterprises to "go abroad"—as part of the "two-way opening up" of attracting foreign investments and investing overseas.[54]

Where does Chinese overseas investment go? Excluding the large share that continues to go to tax havens (especially the Cayman Islands and British Virgin Islands) and through Hong Kong to other destinations, Asia is the most important destination. In 2014, the country's total direct investment in Asian countries was $116 billion, about a quarter of its total.[55] Within the region, again excluding Hong Kong, Singapore is the largest recipient, followed by Vietnam and Pakistan. In recent years, there has been an increase in the flows to Burma/Myanmar, Indonesia, Cambodia, and Thailand. Outside Asia, Germany, the United States, and the United Kingdom are the largest recipient countries, with 12 percent, 9 percent, and 5 percent, respectively, of total Chinese foreign direct investment since 2003.

Among the industries that are attracting the most Chinese investment, the service sector—including trade and finance—stands out, with almost 60 percent of the total. Investment in manufacturing is also significant, with almost 40 percent of the total, whereas investment in agriculture is tiny. Investment in the service sector is concentrated in high-income countries, consistent with the investment motivation that focuses on the importance of acquiring market share and nonfinancial assets such as innovative technology and international brands. On the other hand, the majority of Chinese investment in the natural resources sectors (metals, coal, oil, and natural gas) goes to low-income countries.

Over the years, Chinese companies have acquired stakes in a number of businesses abroad, from banks to shipping companies. In 2015, their merger and acquisition activities overseas totaled almost $67 billion, with 382 total transactions—a 21 percent and a 40 percent increase, respectively, from the previous year.[56] However, Peter Nolan argues that these firms have not taken part in major acquisitions (the acquisition of Volvo Cars, at approximately $1.8 billion, is tiny)—and even their efforts to acquire companies in developed economies have often ended up in failure.[57]

The exception that confirms the rule is the 2004 acquisition of the struggling personal computer division of IBM by Lenovo, a computer technology company based in Beijing. Lenovo paid $1.25 billion for the acquisition, which included the business that manufactured the ThinkPad laptops, and absorbed $500 million of IBM's debt. The deal was hugely symbolic: an obscure Chinese company had managed to acquire an iconic American brand. It also propelled Lenovo onto the international stage, making it the third-largest computer manufacturer in the world by volume. The *Financial Times* welcomed the deal as "a symbol of a new economic era."[58] However, the low profitability of IBM's personal computer division in an increasingly competitive market raises the question of whether the acquisition would have been more politically controversial if the target company had been more successful.[59] In the same league is Geely's acquisition of money-losing Volvo Cars: the takeover of this iconic Western company would have been politically more controversial if Volvo Cars had been a profitable company. In any case, Nolan convincingly argues that the acquisitions that the large Chinese firms have made are small in scale, compared with the deals that the world's leading companies routinely make. For instance, around the time of the Volvo Cars deal—for $1.8 billion—SABMiller, the multinational brewing and beverage company headquartered in London, announced the $10.4 billion acquisition of the Australian brewing company Foster's.[60] More recently, in 2015, SABMiller was taken over by Anheuser-Busch InBev NV in a deal worth $106 billion.[61] In February 2016, ChemChina offered to buy the Swiss agricultural giant Syngenta for about $43 billion; if the deal goes ahead it will be the largest foreign acquisition by a Chinese company and could mark the beginning of a new era of larger deals for Chinese going abroad.

Chinese overseas investment has recently turned to the banking and financial sector. Once again, however, these acquisitions have been of limited size. In December 2014, for instance, the Chinese brokerage firm Haitong Securities acquired the investment banking arm of Portugal's defunct Banco Espirito Santo in a €379 million deal. A few months later, in February 2015, the Industrial and Commercial Bank of China finalized the $690 million purchase of a controlling stake in the UK arm of South Africa's Standard Bank. For the first time, a Chinese bank now has a significant trading floor operation in London.[62]

Many countries—industrialized and developing alike—have expressed concerns about being too closely entangled with China through commercial and financial links. They worry about the exploitative attitude that is often displayed by Chinese firms and the loss of key technological capabilities. In addition, as episodes like Chinese National Offshore Oil Corporation's losing bid for Unocal show, there is strong political resistance in Western countries to letting state-owned Chinese companies acquire significant stakes in strategic domestic companies.[63] The influence of the country's Communist Party in the governance of these state-owned companies is a major source of discomfort for Western governments and their citizens,[64] who feel that China's strategic interests are often at odds with their interests and those of their neighbors.

LENDING TO DEVELOPMENT

Over the years, China has become the world's largest provider of development finance, and this has created even more anxiety, especially in the recipient countries, around the way Beijing deploys development finance. This support comes, in some cases, with particularly favorable conditions and "no strings attached," which often translates to de facto support for undemocratic and repressive regimes.

Figures are murky, but sources estimate that in 2009 and 2010, for instance, the China Development Bank and Export-Import Bank of China signed agreements to lend approximately $110 billion to governments and enterprises based in countries such as Russia, Venezuela, and Brazil. China is also estimated to have supplied more than $119 billion in loan commitments to Latin American countries and firms since 2005. In 2010, it loaned Latin America more than the World Bank, Inter-American Development Bank, and U.S. Export-Import Bank combined.[65] It also provided $10 billion in repayable long-term loans to Africa from 2009 to 2012—and during his first overseas trip to Africa in March 2013, President Xi Jinping pledged to double this to $20 billion by 2015. In November 2013, the head sovereign risk analyst of the Export-Import Bank of China announced that by 2025, "China will have provided Africa with 1 trillion dollars in financing, including direct investment, soft loans and commercial loans."[66]

This financial diplomacy has helped Beijing's relations with many developing countries and has cemented China's role as an alternative to U.S.-led economic diplomacy and the "Washington consensus." Although many countries welcome China's investment as an important trigger for their own development, some have expressed concern about getting too close to China, as they see the imbalances in the relationship—in terms of economic size, financial resources, and geopolitical standing—and therefore the potential risks.

With the creation in 2014 of the Asian Infrastructure Investment Bank (AIIB) and New Development Bank (the new multilateral development banks led by emerging economies; they are both headquartered in China, and China is a founding member of the latter), there is no sign that the country's going out will slow. And the Belt and Road Initiative, formally announced in 2013 and then promoted by the Chinese leadership through 2015 as a modern version of the ancient Silk Road, which connected China to Europe, will provide further stimulus. It is increasingly clear that the country intends to use its significant financial resources to strengthen and expand its presence in Asia and Europe—both offer China important markets and also potential partners to counterbalance the geopolitical influence of the United States in both regions. (It is worth noting that the United States is currently finalizing two megaregional trade agreements: the Trans-Pacific Partnership, or TTP, with many Asian countries but not China; and the Transatlantic Trade and Investment Partnership, or TTIP, with the European Union.) But does it make sense for China to deplete financial resources overseas when it has an immature financial system at home, a dwarf currency, and a significant number of people who still live below the international poverty line? In the next chapter, I will discuss how the country has managed its transformation and the accumulation of significant financial resources, but at the cost of developing a system of financial repression and inefficient allocation of capital.

3

A FINANCIALLY REPRESSED ECONOMY

THE TRANSFORMATION OF China within the context of a more integrated world economy has resulted in a substantial increase in annual income per capita. With approximately $8,500 per person in nominal terms, China is now a middle-income country. And, as people who have experienced deep poverty normally do, the Chinese save a lot. Over the years, the monetary authorities have channeled these savings toward the country's industrial transformation, making sure, however, that the costs for borrowers have remained low. As savers began to feel squeezed, they started to look for better returns than those usually offered on bank deposits: first in the real estate market and then increasingly in so-called shadow banking instruments—unregulated borrowing and lending presented as wealth management products.

But better returns bring more risk and volatility. Many Chinese investors are not sufficiently acquainted with this trade-off, as is clear from the case of Shanxi Platinum Assemblage Investment, a small asset-management firm that collapsed at the end of 2014. In early December, following rumors that the company was in dire financial straits and executives had fled, angry investors gathered at its Taiyuan office, in northern China, to pressure the authorities to intervene and help them recover their money. Individuals and households had put their savings in Shanxi wealth management products that offered interest rates of 14–18 percent annually and were now at risk of losing a combined 100 million renminbi.

The pressure wasn't enough. A few months earlier the People's Bank of China and the Commerce Ministry had warned investors about "problems with chaotic business," adding that "a large number of non-financial guarantee companies are not engaged in guarantee business. They even engage in illegal deposit-taking, illegal fundraising, illegal wealth management and high-interest loans."[1] In the end, the authorities allowed Shanxi Platinum Assemblage to fail, making it clear that the central government would not be there to bail out financial institutions.

Episodes like this, along with the Chinese stock market's steep downward adjustments in 2015 and 2016, brought international attention to the intrinsic contradiction between the state of the country's financial and banking sector and its ambitions to develop the renminbi in one of the key international currencies. Shadow banking, of which Shanxi Platinum Assemblage was a part, is the result of the limited range of regulated savings products in China's financial sector and savers' quest for investments with higher returns than bank deposits provide. Poor options for savers are in stark contrast to the robust and growing array of financial resources that feed the country's manufacturing sector and grow its economy, as described in the preceding chapters on trade and investment. And both these trends are the result of the distinctive feature of China's model of development: financial repression.[2]

Under China's system of financial repression, the government directs and controls where savers invest their money, and depositors don't have many options other than local banks (they can't, for instance, easily take their money out of the country). Typically, policies constrain the returns savers earn on their savings—notably, in bank deposits—so that banks can provide cheap loans to state-owned companies and to the private sector. Therefore, these policies result in a transfer of resources from depositors to borrowers. Financial repression occurs when "governments implement policies to channel themselves funds that in a deregulated market environment would go somewhere else."[3]

The term *financial repression* was coined in the 1970s to indicate growth-inhibiting policies in developing countries, and in recent years, it has

been extended to advanced countries. In the case of China, fina
sion, instead of inhibiting growth, has for years provided ar.
resources to underpin economic activity. Policies include caps on inu.
rates, constraints on cross-border capital movements, and high reserve
requirements.[4] In this sense, financial repression has been an intrinsic component of China's model of growth; it has enabled the country to move
from plan to market, to transform the economy, and to become a global
heavyweight within a single generation.

However, financial repression has created a massive misallocation of
financial resources, with too many money-losing projects being funded
while more promising projects in the private sector can't raise capital. It has
held down living standards, as many savers get poor returns for their money
and thus are pushed to save more. It has inhibited the development of an
efficient and transparent banking sector as well as liquid and diversified
capital markets, leaving savers with limited options and thus fostering the
expansion of shadow banking. It has also led to a paradoxical situation in
which China is a nation of savers with large indebtedness. Ultimately, it has
constrained the development of the renminbi as an international currency.
To understand why, in this chapter, I take a closer look at financial repression
and how it has operated over the course of China's spectacular growth—
notably, both creating and maintaining the link between state-owned enterprises and banks—and how it has allowed shadow banking to thrive.

LOW INTEREST RATES AND LENDING QUOTAS

Financial repression has been motivated by the need to have plenty of
cheap capital that can be used to fund projects that are important to China's economic development strategy or to dispense favor and "buy" consensus. The main organizing mechanism for financial repression in China is
interest rates, which don't function as a market mechanism to allocate savings to investments but to ensure plenty of cheap capital for state-owned
enterprises.

For years, the authorities have controlled both the maximum deposit rate (the rate that banks offer to depositors) and the minimum lending rate (the rate that banks offer to borrowers), with the deposit rate set low enough to allow banks to make a profit by squeezing depositors—in particular, because rates have lagged behind inflation. This was a change from the years before 2004, when the People's Bank of China used to adjust the nominal deposit rate to the rate of inflation.[5] Setting rates centrally has ensured that banks do not compete with each other for deposits and that they can offer very favorable lending conditions (in addition, banks do not ask for stringent guarantees against the loans). The result has been a system in which depositors have subsidized borrowers, with the former effectively transferring a large share of resources to the latter. This has been reflected in a substantial decline in the cost of borrowing—especially after 2008, when interest rates were cut in response to the global financial crisis. Between 2004 and 2011, for example, the average real cost of borrowing was pushed down to only 3.2 percent, compared to 6.2 percent between 1997 and 2003. (It is currently 2.9 percent.[6])

The pursuit of low interest rates as part of a system of financial repression has had serious consequences for the development of a market-oriented economy in China. First, for several years, China has had interest rates that were too low vis-à-vis the growth rate of its economy and fueled strong credit growth. In 2004, credit as a share of the country's gross domestic product (GDP) was approximately 140 percent; in 2014, it was 170 percent.[7] Household bank deposits expanded at a slower pace over the same period—they were approximately 75 percent of GDP in 2004 and 77 percent in 2015—but they are much higher than in other countries—both advanced economies and emerging markets.[8] This system results in the paradox of generating excessive savings even though it penalizes returns on savings. Because savers have limited options, banks can rely on a "captive" group of depositors and thus can cut the interest income that savers receive without risk of losing depositors. At the same time, because of the poor returns that they get from deposits, individuals and households tend to increase their savings in order to achieve their financial goals—for instance, to pay for a child's education or provide for comfortable retirement. So the pool of savings continues to expand—and continues to constrain household consumption growth.[9]

Low interest rates also create an abundant supply of cheap credit, leading to serious distortions in its allocation. Banks have found themselves saddled with excessive numbers of low-quality and nonperforming loans, making them vulnerable to insolvency or a liquidity crisis if the economy turns sour. To preserve their capital base, they shift the burden to savers by imposing low deposit rates—perpetuating this system.

Nobody seems to win, not even firms that borrow at extremely favorable conditions. Either because the interest rate is so low or because financial losses are covered by subsidies, these firms tend to borrow excessively, with little consideration for efficiency and profitability. Many of them end up with highly leveraged and unsustainable financial positions.

The final consequence of China's system of low interest rates and financial repression is that it builds on and maintains the link between state-owned companies and big banks. The link between these organizations is a pillar of the country's system of state ownership and a key feature of its mix of plan and market—and the state-owned enterprises themselves are embedded in China's system of economic planning.

STATE-OWNED ENTERPRISES AND THE GOVERNMENT'S ROLE IN THE ECONOMY

Mao Zedong introduced central economic planning in the mid-1950s, and in the following decades, state-owned enterprises became a crucial component of China's economic system. By 1978, state-owned enterprises accounted for 80 percent of the total industrial output, provided 70 percent of total industrial employment, controlled most industrial fixed assets, and dominated most components of the tertiary sector.[10] These firms were inefficient and lost money, acting as a constant drag on public resources and keeping in place a dual-track price system that, among other problems, created enormous incentives for corruption. (A good sold outside the plan's pricing system could fetch, for example, 50 to 100 percent more than the plan-determined price.[11]) The firms had no financial autonomy and, in fact, had to remit most of their profits to the state treasury. In return, they received state budgetary grants to finance most of their fixed investment and to meet a significant portion of their working capital needs.

Reformers looking to transform China's economy in the late 1970s faced the challenge of improving the efficiency of state firms, expanding the nonstate sector (urban collectives, private firms, and foreign-funded enter-prises), and enhancing the role of the market without, however, significantly reducing state ownership; political, social, and institutional constraints—particularly the absence of property rights—prevented a full program of privatization. Forced to preserve state ownership as a major feature of the institutional landscape, their strategy was to substantially reduce the num-ber of state-owned enterprises, curtailing the ones that were losing money and offering incentives to those that were performing well. Thus, while they were working to develop a group of giant, globally competitive firms to match those in developed countries, they were also ensuring that China's key industries and firms remained firmly under state ownership.[12]

It was only in the early 1990s that Chinese policy makers came to rec-ognize forms of ownership that did not feature the state. In 1993, the Third Plenum of the Fourteenth Chinese Communist Party Congress endorsed the creation of a modern enterprise system, paving the way for the privati-zation of small state firms and the transformation of medium and large ones into limited liability companies. This led to the elimination, the following year, of some 80,000 firms from the roster of state-owned enterprises. This shift marked the beginning of a critical transformation of China's institu-tional setup into one in which private firms were not only authorized but also allowed to compete in the marketplace on equal terms with state-owned enterprises.

The Ninth Five-Year Plan (for the period 1996–2000) took a further step that led to the expansion of private firms. In 1997—faced with the increasing importance of the private sector in expanding economic activ-ity, supporting growth, and creating new jobs—the authorities allowed banks to lend to private firms.[13] (Eventually, in 2004, the Chinese consti-tution formally recognized, and thus legitimized, private ownership as an important component of China's social market economy and one that was on an equal footing with public ownership.[14]) The next year Premier Zhu Rongji embarked on a bold effort to revitalize core state-owned enterprises, initiating a large-scale reorganization to make them more efficient and profitable.

Until then, these enterprises had been ranked at the ministry level and were under the direct leadership of the State Council. Zhu took a number of them—including Bank of China; China National Cereals, Oils, and Foodstuffs Corporation; and China Railway Engineering Corporation—out of the ministerial system. This was the first step toward formally making these firms more autonomous from the government. Many were then prepared for public listing, going through a substantial cleanup that consisted of moving viable commercial assets to what would become the publicly listed company and leaving money-losing operations in the original 100 percent state-owned company. This unlisted organization would serve as a holding company, controlling over 75 percent of the newly listed spinoff's shares, ensuring that the state remained the majority owner by a huge margin. (Even today, when state firms are listed on the stock market, the state typically retains control because only a minority of the firm's shares are sold.) By 1999, over 10,000 traditional state-owned industrial enterprises (about a fifth of the total) had become state-controlled shareholding companies in which the state was the majority or dominant shareholder. These new companies accounted for almost 40 percent of industrial output.

The way the authorities tackled privatization is paradigmatic of China's approach to the overall reform process. They open to external pressure to bring in good practice, rules and regulations, and market discipline from abroad—but do so while retaining significant state control. In this way, China's political leadership (former Premier Zhu, in particular) was able to indirectly, and almost by proxy, promote politically difficult reforms from within. Thus, "privatization" was achieved without giving up commanding state control over the economy.[15] The state's majority equity share also made it difficult for international firms to expand within China through mergers and acquisitions, as "national champions"—companies such as China Mobile, Sinopec, and Baosteel[16]—had privileged access to government-sponsored projects.[17]

Even today the governance of state-owned companies (and their private-sector spin-offs) remains firmly in the hands of the Communist Party. The Organization Department of the party appoints the top three executives (party secretary, chief executive officer, and chairman of the board) in most important state-owned enterprises,[18] and approximately 80 percent of managers at state-owned companies are appointed by the party.[19] There is also a "revolving door" that connects leadership roles in the government and in large state-owned companies. For instance, before taking up his current role, Finance Minister Lou Jiwei headed China Investment Corporation—China's sovereign wealth fund, with assets worth approximately $600 billion. Similarly, Xiao Gang served as the chairman of Bank of China Limited and Bank of China (Hong Kong) Limited for almost ten years before being appointed chairman of the China Securities Regulatory Commission in 2013 (a position he held until January 2016).

By defining the governance of state-owned enterprises and big state banks, the leadership of the Communist Party has fostered a strong link between these two groups, with both serving various policy goals. This link has been, at the same time, a cause and a consequence of the Chinese system of financial repression.

CHINA'S BANKING SECTOR

Within China's model of development, banks provide the mechanism to feed and allocate investment. Like state-owned enterprises, they are a direct legacy of the system of central economic planning but have gone through some transformation in the last thirty years.

In the late 1970s, China's banking sector was a single, monolithic financial institution that served as both the central bank and the sole commercial bank, with a network of over 15,000 branches, subbranches, and offices.[20] Things started to shift in 1983, when the State Council separated the functions of central and commercial banking. It set up the People's Bank of China (PBoC) as the central bank and established the Industrial and

Commercial Bank of China (ICBC) to handle deposit taking and lending. By the mid-1980s, these functions had expanded to four state-owned banks that controlled almost four-fifths of all deposits, accounted for 99 percent of all bank assets, and were responsible for more than 90 percent of all loans.[21]

In the early days of Deng Xiaoping's reforms, the four "specialized" banks—the ICBC as well as the Agricultural Bank of China, China Construction Bank, and Bank of China—were responsible for allocating credit within the economy. The ICBC lent mostly to state enterprises, operating as a subsidiary of the Ministry of Finance; the Agricultural Bank lent exclusively to support agriculture and rural industrial and commercial enterprises; and China Construction Bank was a principal source of funds for new investment projects. Bank of China, which until 1979 had been a subsidiary of the PBoC, carried out all types of foreign exchange transactions[22] and had branches in Hong Kong, Singapore, and London. The London branch had been established in 1929, and during the Mao years, it played a critical role in managing China's hard currency portfolio and arranging for short-term commercial credit. It also maintained correspondent relationships with many Western banks in order to settle financial aspects of trade contracts with noncommunist countries.[23] Even though China then had limited trade and commercial relations with the rest of the world—in 1974, its total trade was just 6 percent of that of the United States[24]—it still needed international banking facilities to settle trade.

Starting in the mid-1980s, a series of policy measures eased regulatory barriers, helping to open up the banking sector and create a credit channel for private business. Influenced by Deng's reformist zeal, the government began to exercise more tolerance toward private providers of capital and to envisage some degree of competition and openness in the financial sector. The idea was to use the state's financial institutions as a channel to provide funding to private entrepreneurs—to rural entrepreneurs transitioning out of agriculture and even to private entrepreneurs who were trading overseas. This was a significant break with the past and was happening, incredibly, only a few years after the end of the Cultural Revolution.[25]

Between 1980 and 1988, the Chinese financial system became increasingly flexible as the reformers directed banks and rural credit cooperatives (small, rural banks that provided loans and saving facilities to farming enterprises) to lend to the emerging private sector. The main elements of this financial liberalization were the adoption by state banks of an accommodating and supportive credit policy toward the private sector, the availability of financial instruments that were exclusively servicing the private sector, and the tacit permission for the use of these instruments. For example, in 1984, the Agricultural Bank authorized flexible interest rates for individual business owners—allowing it to adjust the costs of servicing the debt to the interest rates set by the central bank—and waived loan-guarantee requirements for those borrowers with a good credit history and a high self-funding ratio.[26] The reformers also proactively transformed a number of financial institutions by reducing state controls on rural credit cooperatives and permitting entry by private players. Through measures like these, the authorities ensured that there was plenty of credit for the rural economy in a way that was consistent with the political guidelines of China's economic transformation. Similar measures were taken in cities, where the PBoC formally authorized networks of urban credit cooperatives.

Throughout the 1990s, the authorities increased the credit offerings by expanding the number and types of banks. A dozen new national joint-stock banks (including the China Minsheng Bank, the first private shareholding bank) were created. Shareholders for these banks ranged from private firms to state-owned enterprises. Urban credit cooperatives, which in the mid-1980s lent primarily to urban collective firms, merged to form urban cooperative banks and became the principal source of formal credit for small private companies. Their lending activity expanded rapidly, with 193 billion renminbi in total credit outstanding by the end of 1995.[27]

In 1997, the Fifteenth Congress of the Chinese Communist Party unveiled measures that formally allowed banks to extend loans to the private sector, especially to small and medium-sized enterprises in fast-rising regions and urban areas. Banks were urged to base their lending decisions on the default risks and business prospects of the eligible borrowers. This spurred the creation of city commercial banks, such as the Bank of Shanghai and Bank of Beijing, which were spun out of urban cooperative banks. These banks steadily expanded, lending to private businesses that were too small for the state-owned banks.[28] By focusing on private-sector depositors—mostly individuals and nonstate enterprises—they were able to compete with the state-owned banks and their vast network of offices in almost every city. (In 1994, state-owned banks operated almost 150,000 branches, subbranches, and other offices of various types, mostly located in cities.[29])

On the whole, as the authorities developed the banking sector and removed some of the existing monopolies in the provision of credit, the approach and culture of Chinese banks also became more business friendly and more supportive of private-sector clients. In addition, the authorities increased private control of existing financial institutions and allowed private players more independence in providing financial intermediation services.

As a result, China's banking sector (along with its economy) has shifted toward a more market-oriented system. But increasing the number and types of banks has not dented the dominant position of the big four commercial banks in the country's domestic economy. They account for 44 percent of the banking system's assets.[30] This share increases to approximately 48 percent if we include the Bank of Communications, which the Chinese now identify as the fifth of the large-scale commercial banks. As Nicholas Lardy points out, this share reflects a concentration that is similar to that of the top five banks in the United States—JPMorgan Chase, Bank of America, Citigroup, Wells Fargo, and Goldman Sachs.[31]

Thus, despite some deep transformation and restructuring that has shifted China's banking sector toward a more market-oriented system,[32] the country has not yet embraced full-scale financial liberalization. Financial repression remains, in the form of lending quotas and interest-rate caps. Even the measures that were introduced in late 2006, when China had to open its banking sector to foreign competition as part of joining the World Trade Organization, did not fundamentally transform the big banks. They remained a tool to support the government's objectives rather than business entities operating on a purely commercial basis.

THE PERVASIVE LINK BETWEEN STATE BANKS
AND STATE ENTERPRISES

Through tight controls on both deposit and lending rates and through credit quotas, the monetary authorities manage the allocation of credit within the domestic economy and ensure that money moves easily from the banking system into state-owned enterprises. The consequences of this link between banks and state-owned enterprises are pernicious and now deeply entrenched.

One predictable consequence is that political connections rather than credit ratings and solid collateral play a significant role in access to bank loans. State banks often extend loans "requested" by local party and government officials to support their favorite projects. In many cases, these projects have not been approved by the central government authorities, and, thus, no central bank funds have been provided for lending. Banks therefore finance these loans from deposits taken from the public rather than from earmarked funds provided by the central bank.

Amplifying this issue is the tendency of these state-owned enterprises to borrow more than they can afford and to borrow even for day-to-day operations, often using cheap money to keep businesses afloat that otherwise would need to close. Under considerable pressure from the government to support state-owned enterprises—even the money-losing ones—banks end up saddled with extensive and growing portfolios of nonperforming loans and solvency concerns. According to Dai Xianglong, former governor of the PBoC, a full 20 percent of state banks' loans were nonperforming in 1994. That proportion increased to 25 percent in 1997 and then to 35 percent in 2000.[33] Lardy reckoned that as of 2013 the nonperforming loan share could have been as high as 25 percent of all loans outstanding, which would have placed the major banks dangerously close to insolvency.[34]

The declining quality of state-owned banks' assets as a consequence of nonperforming loans imposes a heavy tax burden, as the authorities often need to intervene and inject public funds to clean up the banks' balance sheets. Between 2003 and 2005, Central Huijin, a state-owned investment company and subsidiary of China Investment Corporation, used foreign reserves to inject almost $80 billion into the big four banks before they went public: $22.5 billion each into Bank of China and China Construction Bank, $15 billion into the ICBC, and $19 billion into the Agriculture Bank of China.

The banking sector's excessive focus on lending to state-owned enterprises also crowds out private enterprises, making it difficult for private companies and households to access financial resources. Of all bank loans outstanding, approximately 40 percent are to state-owned enterprises and 33 percent are to local governments, leaving less than one-third to private businesses and households.[35] With the banking sector thus unable to fully address their needs, many private entrepreneurs—especially in the rural areas—have shied away from banks and rely more heavily on informal finance. (I discuss this trend toward shadow banking more fully at the end of the chapter.) This has become something of a vicious circle, as neglect of nonstate enterprises has prevented banks from developing the skills necessary to assess the creditworthiness of potential borrowers. They are still figuring out how to correctly decide on loan allocation. In particular, they face the problem of acquiring reliable information on the borrowers' ability to repay the loans, as they lack details about the quality of potential borrowers[36] and do not have the credit history records to back up their loan allocation decisions.

There has been some progress in recent years toward weakening the link between state-owned enterprises and the big banks, and commercial criteria increasingly inform Chinese banks' decisions—including, for example, an assessment of a firm's profitability as a criterion in resolving whether to grant a loan and in determining loan size.[37] As a result of these changes, Chinese private firms now enjoy better access to credit than in any previous period in the reform era. However, it is still the case, even if to a lesser extent, that having some state ownership helps firms gain access to bank finance. And political connections continue to carry weight in the decision to lend to the private sector. The banking sector's bias toward state-owned companies continues to fundamentally distort the allocation of capital and to limit private firms' access to capital. This impedes competition and efficiency, slowing down China's transformation into a more market-oriented economy.

BANKS AND THE CAPITAL MARKET

For firms looking for financial resources, one obvious alternative to banks is the capital market. In China, however, the banks are pervasive even there. As a result, the domestic bond and stock markets have expanded slowly, especially in comparison with the fast growth of the country's real economy.

In the stock market, for instance, the large overhang of government-owned shares constrains the supply. Tradable shares are only about one-third of the total stock market capitalization. In addition, because the government regularly intervenes in the market to respond to political lobbying by the brokerage industry or to stabilize expectations (as in the case of the downturn in the domestic stock market in summer 2015 and then again in early 2016), the common perception is that equity pricing is easily manipulated. The size of the Shanghai Stock Exchange reflects these constraints; in terms of market capitalization, it is 45 percent of the size of China's GDP, whereas the New York Stock Exchange is 91 percent of the size of U.S. GDP.

China's bond market is similarly intertwined with the state. Although the domestic bond market has grown since 1990 (and is now, at about 30 trillion renminbi, the third largest in the world[38]), its development depends on, and is somewhat constrained by, the demand for funding, which comes mainly from the government and from government-related bodies. Because government debt is relatively small (just over 40 percent of GDP), the total stock of government bonds outstanding is only 10.7 trillion renminbi.[39] The market for corporate bonds has developed even more slowly and has remained almost exclusively the domain of state-owned and state-controlled companies. For instance, in the first half of 2015, the value of bonds issued by private nonfinancial enterprises in China's domestic bond market had reached 529 billion renminbi—only about 0.8 percent of GDP.[40] This is insignificant in comparison with the U.S. corporate bond market, which currently stands at almost $10 trillion, or about 60 percent of U.S. GDP.

As in the stock market, banks are dominant in the bond market, where they play three roles: they are the key issuers of bonds, the largest buyers of bonds, and the intermediary institutions. The Agricultural Development

Bank of China, China Development Bank, and Export-Import Bank of China were established in 1994 and are referred to as policy banks because of their role in financing economic development, trade, and state-led projects. Together with the Ministry of Finance and the PBoC, they issue about 78 percent of the bonds on the Chinese market. The policy banks do not have commercial banking functions and are not allowed to hold any private deposits. Issuing bonds is the only way for them to collect sufficient capital to provide loans.

China's largest banks—the policy banks and the four big banks—are the main investors in China's bond market. The latter, in particular, were the first banks to be authorized to operate in the interbank market, and they still benefit from their market dominance. Chinese commercial banks hold about 68 percent of the total outstanding bonds, the three policy banks combined hold about 10 percent, fund managers hold approximately 7 percent, and other market players hold approximately 14 percent. Individual investors, who have little access to the bond markets due to regulatory limitations, account for a mere 1 percent.

Finally, banks act as intermediary institutions and thus have almost complete control of the bond market itself. The interbank market is currently the major trading platform and accounts for over 90 percent of national bond issuance volume and trading volume. Only institutional investors are allowed to participate in the wholesale, quote-driven interbank bond market; for nonbanking institutions and individual investors, tight restrictions remain in place.

The authorities' intention is to develop capital markets and to ease the link between the banks and the bond market. For example, China's interbank bond market has recently opened up to foreign central banks and some foreign financial institutions. But it will take a long time for the country's capital market to reach the point of acting as a true alternative to the banking sector. The fundamental problem with developing and opening up the capital market is that this move inevitably collides with the need to preserve the current system. Although the authorities appreciate how important it is for a fast-growing economy like China's to raise capital outside the banking sector, they fear that the development of the capital market will undermine the big banks (and thus the financial sustainability of many state firms) if households begin to withdraw funds from savings accounts and significantly increase their holdings of stocks and bonds. The risk is that banks will find themselves with less liquidity.

SHADOW BANKING AND THE PARADOX OF A NATION OF SAVERS

Banks are so overwhelmingly dominant in China's economy that they hinder capital market reforms—especially the development of more robust equity and bond markets, which should contribute to better pricing of risks and improved access to financing, as highlighted by the Third Plenum in 2013 and then reiterated in the Thirteenth Five-Year Plan 2016–2020. The current system not only is hard to dismantle but also continues to support financial repression. As a result, China is a nation with high savings rates (Chinese households on average save about 41 percent of their disposable income),[41] and it is also a nation saddled with debt. The high savings rates and high indebtedness are, in fact, the two faces of the same coin and reflect, among other things, distortions in the country's banking sector that have resulted from its link with state-owned enterprises and the limited development of the country's capital markets.

The limited availability of consumer credit forces families to accumulate savings in order to finance the purchase of consumer durables. Moreover, limited public provision for health care, retirement, and other social safety nets, as well as low wages, pushes families to accumulate savings in order to be self-insured.[42] In 1978, the cumulative stock of household savings was about 21 billion renminbi, or 6 percent of GDP.[43] At the end of 2013, it was approximately 14 trillion renminbi, or about 23 percent of GDP.[44]

Families have been actively accumulating savings over the years but so have corporate enterprises. The latter have been able to accumulate high levels of financial resources mainly thanks to the low-dividend policy— or the no-dividend policy, in the case of many state-owned enterprises.

The large pool of savings that has been accumulating in the domestic banks since the early days of economic reforms has been instrumental in generating rapid economic and employment growth. But with interest rates kept artificially low, savers do not get much out of their money.

The limited offer of financial instruments other than bank deposits for savers and private firms has combined with China's rapid credit growth to fuel the rapid expansion of unregulated borrowing and lending, referred to as *shadow banking*. Banks, trust companies, insurance firms, leasing companies, and, more recently, e-commerce companies like Alibaba and Internet platforms like Tencent are all part of China's shadow banking, as are pawnbrokers and other informal lenders (including peer-to-peer lenders). Here, through questionable organizations like Shanxi Platinum Assemblage Investment, savers can get higher interest rates on so-called wealth management products than they get on bank deposits—approximately 6 percent on average, compared with 3 percent on bank deposits. Or they can put their savings directly into funds such as Yu'e Bao through Alipay—the online payment company that is part of Alibaba—or through the very popular mobile chatting app WeChat—which is run by Tencent. (With roughly 580 billion renminbi in 2015, Yu'e Bao is the largest money market fund in China and the third largest in the world.[45])

For banks outside the dominant big four, shadow banking is a way to access liquidity. Funds they raise through these wealth management schemes are then allocated to projects that do not normally qualify for loans with state banks—such as real estate, for example, which regulators deem to have grown too much.

These loans are often made off the balance sheet and therefore are outside the purview of bank regulators—hence the name shadow banking. As long as the borrower repays, everybody gains: the borrower, the bank, and the investors in the wealth management products. But if the borrower defaults on a payment to the bank, then the bank cannot pay the interest to the investors. This undermines investors' confidence, making it difficult to attract new investors with fresh capital. Without that fresh money, the bank cannot return investors' capital—shadow banking instruments tend to have a short duration, sometimes no more than three months—and the whole pyramid eventually collapses. As Xiao Gang, China's former top securities regulator, said, shadow banking is "fundamentally a Ponzi scheme."[46]

Despite sentiments like this—and a name that suggests some kind of murky business—shadow banking entities very often are part of China's main banks in organizational and managerial terms. Banks, for example, create and manage wealth management products and include them in their regular offers to their clients. Savers buy these products from their bank and redeem them through their bank, so they tend to think that the same bank guarantees these products and that they are therefore safe. But this is not the case; the ICBC recently made it clear that it would not protect investors to whom it had sold 3 billion renminbi worth of wealth management products. And yet shadow banking is a booming business, valued at $3 trillion in 2010 and twice that in 2012. In its 2014 report on China the IMF estimated the size of shadow banking as 53 percent of GDP.[47]

The PBoC has been carefully monitoring the expansion of shadow banking—in 2014, before regulators stepped in, the issuance of wealth management products amounted to almost 14 trillion renminbi, or almost 10 percent of total bank deposits.[48] At the end of 2015 4.4 trillion renminbi, or 6.5 percent of GDP, were under management in the money market fund industry in China.[49]

Because shadow banking is below the regulators' radar, authorities are concerned that legitimate banks will use lightly regulated wealth management products to repackage old loans and prop up risky companies and projects that might not otherwise be able to borrow money. To remain solvent, banks need to continue to refinance enterprises and organizations that otherwise would go bust—which could bring banks down, too.

There is reason for the authorities to worry about debt. China's total debt—including government debt as well as the debt of financial institutions, nonfinancial businesses, and households—has quadrupled since 2007[50] and is currently around 282 percent of GDP. This is in line with the debt-to-GDP ratios for G7 countries—total debt in the United States and Germany, for instance, is about 273 percent and 210 percent of GDP, respectively—but it is unprecedentedly high for a developing country.[51] That debt has also been growing at an unprecedentedly high rate—it was only 130 percent of GDP in 2008, when, in the wake of the global financial crisis, the government introduced stimulus measures (including a large infrastructure spending program). As a result, businesses and provincial governments have been piling up debt—local government debt increased from 13 percent of GDP in 2005 to the current 33 percent.

No economy in history has experienced credit growth of such speed and scale without eventually suffering a financial crisis and a protracted period of low growth. Furthermore, private credit has risen to 180 percent of GDP, approximately two-thirds of which is corporate debt—these figures are similar to what the United States and Japan experienced before their most recent financial crises. State-owned enterprises and local governments have piled up so much debt that they increasingly need to resort to shadow banking in order to get enough credit to keep going. (On the other hand, firms with good credit ratings and a solid balance sheet do not need to rely on shadow banks for credit.)

Excessive credit growth, sub-prime investments (especially in real estate), and hence the increase of nonperforming loans provide the breeding ground for a banking crisis. As was the case for both the United States and Spain in the years before the 2007–2008 crisis, easy and cheap access to lending and excessive liquidity conjure a situation in which risk is under-priced, and, thus, imbalances build up. Unlike these countries, however, China can preserve its system by maintaining financial repression—and by carefully controlling capital movements and managing the exchange rate (the subject of the next chapter). Although managing the exchange rate has fueled the domestic economy by keeping exports cheap and competitive, it has also constrained the development of the renminbi as an international currency.

4

CHINA: A TRADING NATION WITHOUT AN INTERNATIONAL CURRENCY

C HINA'S MODEL OF development, with its emphasis on cheap capital (hence domestic financial repression) and low-price exports (hence the importance of managing the exchange rate, as I will discuss later in this chapter), has driven the transformation of the real economy. But this extraordinary transformation has not been matched by a similar development on the monetary and currency front. The international use of the renminbi as a means of exchange, unit of account, and store of value—the functions that an international currency is expected to perform[1]—is restricted by its limited convertibility, which is a consequence of the country's uncompetitive banking and financial sector.

The link between a nation's economic development and its international standing has always been reflected in the world of currencies. Countries that are well integrated at the regional or global level have both well-functioning and relatively open market economies and international currencies—and among them, the largest economies have key international currencies (or reserve currencies). Although China now does have a reserve currency, the footprint of its currency is still tiny compared to its economic heft. To paraphrase Nobel laureate Robert Mundell, China is a great nation without a great currency.[2]

Before the dollar, the pound sterling (or pound, for short) was the world's key currency, widely circulated within the British Empire, and used to invoice, settle, and finance the largest proportion of world trade. Britain was the first industrial nation, the world's largest economy (accounting for about 8 percent of global gross domestic product), a powerful empire, and an international center for trade and finance. Factories in Manchester, Sheffield, and northern England needed commodities and semimanufactured goods to build engines, steamships, locomotives, and railways, and those in the increasingly prosperous and expanding middle class were enthusiastic consumers of sugar, tea, coffee, spices, silver, and silk. Between 1860 and 1914, Britain absorbed more than 20 percent of exports from the rest of the world.

As it was the main international trading and reserve currency, the pound became the pillar of the gold standard, with the currency's value anchored to its convertibility into gold. This was a way to preserve the pound's value for individuals and companies that did not live and operate in Britain but that held pounds for trade and investment. Britain adopted the gold standard early, in 1821; the rest of the world was divided between a monometallic (silver) system (embraced notably by the German states) and a bimetallic system (adopted by the United States and France, among others). Great Britain's dominance in trade influenced other economies that felt the need to harmonize their monetary systems with that of the dominant economy; the newly unified Germany switched to the gold standard in the 1870s.

Most of this trade was handled in London, and this fostered the development of banking and financial activities with the pound as the key currency within the system of international payments. Britain also exported financial capital to the rest of the world. The country's foreign investment began to grow vigorously in the 1880s, with a distinct preference for the two Americas. The rest was shared more or less equally among Europe, Asia, Africa, and Australasia. By 1913, Britain was by far the largest exporter of capital, with a total of 9 billion pounds, and was ahead of France, Germany, and the Netherlands.

Until the outbreak of World War I, when its convertibility was suspended, the pound "bestrode the financial world like a colossus."[3] It kept Great Britain at the center of the world's economy and finance well into the twentieth century, even though the British economy had been overtaken in terms of total national income by the United States by 1870 and in terms of industrial power by the United States around 1880 and by Germany around 1905. Even in 1947, pounds still accounted for about 87 percent of global foreign exchange reserves. It took ten years after the end of World War II (and a 30 percent devaluation) before the share of dollars held in official reserves exceeded that of pounds. By the early 1970s, most pegs to the pound were replaced by pegs to the dollar or to trade-weighted baskets, and the pound's commercial role declined rapidly relative to the dollar during the oil crisis. As Catherine Schenk argues in *The Decline of Sterling*, rising international liquidity, inflation, geographical redistribution, and international cooperation were the cornerstones that eased the retreat of the pound from global to national status.[4]

The intertwined development of Britain and its pound, and then of the United States and its dollar (as discussed in chapter 1), emphasizes the anomaly of China's development. Like Britain in the nineteenth century and the United States in the twentieth, China is now the world's largest trading nation and a powerful country in geopolitical terms. But unlike Britain and the United States, it does not have a currency that reflects and complements its rise to the status of international power. In today's multipolar world economy, in which the relative weight of the United States has decreased while that of China and other developing countries has increased, China's lack of an international currency is as incongruous as the United States' monetary hegemony is anomalous.

In this chapter and the next I delve into the paradox of a great nation without a great currency. I maintain that the current state is a consequence of financial repression and the related policies that promote China's model of development—including the management of the exchange rate to promote economic growth and full employment and the continuation of controls on capital movements. The exchange rate is now a crucial part of China's growth model. The policy of managing the exchange rate has served China well and indeed has been instrumental in the transformation of the Chinese economy. However, it has also cemented the renminbi's status as a dwarf currency. As I discuss below, China has now reached a point in its economic development when managing the exchange rate and accumulating foreign exchange reserves have become too costly to continue.

TRADE AND THE EXCHANGE RATE: DISMANTLING
THE AIRLOCK SYSTEM

International trade needs international money, or domestic money that can be converted into international money, to price and settle transactions. At the onset of its reforms, China had neither. In those years, a system of foreign trade planning dictated the price and volume of goods (mainly producer goods) that foreign trade corporations could purchase, in line with the needs of domestic producers, as specified in the plan. Prices were also centrally fixed for producers, who received the same price for a good regardless of whether it was sold domestically or internationally. Market signals were therefore suppressed, and there was no incentive to produce more for the international market when, for instance, demand was stronger.[5] The World Bank defined China's trade regime in the years before 1978 as an "airlock system" because the separation of domestic prices from international prices kept the former stable vis-à-vis the latter.[6]

This separation was particularly targeted at imports' prices, ensuring that the prices of domestically manufactured goods matched those of imported manufactured goods in order to protect China's domestic industries—in particular, the machinery industry. The import pricing policies supported the resulting trade regime, which was fundamentally oriented toward replacing imported goods with domestically produced goods (import substitution).[7] Imported producer goods, that were essential to manufacturing final goods for the domestic market, were about 90 percent of China's total imports and were made available to domestic producers at relatively low prices. This practice made the foreign price of most imports irrelevant to the domestic end-user. The tightly planned system meant that there was little opportunity for the price of foreign exchange to influence the volume of either imports or exports.

In order to keep import prices low, the central government set the renminbi's official exchange rate artificially high—and kept it there. In 1955, the renminbi's exchange rate was fixed at 2.46 per dollar and remained virtually unchanged for almost two decades—but on the black market, rates were twice as much.[8] The artificial overvaluation of the renminbi created excess demand for foreign exchange that could then be exchanged at a better rate on the black market—a sort of arbitrage between the black market and the official one. Therefore, this demand needed to be managed through a rigid and highly centralized system of exchange controls. These controls, in turn, constrained China's transactions and interactions with the rest of the world, as firms could not easily get foreign money to pay for imports or exchange into renminbi the foreign money that they had earned from exports.

This system was incompatible with Deng Xiaoping's strategy of trade liberalization. When he came to power, exports were money losers in domestic-currency terms, with 70 percent accruing financial losses. As the Chinese economy was increasingly relying on imports (such as commodities and semimanufactured goods) as part of its supply chain, the state could no longer feasibly hang onto its traditional mechanism for currency control. To finance imports to feed its expanding manufacturing sector, China needed to grow exports quickly and thus generate foreign exchange.

Extensive domestic price reforms—and, in particular, the reform of the official exchange rate—were necessary. The first step was to reduce the value of the renminbi to a level that would not undermine the competitiveness of Chinese exports. In 1981, the value of the renminbi was reduced almost by half, but subsequent devaluations over the next fifteen years were much smaller. The slow pace of devaluation was dictated not only by economic considerations (the monetary authorities feared that devaluation would contribute to domestic price inflation) but also by the need to overcome political hostility, especially from the central bank, the State Bureau of Commodity Prices, and the State Planning Commission.[9] In those years, when China's economic model was based on producing what was needed domestically, the exchange rate needed to be strong in order to keep the prices of commodities and other imports low enough for domestic manufacturing. The devaluation shifted the focus from import prices to export prices—buttressing Deng's model of development and establishing the principle that the official exchange rate should cover the cost of earning foreign exchange.[10]

To facilitate demand for and supply of foreign exchange, in 1986, Chinese authorities decided to establish foreign exchange adjustment centers, or "swap centers," in major cities. These centers mediated the exchange of foreign currencies between Chinese firms with an excess supply of these currencies and those with an excess demand for them—at whatever rates these parties found acceptable. This policy marked a very significant step toward establishing a market mechanism to allocate foreign exchange. In subsequent years, these centers were made more accessible and were established in more cities. They proved critical to developing the idea of trading at market rates and to establishing swap markets where Chinese and foreign businesses could trade renminbi for dollars, and vice versa.[11] In other words, within these centers, the Chinese authorities created an embryonic foreign exchange market where firms could trade with each other.

Another devaluation of the renminbi against all foreign currencies—this time by 15.8 percent—was announced in July 1986. Other devaluations followed, with the rate moving from 5.2 per dollar in November 1990 to 8.7 per dollar in April 1994. The exchange rate then stayed steady at around 8.2 renminbi per dollar until July 2005. This was the value of the renminbi when China joined the World Trade Organization (WTO). The stable and predictable exchange rate was a boon to firms involved in foreign trade and especially to exporters, as Chinese exports had become relatively cheap in dollar terms.

PEGGING THE RENMINBI AND MANAGING THE EXCHANGE RATE

Dismantling the airlock system and devaluing the renminbi was a step in the right direction; the next step was to switch to a more flexible system of market-based currency management. For this the Chinese turned to currency pegging.

Central banks and monetary authorities use currency pegging in order to control volatility and to provide a nominal anchor for national price levels. Developing countries and emerging-market economies peg their currencies to an international currency (normally the dollar) to "import" price stability and give credibility to currencies that otherwise would be less credible in their own right. In particular, through pegging, countries reduce the

de facto subsidy to its exports and therefore created an unfair advantage for China, in breach of the WTO rules. In 2006–2007, Senator Charles Schumer, backed by Senator Lindsey Graham, put forward in Congress a proposal to impose "a rate of duty of 27.5 percent ad valorem on any article that is the growth, product or manufacture, of the People's Republic of China, imported directly or indirectly into the US" unless the president of the United States certified that China had ceased manipulating its currency "for purposes of preventing an effective balance of payments and gaining an unfair competitive advantage in international trade."[18] And in 2007, when the International Monetary Fund (IMF) member states were working on new rules for the surveillance of countries' currencies, the U.S. Treasury Department made it clear that it was eager to see the renminbi designated as "fundamentally misaligned."[19]

After a year of back-and-forth, in the summer of 2008 the IMF prepared an Article IV report on China that included an accusation that its currency was largely undervalued. However, Lehman Brothers collapsed just a few weeks before the final report was due to come out, the report was never released, and the issue of the Chinese currency fell off the U.S. agenda.[20] In the meantime, the global financial crisis forced Beijing to suspend the peg of the renminbi to a basket of currencies and switch back to pegging to the dollar in order to enhance the stability of its currency and minimize the impact of the crisis. This change inevitably triggered new skirmishes with the U.S. Congress, especially as focus finally began to shift away from the crisis. In June 2010,[21] as pressure from Congress was mounting, China's monetary authorities switched back to a "managed floating exchange rate regime based on market supply and demand with reference to a basket of currencies" and once again pegged the renminbi to a basket of currencies. The Chinese authorities chose to "reform the exchange rate," as they described this measure, a few days before the G20 summit in Toronto. Even if they hinted that the timing was coincidental and they did not feel "any difference in the pressure on the currency issue from the group of G20 nations,"[22] the move nonetheless defused a potential confrontation with the United States on the matter of the exchange rate as part of the G20 discussion.

Concerns about the manipulation of the exchange rate resurfaced in 2014, when the PBoC widened the trading band and allowed the renminbi to move by 2 percent, up or down, around the exchange rate. The Chinese monetary authorities began to daily fix the value of the renminbi against the dollar, and by enlarging the trading band, they allowed the renminbi more flexibility for appreciation or depreciation. However, the move was not received well in the United States.

In the weeks following this policy measure, the renminbi weakened by almost 1.5 percent against the dollar, and worries that Beijing was manipulating its currency once again surfaced. Officials in the U.S. Treasury Department expressed concern that the "reform" signaled a change in China's policy—moving away from arrangements that had become to resemble those of a market-determined exchange rate.[23] The department's 2014 report to Congress singled out the renminbi as "significantly undervalued." It also stressed the need for sustained progress toward a market-determined exchange rate, adding that "this includes refraining from intervention within the band and adjusting the reference rate if market pressures push the exchange rate to the edge of the band."[24] As before, Congress focused on the drop in the renminbi's value in the weeks immediately after the implementation of the policy change, without considering that the value of the renminbi was trending upward.

Beijing's frequent interventions in the currency markets remain a bone of contention with the United States. However, in fact, the introduction of the trading band was a significant step toward making the renminbi exchange rate more flexible and therefore more able to reflect market demand.

The composition of the currency basket to which China pegs its exchange rate is not officially disclosed; neither is the weight of each currency in the basket. It is likely that the basket reflects the composition of the country's trade, allowing it to achieve some stability around the exchange rate with the currencies of its main trading partners. Because the United States is one of China's main trading partners and the dollar is the most used currency in international trade, the greenback is likely the dominant currency in this basket. In December 2015, after the inclusion of the renminbi in the group of currencies that compose the Special Drawing Right basket, the PBoC felt the urgency to explain in more detail how the system worked, stressing that the exchange rate is not automatically adjusted in line with the currencies in the basket. It also noted that some market participants, "for simplicity," had been focusing on the bilateral renminbi/U.S. dollar exchange rate rather than on the basket. "Going forward, it is plausible for all market participants to shift their focus from the bilateral RMB/USD exchange rate to referring more to a basket of currencies. This adjustment process, of course, takes some time."[25] Although this long explanation reassured market participants about the PBoC's willingness to maintain and even improve exchange rate flexibility, it did not seem to add much to what was already known or give further information about the composition of the basket.

Keeping the exchange rate stable and anchored to a basket of currencies—notably, to the dollar—has for years been a pillar of the Chinese leadership's economic strategy, and this strategy has been consistent with the goal of expanding the country's trade—exchange rate stability is valuable to both exporters and importers. But as the economy keeps expanding and foreign money rolls in, the demand for renminbi has gone up, especially in the two to three years before and after the global financial crisis. Indeed, when economic activities expand, the demand for the currency issued by the expanding economy also increases as more jobs are created, investments build, and consumption grows: money is needed to grease the economy wheel. Foreign investors like to get in on the growing economy, and foreign consumers fuel the demand for goods produced in the growing country. As a result, the currency tends to appreciate.

To avoid exchange rate volatility and excessive appreciation, which would make China's exports more expensive, the monetary authorities have been forced to intervene in the currency markets and buy or sell dollars in a large enough quantity to shift the dollar price of the renminbi. Because the increase in the supply of renminbi threatens price inflation or bubbles in the prices of such assets as real estate properties, the central bank needs to mop up the excess of domestic monetary liquidity that comes from foreign exchange interventions. This practice, commonly called *sterilization*, will be described in more detail in the next chapter. Other methods the PBoC has used to control monetary expansion include increasing the reserve requirement for large domestic banks—the required reserve ratio was increased to 17 percent of a bank's capital in March 2016.[26] Measures like these have allowed the Chinese authorities to control and moderate the renminbi exchange rate, which appreciated about 3 percent a year between 2005 and 2007 and 5 percent in 2008. From 2009 to the end of 2013, the renminbi appreciated by slightly more than 10 percent. (By the same token, it has helped to manage the currency weakness throughout 2015 and 2016.)

A CURRENCY WITH RESTRICTED CONVERTIBILITY

China has other tools for managing the exchange rate beyond pegging and market intervention—notably, restrictions on its capital account. Before explaining how these restrictions help to control the exchange rate, I will describe what the capital account is and how it differs from the current account.

Money moves in and out of a country as a result of trade transactions and investments—for example, a country with a trade surplus (like China) gets currency inflows. The current account registers these currency inflows and outflows that result, for example, from trade transactions, such as payments for the import and export of goods and services; an open current account means that there are no restrictions on capital movements that arise from these transactions. Similarly, the capital account registers currency inflows and outflows that result from foreigners investing (or disinvesting) in the country and residents investing (or disinvesting) abroad; a country's capital account is considered fully open when money moves in and out of a country in order to invest in financial assets.

Whereas China's current account has been fully open since the early 2000s, as a result of the reforms that followed the country's entrance into the WTO, its capital account is restricted. For the Chinese authorities, controlling capital movements is another way to maintain a stable exchange rate and also to ensure financial stability by avoiding sudden shifts in the demand for renminbi. For example, in the years after the global financial crisis—when interest rates in the United States were zero and the dollar was weak, whereas the Chinese economy was very robust—foreign investors would have largely turned to China if capital movements into (and out of) the country had not been restricted. This would have put pressure on the exchange rate, pushing up the value of the renminbi.

Furthermore, unrestricted capital movements would pose a problem for a country like China that has high savings rates but is financially repressed. As discussed in chapter 3, these high savings rates result in a high demand for financial and non-financial assets, but financial repression limits investment opportunities as well as investment returns. In order to avoid destabilizing capital movements, the authorities restrict the amount of money that people can move into and out of the country.

Finally, the policy of restricting capital movements reflects concerns about the vulnerability of the renminbi to external shocks if the currency is held by nonresidents. For example, if a change in external conditions—say, a significant increase in the interest rates in the United States and a stronger dollar—induces foreign investors to dump renminbi-denominated assets for dollar-denominated assets, this could trigger domestic financial instability through a stock market crash or a bank run.

However, although China does have restrictions on the capital account, it is important to bear in mind that the account is not closed—as it had been before 1979. Money can move into and out of the country, but the modalities of these inflows and outflows and, more importantly, how much money is allowed in and out are set by the authorities. They use administrative controls and regulations to manage capital inflows and outflows for both Chinese and foreign parties.

How are these capital movements controlled? Chinese firms are allowed to hold or sell foreign currencies—but only through authorized financial institutions and only with approval from the relevant authorities: the Ministry of Commerce, the National Development Reform Council (NDRC), and the State Administration of Foreign Exchange (SAFE). In addition, if these firms plan to use foreign exchange to invest abroad, they need to get the authorities' permission through a time-consuming process that often involves different government departments; for example, overseas investments that exceed $100 million need to be approved by the NDRC, whereas amounts below this need the approval of the provincial Development and Reform Committee.[27] Individuals also face restrictions. For instance, they cannot exchange renminbi in an amount worth more than $50,000 for other currencies annually. (That many wealthy Chinese have become big buyers of overseas real estate indicates the existence of alternative channels—such as unofficial money changers or fake trade invoicing—through which renminbi can be moved abroad.)

The procedures are even more complicated for non-Chinese companies that want to acquire renminbi-denominated assets or exchange profits or payments in renminbi for other currencies. In addition to SAFE approval, foreign companies need to satisfy a number of conditions: all taxes must be fully paid, all losses from the previous financial years must be repaid, and the transactions must be conducted or guaranteed by a qualified bank.[28] In addition, foreigners—companies and individuals—cannot invest in stocks, bonds, and other financial assets in China. A non-Chinese national who lives in China is likely to encounter obstacles and restrictions when opening a bank account—unlike, for example, a non-American national who resides in the United States. All these restrictions make the renminbi a currency with restricted convertibility and thus with limited circulation outside China.

As with many other aspects of the Chinese economy, recent steps have made it easier for both Chinese and foreign businesses to move capital into and out of the country (although individuals' capital movements remain considerably restricted). These steps have focused on gradually unrestricting long-term direct capital inflows—that is, money that moves into China and goes into long-term capital investment, such as, for instance, foreign direct investment—under the assumption that this type of investment tends to be less volatile and less driven by speculative motivations than are short-term indirect flows, such as bonds and stocks. The opening has been sequenced to start with inflows, direct investment, long-term bonds, and institutional investors.[29]

In particular, arrangements like QDII (for qualified domestic institutional investors) and QFII (for qualified foreign institutional investors), introduced in 2006, have created a small channel for inflows and outflows. QDII allows domestic financial institutions, such as asset managers, to invest in stocks and fixed-income and money market assets overseas and to sell mutual funds that include overseas stocks and bonds to local investors.[30] QFII, in turn, allows foreign investors to buy and sell renminbi-denominated "A" shares that trade on the onshore stock exchanges. These programs were devised in response to growing pressure from external imbalances and fast-growing foreign exchange reserves and to the strong growth of the domestic equity market—although they were suspended in 2008, during the height of the global financial crisis. In July 2015, the China Securities Regulatory Commission increased the QFII quota from $80 billion to $150 billion.

The process of opening China's capital account is a work in progress, and so far it has moved much more slowly than the opening of the current account. Using the IMF definition of categories of capital controls, Chinese economists Haihong Gao and Yongding Yu have shown that half of the cross-border capital transactions (under the capital account) are available for nonresidents and residents and half are subject to controls.[31] The former has increased to about three-quarters in recent years,[32] and in 2015, PBoC governor Zhou Xiaochuan indicated that thirty-five out of forty items are fully or partially convertible.[33] However, the transactions that are the most relevant for capital movement either remain restricted or are subject to cumbersome procedures and permissions. The monetary authorities thus continue to rely on capital controls to shelter the most vulnerable domestic sectors from external shocks. Through market intervention, they rein in excessive liquidity and harness large capital inflows that cannot be absorbed by the market, given the limited diversification of the domestic financial sector. As a result of these controls on capital movements, the renminbi is a nonconvertible currency, and this restricts its liquidity and its ability to function as an international currency.

5

LIVING WITH A DWARF CURRENCY

THE RENMINBI ISN'T yet a full-fledged international currency. As we know from chapter 1, such currencies must be attractive to foreigners for use as a means of exchange and a unit of account to price and settle trade transactions; they must also be attractive to individuals, businesses, and governments around the world to hold as a store of value. The dollar is international money par excellence.

During a recent trip to Zambia, my guide gave me the following ranking of currencies accepted by local traders: first, the dollar, which is recognized and accepted everywhere, even in the most remote villages; second, the euro, used in larger towns and areas with significant tourism from Europe; third comes the British pound, which still trades on Britain's colonial past and is mostly recognized by the older generation; and last on the list, the South African rand and the kwacha, the local currency. China is an important trade and investment partner for Zambia—exports to China are approximately 5 percent of Zambia's gross domestic product (GDP), and Chinese direct investment is 7 percent of GDP. However, the renminbi didn't appear in my guide's ranking of "good money." He described it simply as a problem of demand and market infrastructure: there was no demand for renminbi, and it was not easy to exchange renminbi for currencies on the "good money" list. Hence, nobody was happy to accept them.

This anecdote epitomizes the renminbi's lack of international status. It has limited international circulation, inadequate liquidity, and restricted payment facilities. Non-Chinese are not eager to use it as a means of exchange because of its limited demand, limited network of users, and limited liquidity. Who wants to risk being stuck with a currency no one will take?

Having a dwarf currency carries some costs for China. For years, the Chinese authorities have been aware of those costs—in particular, those that are connected to the large accumulation of dollars. But until very recently, those costs were offset by the benefits reaped from capital control and exchange rate management: quickly growing exports and expanding domestic investment, which, in turn, allowed the Chinese economy to grow at double-digit rates for several years. But since the global financial crisis and the slowdown in the pace of economic growth, the downsides of these policies have become apparent. As the country enters a new phase of its development, does it still make sense to control domestic liquidity and the exchange rate? Answering this question requires a closer look at the costs that the constrained convertibility of the renminbi and its limited international use pose to China and the benefits that international use could bring. Chapters 6 and 7 will then explore the country's renminbi strategy and look at the short-term remedies that the authorities have put together to mitigate the situation while they plan a more extensive and more complex set of reforms.

THE COSTS OF DOING BUSINESS IN DOLLARS

Because China's currency cannot be easily used internationally, the dollar remains the cornerstone of its trade and financial relations. There are significant costs that go along with this. For example, exporters face the challenge of minimizing the differential between the price quoted in dollars and that quoted in renminbi, which they use to pay local costs such as wages, rents, interests on loans, and utilities. When local costs are on the rise, as they have been in the last decade—average domestic inflation has been 3.6 percent a year since 2005, and urban wages tripled between 2005 and 2014[1]—and the value of the dollar is falling, companies that receive dollars for their goods need to be careful not to undercut themselves. A company that used to get 8.2 renminbi for every dollar's worth of exports in 2005 now gets only 6.5 renminbi. For the top 100 Chinese trade enterprises, with an average export volume of $2.3 billion in 2005, this means a potential aggregate loss of about 4 billion renminbi because of the exchange rate.

Another problem firms face is that liabilities (for example, foreign direct investment held by foreigners) are denominated in renminbi, whereas claims on foreigners (i.e., official reserves) are denominated in the major reserve currencies—in particular, the dollar.[2] The People's Bank of China (PBoC), for instance, has assets worth approximately $9 trillion and renminbi liabilities worth approximately $9 trillion. When the dollar weakens against the renminbi, the bank faces a loss, as its liabilities increase in dollar terms but the claims remain the same.[3] For instance, an American firm that invested $1 million and exchanged it into 8.2 million renminbi before 2005 would make a profit of $200,000 from the appreciation of the exchange rate alone if it exchanged the renminbi back into dollars. The gain for the U.S. company is, however, a loss for China. In fact, if we used China's foreign reserve holdings in July 2005 and calculated the value in renminbi, the theoretical loss in January 2014.—at the peak of the renminbi strength—would amount to approximately 1.7 billion renminbi.

Scarcity of dollars to settle international trade is another problem that China can face. The liquidity of this key international currency is indeed critical for international trade—especially for a trading nation like China. During the global financial crisis, the central banks of the major economies were facing a severe shortage of dollars and collectively adopted unprecedented policy measures to ease the liquidity crunch.[4] In the months after the September 2008 collapse of Lehman Brothers, China's trade dropped by approximately 14 percent compared with the same period in the previous year. This contraction mainly reflected the drop in demand in the country's main export markets—notably, the United States and Europe—but it also indicated the difficulties that scarce dollars (because of the bottlenecks in the U.S. banking system) had created in international trade. Such limited liquidity means that exporters cannot easily transform cash letters of credit or bank guarantees into dollars. Not surprisingly, in March 2009, PBoC Governor Zhou Xiaochuan argued for a breakup of the dollar-dominated monetary system and suggested switching to a supranational currency: "A super-sovereign reserve currency managed by a global institution could be used to both create and control the global liquidity."[5] Or, without embarking on a major and complex overhaul of the international monetary system, would a multi-currency international monetary system that revolves around three or four key currencies that could be extensively used in international transactions be a solution to reduce the risk and the impact of liquidity crises?

THE RENMINBI AS AN IMMATURE CURRENCY

Countries, like China, that have a surplus from exports and foreign direct investment offset this excess by investing abroad (through both financial and direct investment). This was the case in Britain in the nineteenth century, when private companies as well as the British state invested pounds all over the world, and is the case in contemporary Germany, which lends heavily to other countries in the euro area (especially the southern ones). Economists Ronald McKinnon and Gunther Schnabl term these "mature" creditors, defined as such because they lend in their own currencies. When a mature creditor denominates capital outflows and the resulting claims on foreigners in its country's currency, debts need to be repaid in that currency, and the creditor avoids the exchange rate risk. [6]

Although China has a significant trade surplus, the limited convertibility of the renminbi means that its use in China's international lending is likewise limited and its external claims are in dollars. Over the years, China has had to offset its trade surpluses by building up liquid dollar claims on foreigners (money or financial assets denominated in dollars, mainly in the form of official exchange reserves) and increasingly by making illiquid foreign direct investment (overseas investments that are used, for example, to build factories, plants, and other physical infrastructure but also that are linked with the receiving country's government-sponsored aid programs and are largely under that government's control). This style of lending is typical of immature creditors and makes China one of them.

These lending patterns reflect the intrinsic restrictions—and self-imposed constraints—of the renminbi. Limits on the capital account and the risk of exchange rate mismatches mean that only the central bank is able to invest in foreign financial assets and take the risk of building up dollar claims on foreigners and of accumulating U.S. Treasury bonds. Even if Chinese commercial banks were allowed to invest abroad freely, they would have to face the risk of a currency mismatch between their deposit base in renminbi and the claims on foreigners in dollars or other foreign exchanges.[7]

There are significant costs that arise from having an immature currency—and significant benefits from having a mature one. First of all, many countries—especially developing ones—with immature currencies are affected by the "original sin" of not being able to borrow abroad in their currency. They can borrow only in hard currencies, such as the dollar, as potential creditors are not prepared to accept the exchange rate risk as well as the default risk (or, if they are, they require a high premium for it).[8] Unlike countries with full-fledged international mature currencies that are able to borrow in their own currency, those with immature currencies experience a currency mismatch between revenues generated in the domestic currency and liabilities denominated in the international currency—as, for example, when a domestic project produces revenues in renminbi but is financed internationally in dollars. This puts a further burden on countries with immature currencies in terms of the costs for the loan if the domestic currency depreciates because the risk of default increases.

Second, countries with immature currencies find it difficult to diversify away from domestic credit risk if they cannot take on foreign currency risk. This is particularly problematic for pension funds and insurance companies with long-term liabilities. In the case of a mature creditor, foreign firms and sovereigns can issue securities that are denominated in the creditor country's currency. This helps the mature creditor's financial providers to diversify their risk. For example, a U.S. pension fund can decide to invest in dollar-denominated bonds issued by a large manufacturing company based in France. In this case, the investor has access to a foreign market without, however, taking on the exchange rate risk, as interest is paid in dollars.

Third, countries with mature currencies can reduce their aggregate exchange rate risk by denominating more of their official claims on the rest of the world in their own currencies, but countries with immature currencies do not have this option. As China is expanding its aid operations in Asia, Africa, and Latin America, it continues to take on this risk—especially because, as discussed in chapter 2, China's debtors include countries with poor economic and political governance. As I have discussed in chapter 2, Venezuela, for example, despite its large reserves of oil, has been struggling for years to keep its economy on track. Even if supporting Venezuela entails considerable risk, China remains committed to continue to provide loans and grants to this Latin America country.[9] But prolonged low oil prices expose China to a considerable risk of late payments or even default, in addition to the exchange rate risk. A loan denominated in renminbi, by removing the exchange rate risk, would considerably mitigate China's risk vis-à-vis Venezuela (and other borrowers in similar conditions)—in other words, China would face the risk of its debtor defaulting but not the additional risk of seeing the value of its credit drop in terms of renminbi.

THE COST OF ABSORBING THE TRADE SURPLUS

In addition to problems that stem from China's status as an immature creditor, there are some further costs that arise from its policies of managing the exchange rate and retaining control of capital flows. We have seen already in chapter 4 how these two policies are related: given the country's trade surplus, capital controls are necessary to avoid an appreciation of the renminbi, as non-Chinese would be eager to invest in the country because of the strength of its economy. In addition, this trade surplus (the current account, it is worth repeating, is fully liberalized, which means that foreign exchange gets into the domestic market through exports and imports and is converted into renminbi, and vice versa) needs to be absorbed in order to keep the exchange rate consistent with the economic objectives set by the Chinese leadership.

How does foreign exchange intervention work? The PBoC holds the dollars that are earned through trade in its foreign exchange reserves and gives the exporters renminbi in return. This equates to injecting renminbi liquidity into the banking system, which, in turn, feeds domestic demand and puts upward pressure on consumer prices and asset prices (this could ultimately lead to the creation of asset bubbles because of the limited diversification of China's capital markets, as discussed in chapter 3). To avoid undesired effects on prices and dampen domestic credit expansion, the monetary authorities then need to mop up, or sterilize, excess liquidity by, for example, selling financial securities (notably, bonds) to the commercial banks and/or by imposing high reserve requirements upon banks. (The opposite dynamics work in case the central bank intervenes to support the currency's value.)

Over the years, through foreign exchange intervention, China's monetary authorities have managed to keep a cap on the external value of the currency and thus have avoided excessive appreciation of the exchange rate, which could undermine the country's competitiveness, harm exports, and hence slow down economic growth, domestic development, and job creation. From 1999 to 2005, the PBoC bought nearly all the incoming foreign currencies, invested them, and then sterilized them to lessen the monetary impact on the domestic market by issuing local currency bills to take the funds—mainly dollars—out of circulation. Around 90 percent of China's accumulation of reserves has resulted from the joint process of foreign exchange intervention and sterilization.

Sterilization, however, carries significant costs. First, it does not have a selective impact. Sterilization measures tend to affect the whole economy rather than only those sectors that are cash rich—such as, for example, manufacturing, which benefits from strong exports. They are therefore the equivalent of a monetary policy tightening, which makes borrowing more expensive as interest rates go up and tends to slow down economic growth.

A related problem is that, given the differential between domestic inter-est rates and those on dollar-denominated assets (which I'll discuss fur-ther below), the monetary authorities might be reluctant to increase interest rates and further widen the spread—even when overheating and inflation-ary pressures would recommend such a measure.[10]

Sterilization also leads to the accumulation of foreign reserves as the associated tightening of monetary policy attracts foreign capital inflows. In the case of China, the PBoC has absorbed foreign capital inflows for years, and the official reserves have grown much faster than the coun-try's economy. Its official reserves ballooned from $2.4 trillion in January 2010 to almost $4 trillion in September 2014; they are now approximately $3.2 trillion. This is well above those of Japan (about $1.3 trillion), Switzer-land ($650 billion), and Saudi Arabia (almost $600 billion), the countries with the second-, third-, and fourth-largest reserve holdings.

There is nothing inherently wrong with holding foreign exchange reserves—countries (usually developing countries) with limited capital markets accumulate reserves as a way to cope with payments for imports in case of a sudden dearth of international currencies or as protection against currency crises. Foreign reserves can also be deployed to stabilize the exchange rate. This is what the PBoC did in August 2015 and then again in January 2016 to avoid the rapid depreciation of the renminbi against the dollar; as a result, official reserve holdings shrank by $700 billion from their peak in September 2014. In other cases, such as Thailand around the time of the Asian financial crisis in 1997, intervention was less successful. In fact, when the Thai bath came under a massive speculative attack in spring 1997, more than 90 percent of Thailand's foreign reserves were used to defend the value of the currency—but to no avail. The bath lost more than 50 percent of its value, and the country eventually had to switch to a flexible exchange rate regime in July 1997.[11]

Although there is a case for holding large reserves for market intervention—and even to fend off speculative attacks—the accumulation of official reserves in China is now well above the level considered necessary for precautionary reasons. The benchmark widely used by central banks is to hold reserves commensurate with their countries' total stock of outstanding short-term debt. China's total stock of outstanding short-term debt currently amounts to $500 billion. By this measure, foreign exchange reserves are well off the mark, at about seven times higher than normal practice. An alternative measure suggests that a country should retain the equivalent of three to four months' worth of imports in its official foreign exchange reserves. This amount is deemed adequate to provide protection in case of a sudden large drop in liquidity. For China, this equivalent is approximately $600 billion. Once again, the current reserves look to be far too high.

Unnecessarily high foreign exchange reserves, when coupled with sterilization policies, can distort the economy as a whole. For instance, commercial banks may need to reduce the quantity of funds available to lend if they are required to increase the reserve ratio and to buy sterilization bills. Investments that are critical for economic growth over the long run may be crowded out.

CHINA'S DOLLAR TRAP

Having foreign exchange reserves so far above the amount that is deemed necessary for precautionary reasons suggests that China has reached the point where its currency arrangements are inefficient and a waste of resources. Influential Chinese economists—notably, Yongding Yu, a former member of the PBoC's monetary policy committee—have argued that this reserve accumulation (especially the excessive accumulation of dollars) has a significant adverse impact on China because it increases the country's already significant dollar holding, generates speculation and potential instability in the domestic financial sector, and subtracts capital from productive investment.

Even though China has not disclosed the composition of its official reserves—and treated this information as a state secret until September 2015, when China agreed with the International Monetary Fund that it would begin to disclose its reserves' composition—it is reasonable to assume, based on the composition of China's trade, that they are held mostly in dollars and in U.S. Treasury bills.[12] Among the costs associated with holding massive dollar reserves are the potential losses that arise from the appreciation of the exchange rate. The losses resulting from a weaker dollar (or a stronger renminbi) became evident in the years after the global financial crisis. The Bank for International Settlements in December 2010 estimated that China's potential losses on the official reserves—at the time only $2.7 trillion—would approximate 1.8 trillion renminbi in case of a 10 percent appreciation of the renminbi.[13] This meant that if the renminbi had strengthened, the country would have seen a reduction in the value of its dollar reserves—a reduction in the "wealth of the nation." Of course, the value of a currency can go down as well as up, and the renminbi, in fact, has been on the downward trend since late 2014, after a strong appreciation between 2010 and 2014. Large foreign exchange reserves tend to magnify these movements and the exchange rate risk.

There are also considerable costs that arise from holding dollars and dollar-denominated assets, especially after 2008, as the monetary policies of the United States and China took opposite paths. The United States needed very low interest rates to stimulate the growth of the domestic economy. China, on the other hand, needed a more restrictive monetary policy to contain inflation and cool off excessive demand in some markets—in particular, the real estate market. As a result, the return on the U.S. Treasury bills held in China's reserves was suddenly lower than the return that could be earned on domestic bonds. Thus, the PBoC ended up paying more on bonds that were issued to absorb dollar inflows than it made from holding dollar-denominated assets. In 2010, for example, China's loss on sterilization was estimated at about $40 billion.[14] Compare this with the profit of about $60 billion that the country used to make annually on its sterilization operations in the years before the financial crisis, when the difference in interest rates worked in its favor. In August 2014, the one-year U.S. Treasury bill was almost a zero-return investment, with a yield at 0.11 percent. In the same period, the PBoC offered a rate of 3.7 percent for its one-year bills. The United States, on the other hand, earns more from investments abroad than it has to pay to foreign investors for holding assets domestically. In 2011, for instance, the United States paid slightly more than $500 billion in interest and dividends to foreign investors. This was less than the $740 billion that American investors received on the assets that they held overseas.[15]

Being overexposed to the greenback is problematic not only because China's dollar holdings are subject to loss in value but also because holding dollars equates to a subsidy to the United States. Among emerging and developing countries, China is the one that feels most intensely the contradiction between the excessive accumulation of dollars in its official reserves and the needs of domestic development. Despite its rapid growth in recent years, it is still a country, with approximately 150 million people, or 11 percent of the total population, living on less than $1.90 a day (the World Bank's poverty threshold) and an urgent need for basic infrastructure in the rural regions.[16]

The Chinese leadership has acknowledged on many occasions the need to slow the accumulation of dollars and invest and allocate liquidity wisely and efficiently. In 2009, former Premier Wen Jiabao expressed his worry about the safety of China's holdings of U.S. debt. In 2011 Zhou Xiaochuan, the Governor of the PBoC, voiced his concerns regarding the overaccumulation of China's foreign exchange reserves, describing them as having exceeded a "reasonable" level. He said that excessive reserves should be professionally managed and suggested that the holdings be diversified. The Chinese authorities took action (at least according to media sources, as no official information is available), selling U.S. government bonds worth $34 billion in 2009 after Wen Jiabao's speech. This was followed by another sale of bonds worth $36.5 billion when the long-term sovereign credit of the United States was downgraded in August 2011. This brought the total holding of U.S. bonds down to $1.137 billion.[17] Between 2012 and 2014, nonetheless, dollars accumulated more quickly, as the Chinese monetary authorities continued to actively manage the exchange rate and needed dollars for intervention. Since the beginning of 2015, these authorities have moved in the opposite direction, with interventions aimed at supporting the exchange rate. China's dollar reserves, as a result, have begun to shrink.

THE CHALLENGE OF CHANGE

All in all, China incurs significant costs from using a dwarf currency. There are the opportunity costs that arise when individuals and firms forfeit the benefits of using the domestic currency in international transactions, the transaction costs that firms pay on foreign exchange operations, and the costs of hedging against exchange rate risks that domestic firms face when they engage in overseas trade and financial transactions. At the macro level, using a dwarf currency can lead to liquidity shortages and puts China at a disadvantage as an immature creditor. The related sterilized intervention policy has led to excessive reserves (especially of dollars), bringing with it a host of other costs and risks.

These costs would be reduced if China could use the renminbi extensively in international transactions. In addition, China would earn from seigniorage—the difference between the value of money and the cost to produce that money (for example, if the cost of producing one dollar note is ten cents, then seigniorage is ninety cents).

There would also be a global upside to an increased use of the renminbi. Expanding the use of the renminbi as a means of payment in international transactions would help to reduce the risk of excessive exposure to liquidity shortages within the world economy (and the associated adverse impact on international trade) and reduce the burden on other central banks of providing liquidity to international financial markets.

But greater international use of the renminbi is easier said than done. Even if China was to introduce policies to make its currency more attractive and open for use worldwide, the choice of the invoicing currency ultimately is a decision taken at the micro level by each exporting or importing company and depends on that company's cost structure. For an exporter whose costs, from labor to raw material, are mainly domestic, it is better to invoice exports and be paid in the home currency—the same currency in which costs are denominated. This allows the company to reduce or even eliminate currency mismatches and the exchange rate risk. On the other hand, for a company that locates most of its production overseas and needs to import raw material, it is preferable to invoice and settle exports in dollars in order to acquire foreign exchanges, which will then be used to pay for imports and, again, avoid currency mismatches. Chinese firms are used to dealing with dollars, and invoicing and settling international transactions in dollars is common practice. Foreign buyers also prefer to pay for Chinese imports in dollars because of the greenback's greater liquidity in international markets, lower transaction costs, and lower foreign exchange risks.

Such habits and network externalities can keep companies from switching the currencies they use to invoice and settle trade. Habits tend to become deeply ingrained, generating inertia and thereby preserving the status quo. Thus, many companies prefer to face higher transaction costs rather than changing the currency they use in international transactions to the home currency. A firm that decides to change its invoicing pattern risks being out of sync with partners and competitors. Because foreigners have been using dollars over the years, they are now reluctant to change.

Of course, restrictions on the movement of renminbi funds from and to China make foreign companies even more reluctant to change their habits. Chinese firms also use dollars for their imports—in particular, energy imports. In the commodities market, oil and mining companies can hardly avoid settling the deals with their global partners in dollars. The same applies to soft commodities such as soybeans and cotton. For large Chinese companies like Baosteel, China's largest steelmaker, and China National Cereals, Oils, and Foodstuffs Corporation, China's largest food-processing company, dollars are also needed for overseas mergers and acquisitions.

In addition, there is a preference for dollars among families and individuals, who use them to travel overseas, pay for their children's education abroad, and buy overseas luxuries and other goods not easily available (or very expensive) in China. In addition, they need dollars to buy overseas real estate properties, popularly used as a fast track to permanent visas and foreign passports for rich Chinese. Dollars have played a critical part in these lifestyle choices.

Given inertia, network externalities, and other constraints, change won't take place unless it's seen as extremely worthwhile. The volume of sales and purchases should be large enough to justify the upfront costs that a firm faces when it switches to using its own domestic currency. Thus, the country that aims to expand the international use and acceptance of its currency and its currency's share of global trade needs to generate enough economic activity to create critical mass and produce traction—at least at the beginning of the process of internationalization. In this sense, China is at an advantage, being the largest or the second-largest economy in the world—depending on which measure is used.[18]

Even then, changing people's habits is difficult. The case of Japan, which until a few years ago was the world's second-largest economy and second-largest exporter, is paradigmatic. In the late 1970s and early 1980s Japan, like China today, experienced strong economic growth, thanks to a successful exports-led strategy, and was emerging as a potential rival to the economic dominance of the United States. As Japanese firms expanded their international outreach and exported cars, television sets, computers, VCRs, and cassette tape players (remember, this was the 1980s!), they began to use the yen, instead of the dollar, in international transactions. The international use of the yen for invoicing and settling Japan's exports expanded from a mere 2 percent in the 1970s to almost 30 percent by the early 1980s.[19] However, this share has remained roughly unchanged in the following thirty years—the yen is currently used for less than 40 percent of Japan's exports and slightly more than 20 percent of its imports.[20] Habits, network externalities, and the malaise of the Japanese economy caused the use of the yen to plateau.

China's policy makers are aware that the renminbi faces a powerful incumbent and the difficult challenge of overcoming inertia and habits. Recognizing the need to capture some of the advantages of an international currency, they have put a policy framework in place to surmount these obstacles and increase the international use of the renminbi. This framework goes beyond just the need to reduce the costs for Chinese firms, businesses, individuals, and even the government from having to use, and accumulate, dollars instead of renminbi. The significance of having a dwarf currency extends to, and encompasses, China's standing in the world: "great nations have great currencies." Thus, China has put together a strategy to create an international currency, as I discuss in the next chapter.

6

CREATING AN INTERNATIONAL
CURRENCY

N JUNE 2009, People's Bank of China (PBoC) Governor Zhou Xiaochuan and Central Bank of Brazil President Henrique Meirelles met
during the annual general meeting of the Bank for International Settlements in Basel, Switzerland. They both felt that their countries were too
dependent on the dollar and were eager to discuss the use of their respective
currencies, the renminbi and the real, in bilateral trade. This was a follow-up
to a meeting a few months earlier, during the G20 summit in London, during which the president of China, Hu Jintao, and that of Brazil, Luiz Inacio
Lula da Silva, explored the idea of Brazil using the real to pay for Chinese
goods and China using the renminbi to pay for Brazilian goods.[1] In Basel,
Zhou and Meirelles agreed that "China and Brazil would work on a currency arrangement to allow exporters and importers to settle deals in their
local currencies, bypassing the US dollar."[2]

This might not have looked like a hugely innovative idea—discussions
about replacing the dollar as the key international currency have been recur-
rent since the end of the Bretton Woods system in 1971—but it came at
the right time. In the aftermath of the global financial crisis, policy makers
and experts were eager to consider the future of the international monetary
system and its excessive dependence on the dollar. In addition, trade and
financial links between China and Brazil were strong (the value of bilateral

trade between these two countries was approximately $43 billion) and grow-
ing. Action followed a few years later when, in June 2012, China and Brazil
agreed to exchange 60 billion reais and 190 billion renminbi. The agreement
was then signed in March 2013, "so there would be no interruption of trade,"
as Guido Mantega, Brazil's economy minister, explained.[3] Today trade has
doubled from what it was in 2009 to almost $90 billion, and Brazil's main
trading partner is China, ahead of the United States.

This arrangement with the Brazilians is evidence of China's attempt to
address the limitations of its dwarf currency and the overreliance on the dollar. Since 2009, the Chinese monetary authorities have built on the country's
prominent position in the international trade system to design a scheme
to facilitate the settlement of transactions between its domestic companies
and their foreign counterparts. This policy experiment was designed with
the interrelated goals of promoting the international use and acceptance
of the renminbi and, at the same time, of keeping control of movements of
money into and out of the country in order to contain the risk of external
shocks to the domestic financial sector. To succeed, however, the monetary
authorities face a challenging obstacle: If they continue to manage the flows
of money into and out of the country, how can they ensure that there are
enough renminbi in international markets to encourage foreign investors to
hold them for trade and investment purposes?

In this chapter, I look at the complex policy framework that the Chinese
authorities have begun to put together in order to develop, under restricted
conditions, a currency that matches, even if only partially, China's economic influence. I call it the renminbi strategy, although this is not an
expression in the official documents or used by the Chinese officials. They
are aware of and concerned about unfettered capital movements, and these
concerns constrain the liberalization of capital markets and therefore
the market development of the renminbi. Thus, the only way to develop
the international use of the renminbi is through policy measures that are
aimed to encourage market demand. This strategy is truly an experiment,
in which policies are gradually implemented and tested before the next
step is taken. As Deng Xiaoping said, it is like "crossing the river by feeling
the stones." To understand the challenges the country faces in developing

an international currency, we can look to the experiences of its neighbor Japan, which has also pushed for currency internationalization in the context of a dollar-dominant system.

THE INTERNATIONALIZATION OF JAPAN'S YEN

The case of Japan and the yen illustrates well the difficulties that are intrinsic to the goal of developing an international currency. In the 1970s, the Japanese financial system resembled that of today's China. It was tightly regulated through controls on credit and interest rates, which were too low to allow the market to properly function and to attract enough supply—that is, deposits—to meet the existing demand. It was rigidly segmented and designed to encourage personal savings so that the investment needs of private industry and the rebuilding of public-sector infrastructure could be financed at low interest rates.

As in China, financial repression was part of Japan's development model. For example, there were controls on foreign deposits held by its residents. Its authorities had introduced these controls and further asked Japanese financial companies—banks, securities companies, investment trusts, and insurance companies—not to increase their foreign investment in order to manage the risk of capital outflows.[4] The yen fluctuated in an extremely narrow range (centering on 265 yen per dollar) and was not a particularly attractive currency. If investors and savers had had the option, many would likely have moved their money abroad.

It was during this time, in the wake of the collapse of the Bretton Woods system and the following talks about the reform of the international monetary system, that discussions about the yen's role in the world began. Through the two subsequent oil shocks—in 1973 and 1979—massive amounts of oil dollars were accumulated by oil-exporting countries, and international financial markets started on a path toward major liberalization. The euromarket expanded, and international monetary flows increased in size and speed. Like China after 2008, Japan emerged from those shocks as a stronger economy with the potential to play an increasingly important role in the global economy—whereas the United States suffered a decline in its global economic standing and a loss of international confidence in the dollar. This combination—a stronger Japanese economy and a weaker U.S. economy—generated growing interest in the international role of the yen. In December 1980, a thoroughly revised Foreign Exchange and Foreign Trade Control Law went into effect in Japan. This was the first step in a policy framework to promote Japan's integration into the world economy through trade and investment. And in October 1983, the Japanese minister of finance identified "the internationalization of the yen and the liberalization of financial and capital markets" as major policy objectives.[5]

Coinciding with President Ronald Reagan's visit to Japan in November 1983, the Yen-Dollar Committee was established and, together with the Council on Foreign Exchange and Other Transactions, eventually reached an agreement for how to achieve these goals. The U.S. government had, in fact, put strong pressure on the Japanese because of large bilateral current-account imbalances and Congress's campaign to "retaliate" against Japan. Economists and politicians in the United States maintained that financial-sector liberalization and internationalization of the yen would help to rebalance the Japanese economy.

Specific measures included the lowering of barriers to access for foreign financial institutions,[6] financial liberalization (particularly the continued liberalization of interest rates and the further development and expansion of open short-term capital markets), the liberalization of the euro-yen market as the first step toward making it more convenient for nonresidents to use and hold the yen, and the establishment of an offshore market to facilitate euro-yen transactions in Tokyo. The program for financial liberalization was steadily developed through the second half of the 1980s and the 1990s. Regulations were eased and eventually abolished, interest rates were gradually deregulated, and in December 1986 the Tokyo offshore market was formally established.

The Japanese monetary authorities were following the conventional route in their plan to internationalize the yen by liberalizing the financial sector and opening the capital account. The convertibility of the current account, on the other hand, had been largely achieved by the mid-1960s, at the onset of Japan's large economic expansion. This pattern is similar to the one China has been following so far—China had fully opened its current account by the time it joined the World Trade Organization (WTO), and work is now in progress to open up the capital account. By the mid-1980s, Japan's financial sector and capital account were substantially more open than is currently the case for China,[7] and by the early 1990s, they were largely liberalized.

Unconstrained capital account movements attracted foreign banks and securities firms into Japan while over the same years Japanese banks and securities firms expanded their presence abroad. They opened branches in the main financial centers, acquired existing foreign banks, and began to engage in new activities, such as underwriting euro-yen bond issues. By 1990, the five largest banks in the world, measured by total assets, were Japanese (as now the largest banks are Chinese). Investment firms also increased overseas activities—especially their participation in the U.S. Treasury bond market, with the purchase of a 25–30 percent share of each new issuance in the late 1980s. In the same years, Japan's securities market increased its volume of dealings. Four of the world's largest securities houses were Japanese (Nomura, Daiwa, Nikko, and Yamaichi). In 1986, Nomura, the world's largest securities firm, with net capital in excess of $10 billion, became the first Japanese member of the London Stock Exchange. In 1990, Japan was the world's second-largest economy[8] after the United States, with a 10 percent share of total world gross domestic product and an almost 7 percent share of total global trade.[9]

Then, at the beginning of the 1990s, Japan experienced a banking crisis that ushered in a long period of economic stagnation and deflation. Its economic malaise dampened foreigners' confidence and hindered the internationalization of the yen. The share of the Japanese currency in global foreign exchange reserves dropped from almost 7 percent in December 1995 to 4 percent in December 2015, and the use of the yen as a percentage of global foreign exchange transactions dropped from 20 percent to 5 percent over the same period.[10] As a consequence of the banking crisis and the subsequent "lost decade," the Japanese economy has shrunk. Its share of total world gross domestic product is now a bit less than 6 percent,[11] and its share of total global trade is approximately 4 percent.

SOME LESSONS AND A STRATEGY FOR THE RENMINBI

There are some lessons that can be learned from Japan's experience in currency internationalization. First, economic fundamentals—an economy and trade sector of sufficient size; a foreign exchange market with appropriate liquidity; an open, deep, and diversified financial sector; credible institutions; and the rule of law[12]—are essential to support the internationalization of a currency. Scale and scope matter because it is the volume of a country's trade that can push the international use of that country's currency, create traction, and help reduce inertia. But as the case of Japan shows, these conditions on their own are not enough to push a currency's international use. Although Japan was the world's second-largest economy in 1990, only about 5 percent of world trade was invoiced in yen[13]—partly because internationally traded commodities and raw materials were, and still are, invoiced and settled in dollars.

Second, the opening of the capital account is a necessary but not a sufficient condition for the expansion of a currency's international use; again, on its own, this is not enough to create a deep and well-functioning market for that currency. Policies that support and encourage the currency's international use, or at least that do not hinder it, are equally important. Although Japanese authorities promoted policies to liberalize the capital account during the boom years, they still remained somewhat hesitant about opening up to the rest of the world because they were concerned about the impact of a strong yen on Japan's exports-dependent economy.[14] Their approach was broadly informed by the idea that the internationalization of the yen would happen "naturally" as a result of liberalizing the capital account, and as a consequence, they adopted a relatively passive stance rather than pursuing further policies to push or accelerate the internationalization of their currency.

Third, for a country to support its currency's international use, it is important to have a well-developed international financial center with good financial infrastructure—payment system, clearance, and so on—and liquid capital markets. This was clear in the case of Britain, where the financing of international trade became core to London's international expansion as a financial center. For example, the volume of acceptances on the London market grew from approximately £50 million or £60 million in 1875 to some £140 million in 1913. At the same time, a whole range of pound-denominated activities—from debt securities to trade-related funds and deposit accounts—was developed. British firms' foreign suppliers opened and held deposit accounts in London, where receipts from transactions settled in pounds could be held safely for short periods. This robust and diverse financial system was a major driver of the pound's dominance.

Finally, the regional context is essential in providing traction for the currency. This was true for Britain in the nineteenth century, for instance— France and Germany were similar in terms of economic size and development. However, this was not true for Japan in the 1980s. At that point, Japan was the only advanced economy in Asia, so most of its trade and financial relations were with other developed countries—notably, the United States. The considerable development gap between Japan and its neighbors constrained regional integration and limited the options for expanding the use of the yen within the region.[15] The yen therefore ended up developing as an international currency in a broader context, whereas Japan's trade partners were locked into a de facto dollar bloc. Network externalities and inertia, and the consequent transaction costs, acted as disincentives for firms and other market participants to switch to using the yen. As a result, the Japanese currency never developed into the widely used international money (like the dollar) that many expected at that time.

Even if the regional context for today's China is fundamentally different from the one that Japan faced in the 1980s, Chinese scholars[16] look at Japan's experience for lessons relevant to China's own currency internationalization—especially for what the authorities should not do. The Plaza Accord of 1985, in which the G5 governments (France, Germany, Britain, the United States, and Japan) agreed to depreciate the dollar against the yen and German mark, is seen as the turning point for Japan. American pressures on the Japanese government to appreciate the exchange rate ushered in inappropriately low interest rates to counterbalance the currency's strength. This resulted in excessive indebtedness, which caused the bank to collapse, which, in turn, resulted in a long stagnation. The appreciation of the yen stopped only in 1995, when the U.S. government announced the "strong dollar" policy.[17] Chinese commentators and scholars regard the sharp appreciation of the yen after the Plaza Accord as a compromise that was forced on Japan in the name of international policy cooperation—and that worked to the benefit of the United States. It damaged the country's export-oriented economy and dragged it into a deep recession, the "lost decade" referred to earlier.[18]

This debate is often biased and not entirely grounded in facts. However, it is emblematic of the concerns that surround China's currency development. There are indeed many challenges ahead for the Chinese authorities. But as the Japan case demonstrates, the strategy of pushing the use of the renminbi in the region where China is highly integrated seems the right one, as it puts the whole process of currency internationalization on the path of least resistance. China isn't yet in a position where it can open the capital account and let the market drive the international use of the renminbi. More policy action is needed.

"CROSSING THE RIVER BY FEELING THE STONES"

The aim of China's renminbi strategy is to drive the international use of the currency and to circumvent or revise the existing constraints on its circulation. It is a supply-side strategy; the idea is that having the relevant infrastructure in place to underpin the development of the market for renminbi will drive demand, which, in turn, will expand the market.

The success of China's renminbi strategy therefore depends on a combination of well-designed policies and market forces. Beijing has been developing the strategy in a cautious, step-by-step way, through a sort of learning by doing, and will continue to do so. Reforms in China do not happen overnight but rather progress along a steady and gradual path—the process of crossing the river by feeling the stones that Deng Xiaoping described. The approach to internationalizing the renminbi is no different. The Chinese authorities are looking to make incremental progress, leaving ample scope for policy experimentation and trying to avoid unexpected disruption to the economy.

Thus, policies are gradually implemented and tested, often under controlled conditions. Then, if they work, they are put into effect across the whole country.

Although the authorities have maintained a low-key approach and seem to prefer not to give too much emphasis to this initiative, the Chinese press has welcomed it. Upon the launch of one of the first major renminbi policies in July 2009—the trade settlement pilot scheme, discussed further below—Xinhua, China's official news agency, commented: "The new service is bound to help warm up international trade, further push the yuan around the globe and alleviate the world's overreliance on the US dollar."[19] But both the expansion of the settlement scheme and the reform of the exchange rate that anchored the renminbi to a basket of currencies (chapter 4) went almost unnoticed in the international, non-Chinese press when they were implemented in June 2010.

This lack of attention suited the Chinese authorities, who prefer not to bring attention to the strategy. There is, in fact, very little in the officials' words and documents about the internationalization of the renminbi. The PBoC and other authorities have never published any formal document that presents their plan for the currency or that defines and explains what the internationalization of the renminbi is and what their associated goals are. At the UK-China Financial Forum that was held in London in June 2014, senior Chinese officials stressed that the so-called internationalization of the renminbi was a much more low-key affair for the Chinese, with a less grand name: "In China we called it cross-border use of the renminbi."[20] A few weeks earlier, at the Boao Forum, PBoC Governor Zhou carefully avoided the term *renminbi internationalization*. Instead, he referred to "the cross-border use of the renminbi," using that expression six times in his ten-minute keynote speech.[21] I personally experienced the Chinese authorities' prudent stance in a meeting at the PBoC in late 2010. I had just published a paper on China's renminbi strategy,[22] and I used this expression during the discussion with a group of senior officials; they gently corrected me and explained that there was no such thing as a renminbi strategy.

The authorities' reticence regarding the renminbi strategy is hardly surprising. They have embarked on a complex initiative that requires them to plan for the long term through a series of gradual steps, to anticipate market reaction and determine how to respond, and to foresee short-term and long-term effects both domestically and internationally. They even need the political courage to backtrack to a previous step, if necessary. Crossing the river by feeling the stones, then, is a great way to characterize this process.

China's renminbi strategy has been unfolding along two tracks. The first one, which I discuss next, is the cross-border trade settlement scheme to encourage the use of the renminbi in China's trade. The second track, which I discuss at the end of the chapter, is the establishment of the offshore market to develop the renminbi into a currency that foreigners are willing to hold as a way to store their wealth.

THE TRADE SETTLEMENT PILOT SCHEME

China's "long march" to internationalize its currency began, almost unnoticed, in April 2009, when the Standing Committee of the State Council—China's equivalent of the Cabinet in the United States and the Cabinet Office in Britain—approved a pilot scheme to allow the use of the renminbi for pricing, invoicing, and settling international trade transactions. This plan aimed to "boost China's trade with other trading partners, improve trading conditions, provide liquidity that had been severely curtailed by the financial crisis, lower exposure to foreign exchange fluctuations and maintain a high rate of growth in the trading sector."[23]

The new policy was intended to encourage the use of the renminbi to settle trade transactions with countries around China's border. Under the scheme, a firm that imported goods from China could now decide to pay for these goods in renminbi instead of U.S. dollars. Ambitions were modest; the goal was to leverage the policy scheme on the existing informal use of the Chinese currency in the region.[24]

How does the scheme work? To use renminbi to pay for goods imported from China, the foreign firm asks an authorized overseas bank to wire the payment to a designated clearing bank in Hong Kong (or in another offshore financial center). The clearing bank channels the funds to a settlement bank in mainland China, which, in turn, transfers the funds to the bank account of the exporting company. Alternatively, the firm can use a commercial bank in mainland China as an agent of the overseas bank. In this case, the firm has to open an offshore renminbi bank account at the agent bank so that funds can be transferred interbank.[25]

Building as it does on the circulation of the Chinese currency in neighboring countries, the scheme institutionalized a de facto situation that had existed for many years. Renminbi have been moving between the mainland and bordering countries—in particular, Hong Kong. To address this situation, controls on currency exports were slightly relaxed in the early 1990s—but for relatively small amounts.[26] Starting in 1993, individuals were allowed to take a maximum of 6,000 renminbi into or out of the mainland each time they traveled. This limit was raised to 20,000 renminbi on January 1, 2005—and remains at that level today.

For years, mainland Chinese have been taking their money abroad—even if just as far as Hong Kong. Throughout the 1990s, thousands of mainland Chinese literally carried bags of money into Hong Kong.[27] Consequently, many Chinese residents began to accumulate renminbi outside mainland China—knowing, however, that there was no official channel by which to bring the renminbi back to the mainland. The slow, steady leak of money out of China was evidence of the common mindset among individuals that their money was safer in other currencies. Firms had similar beliefs. To sidestep foreign exchange controls, legitimate Chinese companies often doctored invoice statements to show that they had paid a foreign supplier or partner more than they actually had. The companies then siphoned off the difference into offshore accounts.

To absorb and use this pool of renminbi, informal renminbi exchange markets were established in neighboring countries. Many of these were dominated by money changers that were generally subject to less stringent supervision than banks.[28] This explains why, despite its limitations as an international currency, the renminbi was, in fact, widely used in countries such as Mongolia, Cambodia, Vietnam, Burma/Myanmar, and Laos— to the point of overcrowding local currencies and even other dominant international currencies. For example, in northern Laos, the renminbi was more popular than the U.S. dollar and was called "small dollar."[29] In Indonesia, Malaysia, the Philippines, Singapore, Thailand, South Korea, and Taiwan, local currencies tracked the renminbi more closely than the dollar.[30]

The new policy scheme would legitimize many of these existing informal networks. Within the pilot scheme, qualified companies based in five pilot cities—Dongguan, Guangzhou, Shanghai, Shenzhen, and Zhuhai— were allowed to use renminbi to price, invoice, and settle their international trade transactions with counterparts in Hong Kong, Macao, and countries belonging to the Association of Southeast Asian Nations (ASEAN).[31] Banks in those areas were allowed to provide services, such as deposits, currency exchange, checks, remittances, and trade finance, to those companies that chose to use renminbi to settle trade transactions with the designated enterprises in China.

On the day the pilot program was launched in July 2009, the Bank of China transacted the country's first cross-border renminbi trade settlement deal, with HSBC (in partnership with the Bank of Communications). The deal was completed in Hong Kong, with the remittance for trade settlement coming from Shanghai, in the form of a renminbi documentary credit transaction.[32] It was a symbolic moment as two major banks—one Chinese and the other foreign—stepped in as key stakeholders in the new scheme, linking China's key financial centers (Hong Kong and Shanghai) and showing the business community what the scheme entailed.

Business reacted positively to the new initiative. According to a survey of more than 1,000 exporting enterprises published by the Beijing-based China Academy of Social Sciences in 2009,[33] over 80 percent of the respondents welcomed the use of renminbi for cross-border trade settlement, seeing it as a way to minimize exchange rate risk and transaction costs. The same survey indicated that the scheme could provide an incentive for small and medium-sized enterprises to engage in international trade; it is more difficult for firms of that size to obtain approval to open a U.S. dollar account for trade settlement.

All the big banks—Chinese banks as well as leading international banks such as Standard Chartered, JPMorgan, and HSBC—saw this as an opportunity to develop products for the small, but potentially huge, renminbi market. They enthusiastically embraced the new scheme and set extremely optimistic expectations. For example, HSBC China estimated that the demand for trade settlement in renminbi could reach $2 trillion in 2012, accounting for 40–50 percent of China's foreign trade. "If 40–50 percent of the settlement volume is converted to renminbi, there will be more diverse options in terms of trade, costs of trade and trade finance, thus reducing foreign exchange risks and transaction costs to effectively promote regional trade," said Ben Shenglin, the head of HSBC China commercial banking, in August 2009.[34]

The main banks began offering trade services in renminbi to their clients. In March 2010, as part of the scheme, renminbi-denominated bank current accounts and a standard lending rate were launched in Hong Kong, providing more flexibility to businesses to transact in renminbi. The big international banks began to actively encourage the use of the renminbi among trade customers as an integral part of their commercial services in Hong Kong. For clients, the option of directly settling trade in renminbi was particularly attractive because of the strength of the Chinese currency against the U.S. dollar.

Enthusiasm was not confined to banks and financial institutions in Hong Kong. An array of new services sprang up on the back of the pilot scheme in countries that traded intensively with China. By the end of July 2009, for instance, in Vietnam more than 6,000 dealers had registered to offer assistance to firms in settling their trade transactions in renminbi. Such businesses were concentrated in the region alongside the Beilun River, which connects the Guangxi Province in southwest China and the Quang Ninh Province in northeast Vietnam.[35]

The scheme was also a useful innovation for companies involved in importing and exporting manufactured and semimanufactured goods to and from China, as it helped to simplify the process of invoicing and paying for trade and reduced the exchange rate risks. Not surprisingly, then, many businesspeople were happy and willing to join the scheme. Huang Yifan, the executive director of Vietnam Charity Trading Company Ltd., a Vietnamese furniture trading company that exports 70 percent of its products to

China, went on record to express her support for the scheme: "I really hope there is a single currency like the euro in Asia to cut off the cost of exchanging currencies and make the whole process easier. . . . I hope the yuan could be the one as it has been stable and welcomed by the ASEAN people." She added that renminbi were very popular in Vietnam, Cambodia, and Laos.[36]

"Opening a renminbi commercial current account provides corporates with more flexibility when doing trade settlement," added Albert Chan, head of commercial banking at HSBC in Hong Kong.[37] He explained that traders could now use checks in addition to remittances when settling trade locally in the Chinese currency. "With the introduction of the pilot scheme for the renminbi cross-border trade settlement, there are many opportunities presented to both importing and exporting companies to increase their sales, reduce costs and manage their risks," echoed Neil Daswani of Standard Chartered.[38]

In June 2010, the renminbi pilot scheme was widened to cover twenty provinces[39] and cities in mainland China.[40] A year later, it was expanded to the whole country. In October 2011, the PBoC issued guidelines to allow foreign direct investment to be denominated in renminbi. Since then, the scheme has further evolved into a formal program through which all of China's international trade can, in principle, be settled in renminbi. Indeed, since March 2012, all companies with import and export licenses that have been incorporated in mainland China have the option to join the scheme and can settle trade in renminbi not only with ASEAN countries, Hong Kong, and Macao, as previously allowed, but also with the rest of the world.[41] Administrative procedures and the red tape have been simplified, and all restrictions and requirements for administrative approval have been lifted.

However, even if Chinese businesses switched to the renminbi to reduce exchange rate risks and transaction costs, this would not necessarily mean that their overseas counterparts would be equally happy with the change. A currency subject to restrictions on international financial transactions was unlikely to suddenly become widely used, even if only for trade in goods, because such trade still involved financial considerations, such as trade financing and the hedging of exchange rate risk.[42] This meant that, if non-Chinese holders did not have the option to invest their renminbi in financial and nonfinancial activities, then their cost to hold renminbi was high because, first, they could not gain interest by trading the currency on capital markets and, second, if the currency depreciated, they would not be able to quickly and easily dump their holdings and switch to other currency assets. This inevitably limited the scope of the renminbi's international use and, at the same time, reduced its potential.

Given the renminbi's restricted convertibility, non-Chinese firms and investors had no incentive to hold Chinese money. As Datuk Bong Hon Liong, deputy president of the Malaysia-China Chamber of Commerce, put it when he was asked to comment on the renminbi trade settlement scheme: "Current conditions are not conducive for renminbi settlement. With the Yuan trending upwards and the dollar weakening, there is no incentive for importers to use renminbi. As for exporters, they were very comfortable with the present rates."[43] Because restrictions on the capital account prevented non-Chinese businesses that trade with Chinese firms from holding renminbi in domestic bank deposits, the best solution was to hold enough Chinese money to settle the day-to-day transactions and convert the remaining renminbi into a more desirable currency. If foreign businesses and investors were not willing to hold the currency, then renminbi flows would simply move in a loop, with importers and exporters exchanging renminbi to settle their transactions but without expanding the currency's use and circulation. So the trade settlement scheme could, at best, help develop only one function of international money—that of means of exchange. Using the renminbi to invoice and settle trade therefore was a necessary but not a sufficient condition to promote the currency's international use.

The limited impact of the renminbi trade settlement scheme became apparent a few months after its launch. By mid-2010, the Chinese monetary authorities realized how difficult it was to internationalize a currency with restricted convertibility. Without policy intervention to support the internationalization of the currency, the limited liberalization of long-term capital flows was likely to constrain the international use of the renminbi in the years to come, even if just for trade transactions.

The authorities understood that they needed to ensure that renminbi were largely available outside China to overcome the constraints that come from the currency's limited convertibility. With sufficient liquidity, market participants could buy and sell the renminbi as cheaply and predictably as they did the dollar and therefore feel more comfortable about holding the Chinese money. To achieve this liquidity, the Chinese government concluded that it had to create a market for renminbi-denominated assets, and incentives for foreign firms to participate, in order to generate enough renminbi liquidity in the international payment system. Liquidity was indeed the key condition for foreigners to happily and willingly hold renminbi despite the existing restrictions.

Of course, the Chinese authorities could have chosen to create liquidity by easing these restrictions, following the route Japan took in the 1980s by fully opening the capital account and liberalizing capital flows. But without a thorough reform of the domestic banking and financial sector and a change in the exchange rate regime, the risk of exchange rate shocks and the adverse impact on the domestic financial system of unmanaged capital flows was too high. The abolition of capital controls therefore was not (and still is not) in the cards.

Instead, China's policy makers began to experiment with the idea of developing a special market, separate from the domestic one, in which the renminbi and renminbi-denominated assets could be freely traded. Not only would this market need to be liquid, but also it would need to have robust infrastructure, trustworthy institutions, credible regulations, and the capacity to eventually develop new products (like the renminbi-denominated bond).

THE OFFSHORE MARKET SOLUTION

To make the renminbi more attractive, the Chinese monetary authorities designed an ingenious, albeit burdensome, solution—the offshore market. This market would allow renminbi to be traded outside China, under unrestricted conditions, and would provide support for Chinese companies that were investing abroad, or were planning to do so, as well as for those companies that wanted to raise funds in overseas capital markets. By moving all these transactions offshore, the monetary authorities hoped to protect the onshore market in mainland China from undesired and potentially destabilizing capital movements that could undermine the country's domestic financial stability. Thus, they began to develop a series of policies, parallel to the trade settlement scheme, that would enable them to build a pool of liquidity outside mainland China and away from Beijing's jurisdiction.[44]

In the offshore market, nonresidents would have access to renminbi for the purpose of trade and investment and could hold renminbi funds. These funds could be moved to and from mainland China through complex channels that provided, at least in theory, a mechanism to control capital movements and thus to reduce the risk of financial instability. Those wishing to convert payments into another currency could do so in the offshore market, with offshore renminbi—or CNH, to use the technical abbreviation that is commonly employed in the foreign exchange markets—which would be converted into any foreign currency at free-floating market rates. Thus, in the offshore market, the renminbi—or, to be precise, the CNH—could become a fully convertible currency with a flexible exchange rate. In practice, this meant the creation of two parallel currencies: the offshore fully convertible renminbi (CNH) and the onshore nonconvertible one (CNY).

The aim of establishing the offshore market was to allow the renminbi to be used internationally as a financial asset—and thus to achieve the function of money as a store of value, which would support its internationalization. In the meantime, China's monetary authorities would retain control over capital movements into the domestic (or onshore) market and over the pace of the capital account liberalization.[45] The development of the offshore market would also open up opportunities for international financial centers, especially Hong Kong, that were involved in the renminbi business. They could offer a wide range of renminbi-denominated assets and investment instruments as well as banking and trade-related business services.

The renminbi cross-border trade settlement scheme and the renminbi offshore market have become complementary aspects of China's approach to internationalizing the renminbi. This two-track strategy includes measures specifically designed for each track. The goal of the first track is to increase the use of the renminbi in international trade and thus to promote its use as an invoicing currency for trade. The second track aims to create an offshore market for renminbi-denominated assets, which allows China to avoid opening up its capital account prematurely or increasing the imbalances in its international balance sheet.

These two tracks run parallel to and reinforce each other. The cross-border trade settlement scheme feeds the offshore market because the proceeds of trade can be held in bank deposits or even in renminbi-denominated assets in the offshore market. The development of the renminbi offshore market, on the other hand, provides a way for nonresidents to invest renminbi that they have earned through trade. In turn, these offshore renminbi feed and expand the liquidity pool in the offshore market. Chinese policy makers expect that more foreign firms will use renminbi to settle trade transactions with China if they have viable options by which to hold renminbi and plenty of liquidity. The development of the offshore market therefore addresses their challenge of how to persuade foreign firms and foreign market participants to hold renminbi in offshore bank accounts or in offshore financial instruments.

Thus, within this two-track policy framework, the currency can be used internationally under controlled conditions. Through the development of the offshore market, Beijing can retain control of capital flows into and out of the country and protect China's banking and financial system in case of uncontrollable events and shocks. However, as I will discuss in the following chapters, the offshore market cannot act as a complete substitute for the currency's convertibility; until the restrictions on capital flows are eased, the international use of the renminbi will be limited in scale and scope.

7

BUILDING A MARKET FOR
THE RENMINBI

C HINA'S STRATEGY TO develop the international use of its currency
through a consistent and sequenced set of policies is unprecedented.
It is the first developing country to actively drive the process of
internationalizing its currency rather than letting it develop naturally. It is
also the first country to attempt to do this in the era of true fiat money,
when there is no link, even residual, between an international currency and
gold or another physical asset.[1] This means that the renminbi's credibility
cannot be established by comparing its convertibility to gold with that of
other currencies, as happened when the dollar took over from the pound.

Establishing the credibility of and an international reputation for the
renminbi and making it acceptable in those parts of the world where the
dollar dominates—even if just in Asia—are difficult objectives, but they are
what the two-track renminbi strategy (the trade settlement scheme and the
offshore solution) is designed to achieve. Nevertheless, this strategy faces
many interrelated obstacles in building a market for the renminbi.

The first of these challenges is to channel the renminbi into the hands
of foreign holders—a tricky feat, given China's restrictions on capital flows
and on the convertibility of the renminbi. With China's preference for maintaining a surplus in the current-account—presently down to approximately
3 percent of gross domestic product but higher, at approximately 5 percent, at

the beginning of the renminbi strategy in 2010—and managed exchange rate, pushing the overseas demand for renminbi means accumulating dollars on the asset side of the central bank's balance sheet. As I discussed in chapter 5, managing the exchange rate means that the People's Bank of China (PBoC) has to hold dollars in its reserves and release renminbi. In other words, in order to keep the exchange rate stable, it needs to intervene to absorb dollars while supplying renminbi to the market; as a result, it ends up piling up more dollars in the official foreign exchange reserves and thus further enlarges the "dollar trap." (The alternative to accumulating dollars would be moving to a truly flexible exchange rate, but as we've discussed and will consider further in chapter 9, China is not prepared to do this.)

Assuming that China succeeds in creating traction for the renminbi, another challenge is to respond to and expand the foreign demand for renminbi funds and renminbi-denominated assets while maintaining domestic financial stability. The authorities believe that this can be preserved as long as the channel through which offshore renminbi get back to the onshore market is restricted. But restrictions on flows—both inward and outward—curb market demand, thus acting as a counterforce on the internationalization of the renminbi. Also, the Chinese authorities must carefully sequence the policy measures that are part of the renminbi strategy to avoid creating opportunities for arbitrage and carry trade between the offshore and onshore markets.

Finally, there is no guarantee that the market participants will use renminbi, once China has implemented the renminbi strategy and "facilitated" the functioning of the market. The authorities assume that once they have put the critical infrastructure in place, the process can get enough traction to drive the market, and then the internationalization of the currency will follow—especially given the scale and scope of the country's trade. Policies can certainly support currency internationalization, but can they drive it? China can set the stage but cannot force market participants to use the renminbi. For this to happen, they need to feel confident about the currency's liquidity and credibility.

The challenges China faces can be boiled down to liquidity, market infrastructure, and the relationship between the two. Well-designed and well-implemented infrastructure will help ensure that there is plenty of renminbi liquidity outside mainland China, which will in turn support the demand for renminbi and encourage market practice. Therefore, the key element of such market infrastructure is the liquidity channel between the offshore market and the onshore market. In this chapter, I will take a closer look at what has been done in order to build a market for the renminbi and the infrastructure that underpins such a market.

SUPPLYING RENMINBI TO THE OFFSHORE MARKET

Liquidity is critical to establishing a well-functioning renminbi market. Foreign companies that may be able and willing to use the renminbi in their trade with China need to be sure that the currency is easily available in the offshore market when it is needed and, above all, that it is swiftly exchangeable with any other currency. They need to be assured that China's constraints on capital flows will not affect the pool of the renminbi in the offshore market and hinder transactions.

There are two common ways to supply liquidity for the offshore market. First, market participants deposit the money they have earned from trade transactions in offshore bank accounts. This helps create a "reservoir" outside the country that issues that currency. This liquidity can then be used in international transactions outside the jurisdiction of the issuing country. Because of its dominance in the international payment system, the dollar, for instance, is extensively used, accumulated, and intermediated outside the jurisdiction of the United States by people who do not reside in the United States. A German firm that operates in a number of different countries and markets around the world may decide to hold a dollar account in London—the world's largest dollar offshore market—which it uses to make and receive payments around the world without sourcing funds from or deploying funds into the United States. Dong He and Robert McCauley call this a "pure" offshore market.[2]

The second way to ensure plenty of liquidity for the offshore market is for market participants to exchange dollars or other international currencies into the offshore currency, using the clearing bank in the offshore center or a correspondent onshore bank, and for onshore banks to lend to their off-shore subsidiaries through the clearing bank offshore. The German firm in the example above can exchange its euros into dollars and wire that money into its dollar bank account in London.

China cannot pursue either of these common paths. The use of the ren-minbi in international trade is not yet sufficiently developed to provide enough liquidity to the offshore market,[3] and restrictions on China's capital account limit the liquidity that can be generated by market participants. Because of these constraints, the renminbi market—at least for the time being—is not a pure offshore market. It is better characterized as net inter-national lending in renminbi.[4] This means that the renminbi offshore mar-ket works mainly as a conduit of funds from mainland China to the rest of the world rather than as a vehicle for the circulation of renminbi outside China's jurisdiction. Using renminbi bank deposits as a proxy, the size of the renminbi offshore market has been estimated to be around 2.2 trillion renminbi.[5] This is only about one-tenth the size of China's total foreign exchange reserves and approximately 3 percent of its gross domestic prod-uct. This means that the liquidity generated by market participants—that is, the private sector—is not, on its own, sufficient to underpin the devel-opment of a market for the renminbi that is significant enough to, in turn, expand the international use of the Chinese currency.

Thus, the policy of controlling the currency runs counter to China's pol-icy on the development of the renminbi. Foreign holders of renminbi face several restrictions on the repatriation of the funds that they raised in the offshore market in order, for example, to invest them in the mainland, so they may find holding renminbi in the offshore market unattractive.[6] At the same time, relaxing controls on capital outflows may run counter to the need to maintain plenty of financial resources for the domestic banks. As China's economic growth slows and the Federal Reserve's monetary policy becomes less accommodative—providing better returns for dollar-denom-inated assets—outflows have begun to outnumber inflows. In 2015, China's net capital outflows reached a record high of $676 billion.[7]

The PBoC therefore has found a third way to provide liquidity—by actively supplying it. The role of the central bank as supplier of renminbi liquidity is what sets the renminbi offshore market apart from the dollar offshore market. In deciding how much liquidity to inject into the offshore market, the Chinese central bank must consider market demand, policy goals, and the risks to domestic financial stability that excessive liquidity might generate. In line with the country's gradual approach to policy making, liquidity is carefully increased and decreased. With this "proactive, controllable and gradualist" approach,[8] China aims to minimize the risk of developing an oversized offshore market beyond the authorities' control.[9] And by controlling the amount of liquidity in the offshore market, its monetary authorities de facto control the pace of its development.

MANAGING THE SUPPLY OF RENMINBI

Liquidity is largely in the hands of China's central bank, so how does it ensure that there is a sufficient supply of renminbi? One way is through currency swaps, such as those initiated between Brazil and China in 2013. These bilateral agreements are devised as a safety net to ensure the availability of currencies that are critical for a country's trade relations and to avoid disruption to trade from a temporary scarcity of liquidity. Swaps also, crucially, create renminbi liquidity in the offshore market.[10] The argument that currency swaps could be used to provide renminbi liquidity and thus encourage its international use was first put forward in 2009 by Ma Rentao and Zhou Yongkun, two researchers at the Graduate School of the PBoC.[11] Since then, the Chinese monetary authorities have been experimenting with using swap agreements to increase the pool of the currency outside China. As more renminbi become available outside the country and in the foreign exchange markets, it becomes easier for foreign firms to use them to settle trade. Currency swaps should also assist China's trade partners by reducing the many costs that are normally associated with financial transactions—such as commission fees, interest rates, loan origination fees, and taxes.

Currency swap agreements have thus become a key component of China's renminbi strategy. They are a way to deepen its financial and monetary integration with the signatory countries[12] and to create offshore pools of renminbi around the world. Since 2009, more than 3 trillion renminbi have been committed through bilateral currency swap agreements that China has signed with thirty-two countries—most are in Asia, including Thailand, Indonesia, and South Korea, but Britain, New Zealand, Switzerland, and Argentina also have entered into agreements.[13]

The PBoC signed the first of these agreements with the Bank of Korea in December 2008, in the aftermath of the global financial crisis. This agreement allowed the PBoC and Bank of Korea to swap 180 billion renminbi over a three-year period; that is, it allowed these two countries to purchase currencies from each other in case of a liquidity crisis. In 2013, the PBoC signed a 500 billion renminbi swap agreement with members of the Association of Southeast Asian Nations under the Chiang Mai Initiative[14] to promote regional financial stability and a 200 billion renminbi swap agreement with the Bank of England. That China has signed agreements with so many countries despite the fact that the renminbi technically is a nonconvertible currency, is evidence of the leverage that it has, especially with developing countries.

In many countries, these renminbi swap agreements are of limited use because the size of the renminbi business—and trade with China—is not large enough to trigger a liquidity crisis. According to the PBoC, in 2014, only about 81 billion renminbi of the accumulated swap amount of 2.3 trillion renminbi were used.[15] But the situation is different in Hong Kong, for instance, where having a renminbi safety net really matters (Hong Kong, as I discuss later in this chapter, is the key offshore market for the renminbi). In January 2009, Hong Kong set up a three-year swap agreement with the PBoC for a total of 200 billion renminbi. This agreement was then renewed twice, in November 2011 and November 2014, and increased to 400 billion renminbi for the specific purpose of facilitating the development of the renminbi offshore market. Norman Chan, chief executive of the Hong Kong Monetary Authority (HKMA), welcomed the agreement as "crucial in helping us to provide liquidity, when necessary, to maintain the stability of the offshore renminbi market in Hong Kong."[16]

The importance of such an agreement was demonstrated in June 2012, when the swap line was activated to ease the temporary scarcity of liquidity created by strong demand for renminbi from banks in the Hong Kong offshore center and to avoid destabilizing the offshore renminbi market.[17] By allowing banks to obtain renminbi from it, the HKMA, the de facto central bank, sent a strong message that helped calm nerves and relieve market pressure.[18]

China's monetary authorities have not limited the creation of liquidity to the provision of currency swaps. In recent years, they have begun to encourage the policy banks to offer competitive loans in renminbi to countries that have limited borrowing capacity in the global capital market. In March 2012, at the BRICS Summit in New Delhi, the China Development Bank announced the signing of memorandums of understanding with the development banks of Brazil, Russia, India, and South Africa, in which they agreed to make their currencies available for invoicing trade and lending with each other.[19] In addition, in 2011, the China Ex-Im Bank began cooperating with the Inter-American Development Bank for the purpose of setting up a fund denominated in renminbi that would support infrastructure investments in Latin America and the Caribbean and through which China could expand lending in renminbi to commodity-rich countries in Latin America.

The New Development Bank and the Asian Infrastructure Investment Bank, in which China is a significant shareholder, are also seen in Beijing as potentially instrumental in the promotion of the renminbi to large regional and international projects. Although the subscribed capital for both banks is in dollars—$50 billion and $100 billion, respectively—these amounts are rather small for large development projects. The total capital of the World Bank, by comparison, is about $223 billion. It is therefore plausible to think that both banks will eventually need to expand their capital, and China may be eager to contribute with renminbi instead of dollars.

These developments—from currency swaps and bilateral loans to the creation of new development banks—carry important implications for the renminbi offshore markets. Companies in those countries with which China has signed swap agreements can establish entities in the offshore centers—notably, Hong Kong—in order to carry out trade business in renminbi. Ultimately, they can use the offshore centers as hubs from which to conduct back-to-back trade. In this context, swap agreements with the PBoC equate to an "official endorsement," intended to reassure market participants that renminbi will remain available in the event of a shortage of offshore renminbi—the CNH.

BUILDING A PAYMENT SYSTEM

The other key consideration for a well-functioning offshore market is infrastructure—in particular, the payment system. This is the means by which banks and firms in mainland China connect with their counterparts overseas, and, thus, it entails the conversion of the flows of renminbi into and from mainland China (an essential bridge because the China National Advanced Payment System does not support international payments). Designated clearing banks act as conduits with the onshore interbank payment system, and it is through these channels that renminbi are repatriated to China.

How does the system work? Each offshore market has its own clearing bank, designated by the PBoC. Let's take the example of Hong Kong. Here the Bank of China (Hong Kong) is the designated clearing bank. (Other clearing banks include the Industrial and Commercial Bank of China and China Construction Bank, which are the clearing banks in Singapore and London, respectively.) The Bank of China (Hong Kong) maintains an account with the Shenzhen branch of the PBoC, into which it deposits renminbi collected from nonmainland banks that participate in the trade settlement scheme. Through the link between the onshore interbank payment system in mainland China—called the high value payment system (HVPS)[20]—and the offshore renminbi real-time gross settlement (RTGS) system in Hong Kong,[21] the clearing bank settles renminbi payments outside mainland China. Thus, a nonmainland bank can engage with a correspondent bank in mainland China, which, in turn, clears the payment with the clearing bank, or it can engage directly with the clearing bank, or it can use both the correspondent bank and the clearing bank. In addition to taking renminbi deposits from its own customers, a nonmainland bank can obtain renminbi funds by converting or borrowing through the clearing banks or mainland correspondent banks.

The RTGS system allows cross-border payments (for example, in Hong Kong dollars and U.S. dollars between banks in Hong Kong and their counterparts in Shenzhen and Guangdong) to be settled efficiently and safely. It pays interest to participating banks, determined on the basis of the interest rate on deposits that the PBoC, in turn, pays to the clearing bank. The clearing bank is also entitled to a special membership in the China Foreign Exchange Trade System, where it can clear the renminbi positions from the exchange business of participating banks. At the end of April 2016, there were 214 direct participants in the RTGS system that were clearing transactions with a total value, on average, of 700 billion renminbi a day.[22]

Participating banks can set their own conditions on renminbi deposit accounts in the offshore markets. In Hong Kong, for instance, residents—such as Hong Kong identity card holders—face no limit on deposit or withdrawal amounts. They face some limitations, however, on the amount of renminbi they can exchange into Hong Kong dollars, or vice versa,[23] and can remit renminbi from Hong Kong to "personal savings accounts" at banks on the mainland.[24] Participating banks can issue debit and credit cards to Hong Kong residents for use on the mainland, subject to the usual maximum credit limit of 100,000 renminbi. In addition, since 2010, measures have been introduced to facilitate transactions between the onshore and offshore markets—allowing, for instance, transfers of renminbi deposits between banks.[25] Also, firms can set up accounts in renminbi with no limit on the amount that can be held or transferred into and out of those accounts.

There are significant limitations to using the RTGS system to deal with the renminbi payments in the offshore market—notably, the hours of operation and the restricted use of Roman characters—making it difficult for the renminbi's development as an international currency. To advance China's ambitions for its currency, the PBoC has been developing a new payment system—the Cross-Border Inter-bank Payment System (CIPS)—that connects all renminbi users through a single platform, specifically supports cross-border clearing among both onshore and offshore participants, operates twenty-three hours a day (useful for both Asian and European markets), and supports both Chinese and Roman characters. It is intended to provide the infrastructure to facilitate direct international renminbi payment clearing, cut transaction costs and processing times, and put the renminbi on an even footing with key international currencies, thus offering a further incentive to use the renminbi in international payments. A total of nineteen banks have been selected to participate in CIPS, eight of which are Chinese subsidiaries of foreign banks, including Citi, Deutsche Bank, HSBC, and ANZ. In October 2015, Standard Chartered (China) became the first bank to complete a transaction through CIPS, sending a payment from China to Luxembourg for Ikea, the Swedish retailer.[26]

Another benefit for China of using its own clearing system is that it can rely less on the Belgium-based payment system provided by the Society for Worldwide Interbank Financial Telecommunication (SWIFT). Dominated by U.S. and European banks, SWIFT has indirectly become a tool of international politics. For instance, in January 2015, because of the conflict in Ukraine, the European Union threatened to exclude Russian banks from SWIFT. Even without strong geopolitical risks for China at the moment (although there is significant tension between China and the United States and between China and Japan), the Chinese leadership would probably prefer to avoid being in a potentially vulnerable position, in which a retaliatory move due to political pressures could cut off payments in renminbi.

THE DIM SUM MARKET

Along with sufficient liquidity and an infrastructure for payments, sufficient international activity in the Chinese stock and bond markets is especially critical the international use of the renminbi. This is for two reasons. First, by adding another group of financial assets, it further encourages the accumulation of renminbi funds for investments and loans. For instance, Chinese companies can borrow in the debt market and then use the funds that they raise for their overseas investments, or they can even repatriate the funds and invest them domestically. Foreigners, in turn, are more likely to hold renminbi if there is a market for renminbi assets beyond just parking renminbi in deposits in the offshore banks. The more renminbi-denominated instruments available, the less onerous and constraining it is to hold renminbi. Lending and borrowing in renminbi are therefore critical for the development of the Chinese currency.

The second reason for building a renminbi-denominated debt market is that such a market helps "discover" the prices of other assets that are denominated in renminbi, and, thus, it further supports market diversification. As different organizations—sovereign, intergovernmental, and corporate— issue bonds denominated in renminbi, each with its own yield and length, a yield curve and benchmark interest rates are established. Other issuers then follow, each contributing to make the yield curve less blurred. Once a market for renminbi-denominated bonds is established, other financial instruments can be developed—for example, insurance policies that need bonds to cover their policy exposure and investment and pension funds that need bonds to provide an income stream. A well-developed bond market is also critical to the development of the asset management business. They are, in fact, mutually reinforcing: asset management supplies funds to the bond market, and the latter offers investment opportunities through the asset management products. Furthermore, a liquid and diversified bond market supports the development of hedging instruments, such as derivatives. A range of hedging instruments makes it more attractive for foreign companies to use renminbi to invoice and settle trade transactions.

The most developed offshore market for renminbi-denominated bonds is the one in Hong Kong, which is nicknamed the "dim sum" market and issues "dim sum" bonds—to differentiate it from mainland China's onshore "panda" market. The dim sum bond market got its start in 2007 (before the launch of the renminbi trade settlement scheme), when the PBoC and the National Development and Reform Commission made it possible for commercial banks and companies based in mainland China to issue renminbi-denominated bonds in Hong Kong. In the same year, the China Development Bank issued a renminbi-denominated bond in Hong Kong worth 5 billion renminbi. Big commercial banks in mainland China followed suit and issued renminbi bonds in Hong Kong. In 2007, for example, the Bank of China launched a bond offering that amounted to 3 billion renminbi.[27] In October 2009, China's Ministry of Finance issued sovereign bonds worth 6 billion renminbi in Hong Kong, the first such issuance outside the mainland.[28]

These were experiments (all controlled, to some extent, by the state) to test the reaction and the interest of market participants. The real breakthrough, however, came in August 2010, when McDonald's, the multinational fast-food chain, issued a bond worth 200 million renminbi, with a coupon rate of 3 percent and a maturity of three years. It was the first foreign company and the first nonfinancial company to issue a bond in the dim sum market. This marked the beginning of an intense period of bond issuance by Hong Kong–based and foreign companies.

From 2007 to November 2015,[29] the total issuance of dim sum bonds exceeded 443 billion renminbi. Issuers came from a broad range of industries—from consumer goods and financial products to tools and machinery—and countries, including Hong Kong (Hopewell Highway), Japan (Hitachi Capital, Mitsubishi UFJ, Mitsui & Co.), South Korea (Korea Eximbank, CJ Global), Malaysia (Khazanah's Sukuk), Taiwan (New Focus Auto Tech, Solargiga Energy), and the United States (Caterpillar, Ford Motor) as well as a number of European countries (HSBC, Unilever, VTB Capital, Volkswagen, Tesco).

In 2009, in the early days of the dim sum bonds, the Hong Kong bond market was mainly driven by the local currency, with 98 percent of the bonds issued in Hong Kong dollars. Dim sum bond issuances now amount to more than 60 percent of Hong Kong's total bond market.[30] This has shifted Hong Kong's financial center toward more trading in renminbi instruments.

The logic of issuing renminbi bonds is clear. The issuer finds it advantageous to tap into a market with lower borrowing costs—issuing dim sum bonds is cheaper than issuing panda bonds when interest rates are lower in Hong Kong (as has been the case since the global financial crisis). In the case of McDonald's, for instance, fundraising in Hong Kong allowed the multinational fast-food chain to take advantage of cheaper rates than the ones prevailing in the onshore market. Funds raised this way were then repatriated to mainland China through the newly established clearing bank channel.

(Recall that multinational firms like McDonald's that make direct investments in mainland China have significant freedom to move money into and out of the country.)

At the same time, when renminbi-denominated bonds are available in the offshore markets, international investors can diversify their portfolios and—at least until recently—invest in an appreciating asset. The existence of a channel to move these funds between the offshore and onshore markets, and vice versa, makes the whole process easier and thus more attractive.

The forces that have propelled the dim sum market should continue to drive its growth. First among these is China's economic growth and transformation, which is significant even if it is moving at a slower rate than in the past. The push for Chinese companies to "go out" (as discussed in chapter 2) and bottlenecks in the banking sector ensure a steady demand for capital to support existing businesses and to establish new ones. In addition, expectations that the renminbi would steadily appreciate provided some further traction until 2014, when this trend began to change. Furthermore, investing in bonds issued in the offshore market is the easiest way for international investors to gain exposure to China's debt market. Finally, the separation of currency risk from country risk is attractive to foreign investors and other market participants. When buying renminbi bonds in the offshore market, international investors avoid any risk, even political risk, that is related to mainland China. In the offshore market, investors also may be more protected from instability that could arise from operational bottlenecks if the PBoC becomes more active in and reliant on the securities markets for its access to liquidity. This is reflected in yield differentials between the offshore and onshore markets.

Despite the obvious boons, there are significant obstacles that the offshore debt market must still overcome. Although the dim sum bond market doubled its size in its first five years, the yield curve remains limited and the secondary market nonexistent. These two elements (a diversified yield curve that reflects a wide supply of bonds with different yields and different maturities and an active secondary market in which investors can trade bonds before they mature) are essential for a well-functioning bond market. Bond yields are on average just over 4 percent, and the average duration is around three and a half years. That these obstacles remain is not due to lack of efforts to address them—China's Ministry of Finance has been actively selling bonds of different maturities to provide a pricing signal for other issuers, and in June 2013, it even issued the first thirty-year off-shore sovereign bond. The obstacles are also not the result of lack of international investors. International financial institutions issued approximately 7 percent of the renminbi bonds in 2013; and overseas nonfinancial corporations are the largest group of issuers, with a market share of approximately 33 percent. China's monetary authorities are well aware of the need to develop a more liquid and more diversified bond market, and, indeed, the reform and opening of capital markets featured prominently in the plan for reforms presented at the Third Plenum in November 2013 and reiterated in the Thirteenth Five-Year Plan, 2016–2020.[31] Such a development, however, is linked to the reform of the banking sector and, more generally, to the reform of the governance of Chinese companies and provincial governments.

CHANNELS TO MANAGE RENMINBI FLOWS

Once the critical market infrastructure has been created and liquidity has been provided by the PBoC, then international demand for renminbi and renminbi-denominated assets should pick up. But this is where things get complicated. Given the existing restrictions, who is allowed to invest in stocks and bonds listed in Shanghai and Shenzhen—and how can the Chinese invest in stocks and bonds listed overseas? In order to facilitate capital transactions and investments, Beijing's monetary authorities have introduced (or expanded) an alphabet soup of programs: the qualified foreign institutional investor scheme (QFII), which, as described in chapter 4, allows foreign investors to buy and sell renminbi-denominated "A" shares that trade on the onshore stock exchanges; the renminbi-qualified foreign institutional investor scheme (R–QFII), which allows foreign investors to use offshore renminbi funds and invest them in mainland China's capital markets; the renminbi-overseas direct investment program (R–ODI), which enables enterprises in mainland China to invest onshore renminbi funds abroad; the renminbi-foreign direct investment program (R–FDI), the vehicle that "overseas enterprises, economic entities or individuals" can use to make foreign direct investment in the mainland with renminbi; and the qualified domestic limited partnership (QDLP), which launched in April 2015 and allows overseas asset managers to establish qualified domestic private renminbi funds to invest in offshore securities markets.[32]

How do these schemes work? Let's consider the R–QFII. In this case, China's monetary authorities grant an investment quota to financial centers that have a renminbi offshore market. When the scheme was established in 2011, Hong Kong was granted a 270 billion renminbi investment quota; when the scheme was expanded in 2013, quotas of 50 billion renminbi and 80 billion renminbi were assigned to Singapore and London, respectively. The Hong Kong financial center has grown significantly since the launch of R–QFII, with over forty mainland Chinese companies now present there to manage money flowing out of the mainland and to engage in fund advisory businesses. Growth has been so brisk that the HKMA has been discussing the possibility of increasing the quota with the PBoC.[33] Other schemes have been similarly popular—between 2013 and 2014, the R–ODI doubled its size to approximately 187 billion renminbi, and the R–FDI almost doubled to 862 billion renminbi.[34]

New policies are introduced all the time. For instance, the Shanghai–Hong Kong Stock Connect went live in November 2014 (after some delay, which was allegedly due to Beijing's irritation with the ongoing "Occupy Hong Kong" protest). Under this system, China's domestic stock market is, for the first time, directly open to international investors—in particular, retail investors and global hedge funds—without the need for any license or official approval. It also gives China's domestic investors access to international assets through the Hong Kong stock market.

As with the other schemes devised for the offshore market—and more generally with most new schemes in China—there are quotas. Hong Kong can buy up to 250 billion renminbi worth of stocks from the Shanghai Stock Exchange 180 Index and 380 Index and all "A" and "H" stocks listed in Shanghai. Similarly, mainland Chinese investors can buy and sell shares on the

Hong Kong Stock Exchange up to a maximum value of 250 billion renminbi. Each day up to 13 billion renminbi can flow from Hong Kong into the mainland's stock market, and a maximum of 10.5 billion renminbi can move daily from Shanghai to Hong Kong.[35] At the time of the launch, more than 150,000 investors based in mainland China registered their interest in trading Hong Kong–listed shares with the Shanghai Stock Exchange, but on the first day of trading, only 20 percent of the daily quota was used.[36] Demand for Shanghai-listed shares, on the other hand, was so strong that by 2 p.m. on the first day of trading, international investors had exhausted their daily quota.[37]

Despite the strong start, the scheme did not look particularly successful in the first few months of trading, with less than 3 percent of the daily quota for Chinese investors and slightly more than 20 percent of that for international investors used. But since then, activity has picked up significantly, creating a conduit for two-way portfolio investment.[38] In April 2016, more than half of the quota for the Shanghai Stock Market had been used, with total transactions of more than 350 billion renminbi and an average daily turnover of about 3 billion renminbi—down from 4 bn in March 2016.[39] Activity on the Hong Kong Stock Exchange has been less dynamic, with less than 50 percent of the quota used, total transactions of almost 350 billion renminbi, and an average daily turnover of about 2.9 billion renminbi.[40]

Ultimately, this system of gradually introducing new policies (each with its own associated quotas) allows the authorities to retain control of capital movements. It is worth repeating here that the way to make this system of quotas consistent with the policy of internationalizing the renminbi is by developing the offshore market. And which financial center would be a more appropriate renminbi hub than Hong Kong?

HONG KONG: ONE COUNTRY, TWO SYSTEMS

That Hong Kong has been so closely associated with China's renminbi strategy is hardly surprising. The city is the entrepôt of China's trade in the region and a leading international financial center.[41] It handles over 60 percent of foreign direct investment into mainland China, and its banks have been doing business with the mainland for years. But its legal, judicial, and regulatory systems are a legacy of its status as a British colony until 1997, and they are different from the systems prevailing in mainland China—"one country, two systems," to use Deng Xiaoping's description.[42]

Over the years, the Chinese authorities have been trying to combine the capitalist skills of Hong Kong with China's transformation from a planned to a more market-oriented economy. The role of Hong Kong in the development of mainland China was such that Deng explicitly advocated the preservation of Hong Kong's capitalist, free market system, wishing that it should continue for "a hundred rather than fifty years."[43] Since Deng's days, Hong Kong's main strength has been in having an environment stable and free enough to attract and retain the most successful firms and a large number of the most educated and ambitious people—even the "Occupy Hong Kong" protest in 2014 does not seem to have diminished Hong Kong's attractiveness or to have irreversibly damaged its relationship with Beijing.

In the context of China's renminbi strategy, Hong Kong's special status provides the testing ground for the use of the renminbi outside mainland China. In fact, the renminbi offshore market has been developed for Hong Kong and with Hong Kong as a template. Through Hong Kong, Beijing can experiment with the gradual and controlled opening up of China's financial market. And Hong Kong, though an integral part of China's currency strategy and financial reforms, offers the necessary degree of separation between the onshore and offshore markets. Keeping these markets separated—but within the same country—in principle enables China's monetary authorities to monitor the flow of external funds between offshore and onshore accounts and to avoid the huge influx of funds that could create instability in domestic financial markets.[44] At the same time, they provide the necessary renminbi liquidity for the offshore operations—and because of this, Hong Kong is not a pure offshore market.

As a ground for experimentation with the renminbi, Hong Kong has the opportunity to redefine its role vis-à-vis the mainland and shape its financial services sector more around mainland China's renminbi strategy. The 2009–2010 Policy Address—the key policy document that sets out the

Hong Kong government's main guidelines—stated that "we can support the Mainland in promoting the regionalisation and internationalisation of the RMB. In the process, Hong Kong can help the Mainland enhance financial security and develop offshore RMB business." The document resolved that "We should fully grasp the opportunities presented by 'One Country, Two Systems.' We will continue to develop Hong Kong as a global financial centre, asset management centre and offshore renminbi business centre attracting capital and talent from within and outside the country."[45]

The majority of the renminbi business goes through Hong Kong. It handles almost 80 percent of the total renminbi cross-border trade settlement business and about 80 percent of global renminbi payments.[46] Renminbi funds flow in through trade payments or other channels and become renminbi deposits that can then be used, deployed, or exchanged freely with other currencies in the market. This development is not just about banks; over the years, Hong Kong has developed other streams of activity within the renminbi market, such as foreign exchange trading and wealth management. These streams reflect the main components of China's renminbi strategy and are mutually reinforcing. The result has been the rapid development of the renminbi business. For example, Hong Kong's renminbi offshore foreign exchange market has become a major currency market in Asia—after being nonexistent a few years ago. This has deeply affected, and gradually changed, the activities and operations of the city that is one of the world's leading financial centers. According to SWIFT,[47] the renminbi is now the second-most-used currency for cross-border payments between the mainland and Hong Kong—with a share of approximately 12 percent of cross-border payments.[48]

However, despite many breakthroughs in recent years and the large expansion of the renminbi business, bank deposits in renminbi remain a mere 8 percent of total bank deposits in Hong Kong. In March 2016, according to the HKMA, total deposits were worth almost HK$11 trillion: more than half, or HK$5.3 trillion, were held in Hong Kong dollars, and the rest were held in foreign currencies.[49] Compared with total bank deposits in mainland China, which amount to more than 90 trillion renminbi, the size of the renminbi deposits in Hong Kong looks even smaller.[50]

There is clearly room for some further expansion of the renminbi off-shore market in Hong Kong. In any case, due to its special relationship with mainland China, Hong Kong is already well ahead of all other international financial centers—even those that aspire to be a significant part of the renminbi offshore market in terms of the volume of renminbi deposits, as I discuss in the next chapter—and continues to enjoy first-mover advantage, especially in the banking sector. Because of its large offshore liquidity, Hong Kong offers a platform for primary bond issuance and secondary market trading of renminbi products, and this gives it a definite advantage over its competitors.

Hong Kong may not retain its leading position for long, however. The renminbi strategy, as I have stressed, is a work in progress. Beijing's experimentation around the renminbi is already expanding in other directions—in terms of both policy and geography. The risk is that Hong Kong will become less central to this strategy. As I discuss in the next chapter, other financial centers have expanded their renminbi operations and increasingly compete with Hong Kong. This competition is likely to become stronger if and when the renminbi offshore market becomes a pure offshore market—that is, when China eventually fully liberalizes capital movements. In addition, China's monetary authorities have been experimenting with other measures to open the capital account under "controlled conditions." The free trade zones, as I will discuss in the next chapter, are set to develop an onshore renminbi market open to nonresidents, and I wonder whether this will eventually make the offshore market less relevant for China's renminbi strategy. Being able to access China's market directly through the free trade zones will allow many foreign investors and businesses to circumvent the renminbi offshore market in Hong Kong, and make it less critical to Beijing's renminbi strategy.

8

THE RENMINBI MOVES AROUND

W HEN THE POLICIES that comprise the renminbi strategy were first launched, not many people were prepared to bet on the chances of success for a currency with limited convertibility, and thus limited international circulation, that was issued by a country with an authoritarian government and institutions that did not conform to the Western model of democratic liberalism. Many commentators, both in China and abroad, maintained that the trade settlement and offshore schemes were doomed to fail. But market participants, especially those based in Greater China and the surrounding countries, showed enough enthusiasm for this initiative to create the traction needed to keep it going. (To some extent, market participants have been more receptive to this new policy course than Chinese business leaders and scholars.)

In just over five years, what I've called China's renminbi strategy has expanded from the small, low-key pilot scheme that aimed to increase the use of the Chinese currency in cross-border trade to a full-scale operational program that covers a broad policy spectrum. Using China's trade to build a platform for the use of the renminbi and creating an offshore market infrastructure in Hong Kong—with clearing, payments, and other banking facilities to facilitate the use of the renminbi in trade and investment— the Chinese monetary authorities have set up an official channel for the renminbi to freely flow between China and its neighbors and have created a framework for what was the de facto circulation of the currency in the region—especially in China's neighboring countries.

As a result, the renminbi circulation has "normalized," and a well-functioning renminbi market has been created in Hong Kong. To fully appreciate the impact of this initiative, it is worth remembering that for years businessmen hauled suitcases of yuan across the border and deposited this money in banks in Hong Kong in order to be able to pay for international transactions and invest abroad. Opening a formal banking channel and, for example, encouraging Burmese jade dealers who trade in the Yunnan Province, on the border with Burma/Myanmar, to accept renminbi[1] is a positive development. However, it does not turn the renminbi into a key international currency.

The Chinese authorities, even if they continue to maintain a low profile around this initiative, have ambitions for the renminbi that are bigger than just becoming the dominant regional currency. These ambitions were evident in the huge expectations that surrounded the International Monetary Fund (IMF) deliberation in 2015 on whether to include the renminbi in the basket of currencies that provide the basis for its Special Drawing Rights (SDRs). Many in China—from scholars to journalists and businesspeople—were adamant that the renminbi deserved such recognition to cement its status as one of the key international currencies. The IMF concurred, and the renminbi is now one of the currencies in which SDRs can be exchanged (the others are the dollar, the euro, the yen, and the pound). The inclusion of the renminbi in the SDR basket was a "milestone for China," as Christine Lagarde, IMF managing director, stressed.[2] At least formally, the renminbi is no longer a dwarf currency and has become a member of the same club as the other key international currencies.

Where does the renminbi go from here? Hong Kong provides a policy template for establishing offshore markets in other financial centers in Asia and around the world. And, given the existing restrictions on the movement of money into and out of China, it is through this expansion of the offshore markets that the country can support the international circulation and use of the renminbi. Of course, with these markets constrained by the currency's limited convertibility, their size depends on the supply from the Chinese monetary authorities. Collaboration between the Chinese government and that of the country wishing to set up an offshore market is therefore paramount—and these countries must accept that, at least for the time being, there is limited opportunity to develop a pure offshore market. This need for collaboration inevitably adds a political element to what appears to be a mere technical and commercial issue, so it's no surprise that the other renminbi offshore centers are in countries that are in China's sphere of influence (even Taiwan, given the scale and scope of its trade relations with the mainland) or have friendly commercial and diplomatic relations with Beijing.

In this chapter, I look at how China's renminbi strategy has extended beyond China, creating the conditions for greater circulation of the Chinese currency within, and beyond, East Asia—and even beyond the borders of Asia as a whole. The renminbi has increased its international circulation and is now much more firmly on the international map. But the numbers remain tiny outside Asia, and the drawbacks and constraints suggest (as I discuss in the second half of this chapter) that the next development for the renminbi may be beyond the offshore market.

EXPANDING THE OFFSHORE BUSINESS

Hong Kong plays a critical role in developing the international use of the renminbi. The successful development of its offshore market has increased competition and created the incentives—or the push—for other financial centers, in both Asia and Europe, to get in on the growing renminbi market. To date, a dozen financial centers have established renminbi offshore markets. With the exceptions of Toronto and Doha, all are in the Asia-Pacific region—Sydney, Kuala Lumpur, Singapore, Seoul, Taipei, and Tokyo—and in Europe—London, Frankfurt, Luxembourg, Paris, and Zurich. The number of clearing banks has grown as well; there are fourteen across the world, including one that opened in Chile in May 2015, becoming the first in Latin America, and one that opened in Qatar in April 2015, becoming the first in the Middle East.

Given the importance of China in the world economy, being part of the growing renminbi business is critical for leading international financial centers as well as for regional financial centers based in Asia. In particular, financial centers that aspire to be more integrated into China's regional expansion feel the urge to respond to the growing demand for renminbi trading and thus to be active and participate in the renminbi offshore market. This is particularly relevant for Singapore and Taipei, which, for different reasons and with different dynamics, are in competition with Hong Kong. For Singapore the head-to-head competition with Hong Kong is to be the leading financial center in Asia—and one of the most important in the world. For Taipei, the competition is more regional, and the renminbi business is related to Taiwan's trade relations with mainland China. China's renminbi strategy has had an impact on both centers (although to a much lesser degree than on Hong Kong), and they are now the largest offshore markets for the renminbi after Hong Kong. The renminbi banking business is critical to both—Singapore's bank deposits totaled almost 200 billion renminbi at the end of December 2015, and Taipei's totaled more than 370 billion renminbi at the end of January 2016. Both centers have a clearing bank—the Industrial and Commercial Bank of China in Singapore and the Bank of China in Taipei—and this allows banks incorporated in both centers to open renminbi accounts.

Singapore has a strong advantage over other financial centers in the international foreign exchange market and in the commodity trading market. It is also an enclave for Association of Southeast Asian Nations (ASEAN) countries and is part of an extensive trading network in the region—about 55 percent of Singapore's trade consists of transactions within Asia. As a result, it can offer a platform from which Beijing can facilitate a wider use of the renminbi in China-ASEAN trade. Companies and individuals can now open renminbi accounts with participating banks in Singapore, and these banks can make and receive payments in renminbi for cross-border trade transactions. (Before the renminbi clearing services were allowed in Singapore, most offshore renminbi clearing was conducted through Hong Kong.)

According to a survey published by HSBC, approximately 15 percent of companies in Singapore use renminbi to settle cross-border business.[3]

The average daily turnover in renminbi foreign exchange almost doubled over the course of its first year of operation, from $16 billion in March 2013 to $31 billion in December 2013. Singapore has also issued renminbi-denominated bonds worth a total of 7.5 billion renminbi, and several banks now offer renminbi-denominated bonds. HSBC leads the pack with the issuance of a two-year bond, at 2.25 percent, for a total amount of 500 million renminbi.

Taipei is a smaller financial center than Singapore and Hong Kong, but it has a key competitive advantage over these financial heavyweights: deep and extensive trade links with the mainland.[4] The depth and scope of business relations between mainland China and Taiwan drive the renminbi business and generate liquidity for the renminbi offshore market. Improved relations between Taipei and Beijing resulting from three memoranda, including the Cross-Strait Financial Supervision Memorandum of Understanding,[5] and the opening of the renminbi channel have made it easier for Taiwanese companies to access the mainland's capital markets. As of 2013, Taiwanese banks could take renminbi deposits, and the renminbi clearing channel helps banks and trading companies move funds from the renminbi trade settlement scheme faster and at lower costs. As a result, the monthly growth rate of Taipei's renminbi deposits hit a record high at 45 percent in February 2013.[6]

The renminbi can now be traded in other centers in Asia, such as Tokyo and Seoul, where the renminbi exchange rate can be quoted, respectively, against the Japanese yen and the Korean won. The yen and the won are also now directly tradable in the foreign exchange market in Shanghai. In principle, direct trading can reduce the dependence on the dollar in trade between these nations, but liquidity is still limited. (In the case of the South Korean market, this is partly due to the fact that the direct trading between the renminbi and the won was launched only in the summer of 2014.) Market participants that conduct large transactions still prefer to use the dollar as the vehicle currency to settle trade. In particular, the use of renminbi to settle bilateral trade between China and Japan remains very limited because of tensions around the Senkaku or Diaouy Islands in the East China Sea.[7]

MOVING TO LONDON

Trade is the key trigger for the expansion of the renminbi business in Asia. This is hardly surprising, given the depth of China's trade and financial relations with its neighbors. But even though Britain is China's second-largest European trade partner (especially for Chinese exports) after Germany,[8] it is finance rather than trade that explains the development of the renminbi offshore market in London—and outside Asia, in particular. The development of a global market for the renminbi in London means that China is moving beyond its Asian regional strategy and beyond the development of a regional currency.

London, at the crossroads of Asia, Europe, and North America, is the world's leading international financial center. It offers many advantages: its time zone, a sound legal system, a comprehensive regulatory framework, a broad and deep pool of talented professionals, a considerable track record of innovation and risk management, and the experience of developing the eurodollar market.[9] Even better, in China's case, the bulk of Chinese commercial banks have a presence in London. London is already an important center for renminbi foreign exchange trading, with a 67 percent share of the global renminbi offshore spot market at the end of 2014.[10]

London accumulated huge expertise in offshore finance when it developed the eurodollar market in the 1960s and 1970s. The establishment of that market, however, took a fundamentally different path from the Chinese authorities' renminbi development. It was triggered by British banks' attempts to avoid pound exchange controls and by U.S. banks' attempts to avoid domestic regulation—so it was market led.[11] The renminbi offshore market, on the other hand, is policy led, requiring the British Treasury and the City of London (the local authority responsible for developing the financial center) to work in close concert with the authorities in Beijing and Hong Kong.

This joint work kicked off in September 2011, at the Fourth UK-China Economic and Financial Dialogue, when UK Chancellor of the Exchequer George Osborne and China Vice-Premier Wang Qishan announced their collaboration on developing the renminbi offshore market in

London. This was followed by the launch of a private-sector forum to enhance cooperation between Hong Kong and London; this has become a key semiannual event, allowing policy makers at the British Treasury and the Hong Kong Monetary Authority to formulate policy suggestions for Beijing on how the market can be developed. As a result of this dialogue, London's market has developed along the same format as Hong Kong's. It now has checked all the boxes required for the offshore market: a clearing bank, a swap agreement with the People's Bank of China (PBoC), and a bond market.

Although the renminbi business in London is growing at a strong rate (approximately 37 percent annually, fueled by the increase in corporate deposits), it remains relatively tiny. The pool of renminbi—about 50 billion renminbi in bank deposits at the end of January 2016; approximately half of these renminbi are in corporate accounts[12]—is a fraction of the renminbi deposits in Hong Kong and even in Singapore. As for the bond market, HSBC took the lead in April 2012, raising 2 billion renminbi in the first renminbi bond issuance outside mainland China and Hong Kong. Approximately two-thirds of the three-year bonds (paying 3 percent interest) went to European investors; the rest were bought by Asian investors.[13] There were other firsts, from the largest renminbi bond issuance in an offshore market (that bond, worth 2.5 billion renminbi, was issued in January 2014 by the Bank of China) to the first non-Chinese sovereign bond (that bond, worth 3 million renminbi, was issued by the British government in October 2014 to finance official reserves; until then, Britain held only U.S. dollars, euros, yen, and Canadian dollars in its reserves).[14] But so far, these issuances total only about 29 billion renminbi.[15] They have been mainly symbolic, highlighting the joint efforts of the United Kingdom, mainland China, and Hong Kong in creating the renminbi offshore market,[16] the strength of their commercial and diplomatic relationships, and China's financial integration with the West.[17] However, they have done little to drive market demand for renminbi-denominated bonds.

Still, Britain has very little to lose—and much to gain—from being involved in China's renminbi strategy and promoting the use of the Chinese currency in London. These gains are clear—more diversification, a stake in a potentially large market, and stronger commercial and diplomatic relations with China. Above all, there is no threat to the pound. As a British senior civil servant told me, it is not only about supporting the renminbi but also about engaging with China on trade and investment: it is a "joint-up" policy.

THE UNITED STATES TRAILS BEHIND

The same logic applies to many European centers that have recently opened to the renminbi business. Renminbi-denominated bonds have been listed in Luxembourg, Paris, and Frankfurt and have been traded on the over-the-counter market. Luxembourg has built a highly competitive position in this market as host to the European headquarters of the Industrial and Commercial Bank of China, Bank of China, and China Construction Bank. It boasts the largest pool of renminbi in Europe in terms of deposits, loans, listed bonds, and assets in mutual funds. It also serves as the main hub and entry point into the euro area for Chinese investors. As for Frankfurt and Paris, their advantage lies in their countries' close trade ties with China. For instance, German companies now have access to the onshore and offshore renminbi bond markets—Daimler was the first European company to issue bonds on China's interbank market.[18]

The stake for the United States, on the other hand, is much higher. The renminbi is in direct competition with the dollar, and there are geopolitical as well as commercial implications to a rising renminbi. And, as was evident during President Xi Jinping's state visit to Washington, D.C., in September 2015, the relationship between the two countries is rather frosty, especially around issues such as censorship, cybersecurity, and the South China sea. It is not surprising, then, that there is no operational renminbi center in the United States, and the Obama administration did not make any provision for U.S. participation in the renminbi market. As a result, despite having the largest financial markets and some of the biggest banks in the world, the United States accounts for less than 13 percent of renminbi offshore foreign exchange transactions outside China. Individuals and businesses in the United States can trade renminbi in many banks, including Chinese banks—but the Bank of China puts a limit of $4,000 per day (and $20,000 per year) on the amount that a U.S.-resident individual can convert.

The United States has not intervened in the debate about China's renminbi strategy and was especially careful not to openly discuss, in the months preceding the IMF revision of the composition of the SDR basket, whether the renminbi should be included or not. After the rebuff of Britain for having joined the Beijing-led Asian Infrastructure Investment Bank, U.S. policy makers have avoided saying anything that could add more tension to an already strained situation or that Congress could use in its "China bashing." (China's efforts to internationalize its currency had reduced Congress's attacks in recent years, but in 2015, the weakness of the renminbi once again triggered accusations of currency manipulation.) However, in my one-on-one and off-the-record conversations, I have heard these policy makers express concerns about Chinese companies being allowed to raise capital offshore and about the inadequacy of the channels that the PBoC has recently made available to the Chinese market. From their point of view, collaborating with the Chinese monetary authorities to set up an offshore market for the renminbi in the United States does not make sense because of what it would be perceived as a direct threat to the dollar and the possible savage reaction from Congress that this would trigger—even if the impact on the dollar is likely to be negligible.

The conspicuous absence of the United States in the renminbi offshore market has created an opportunity for Toronto (where a renminbi offshore center and clearing bank were created in 2015) to become the leading renminbi center in the Americas. Vancouver could follow Toronto's lead. Like most other economies, Canada sees the internationalization of the renminbi as an opportunity to deepen the bilateral economic relationship with China—its second-largest trade partner—as well as to position itself as North America's premier renminbi financial hub. Engaging with China in the renminbi market is thus a foreign policy issue as well as an opportunity for local capital markets.

ASSESSING THE SCHEME

As this burgeoning global expansion demonstrates, China has had considerable success in developing its renminbi initiative from a small pilot scheme to a much more complex policy framework. As I discussed in chapter 6, one of the objectives of the renminbi strategy is to encourage the international circulation of the renminbi and narrow China's dependence on the dollar. It has indeed been able to increase the international use of its currency without fully liberalizing capital movements. More than 20 percent of China's imports and exports (worth around 1.65 trillion renminbi) are now settled in renminbi,[19] compared with 2 percent in 2010—and zero in 2009.[20] In March 2016, the renminbi unseated the Japanese yen from the fourth position among the world's top ten payment currencies, with almost a 2 percent share of global payments; only a few years earlier, in January 2013, the renminbi ranked thirteenth.[21] The renminbi is now the second-most-used currency, after the dollar, in international trade finance. It is used to settle approximately 9 percent of total trade finance—letters of credit and collections—up from less than 2 percent in January 2012.[22] And at the end of November 2015, the IMF announced the inclusion of the renminbi in the SDR basket.

However, the renminbi's increased circulation has not reduced China's dependence on the dollar. Actually, since the launch of the process of internationalization, the pace at which dollars have accumulated in China's foreign exchange reserves has accelerated. Between the end of 2010 and the end of September 2014, China's reserve holding of dollars grew by 50 percent, reaching a record $4 trillion (although it subsequently dropped by 20 percent to $3.2 trillion in May 2016, due to a rise in capital outflows and the PBoC's need to manage the value of the renminbi). So China has achieved part of its first objective, but its promotion of the renminbi as an international currency has not yet helped it decrease its dependence on the dollar.

China's other objectives with the renminbi strategy are to remove the exchange rate risk and reduce transaction costs, expand the scope of the renminbi business beyond the range of regional trade and support Chinese enterprises that go out, and develop market infrastructure and expand the market for the renminbi. It has had similarly mixed success with each of these goals.

The renminbi trade settlement scheme provides a way for Chinese businesses to remove the exchange rate risk and lower transaction costs. We know how much trade is now settled in renminbi, but when we try to determine how much of China's trade has been priced and invoiced in renminbi, the figures are murky. The majority of Chinese firms continue to price trade transactions in dollars—meaning that the exchange rate risk remains. It is also difficult to measure whether transaction costs for Chinese businesses have fallen—it may even be the case that the renminbi trade settlement scheme pushes them up because (as often happens with China's policy experimentation) the scheme is heavy on rules and requirements, which can generate extra costs. For instance, applications to schemes such as QFII take two to four months to be processed; many enterprises regard the time and money spent preparing these as an unnecessary burden.

As for expanding the scope of the renminbi and helping Chinese firms to go out, success has mainly been regional, with a significant increase in the use of the Chinese currency in both trade and financial transactions within the region. Seven out of ten countries in Asia—including South Korea, Indonesia, Malaysia, Singapore, and Thailand—have tracked the renminbi more closely than the dollar in the past three years.[23] This is consistent with China's position as the center of East Asia's production and investment and as the key hub within the regional supply chain. China trades about $1.4 trillion worth of goods a year with neighboring countries.[24] About 22 percent of its manufacturing trade is now with East Asian countries, up from 2 percent in 1991. For some of these countries, China is the largest trade partner. For instance, 20 percent of Vietnam's trade is with China, although Vietnam accounts for less than 1 percent of China's trade—and the country's trade deficit with China is rising.[25] New initiatives, such as the New Silk Road (also known as Belt and Road), are designed to help Chinese firms "go out" and to expand the international use of the renminbi. The impact of these measures is evident in China's overseas investment, which increased by more than 70 percent in the first two months of 2016, to a total of approximately $30 billion (within this, investment in the New Silk Road increased by 40 percent, to $2 billion).[26]

Finally, although the renminbi market has grown rapidly, it still remains quite limited in terms of size and scale. Growth has been concentrated mainly in Hong Kong. The outstanding stock of renminbi lending there is approximately 35 percent of total lending—or about half a trillion renminbi. The outstanding stock of renminbi liquidity in Hong Kong (bank deposits) is approximately 800 billion renminbi. The other centers significantly trail behind.

All in all, the renminbi is mainly a regional currency. China's trade in the region provides traction for the renminbi offshore market, which builds on the renminbi circulation in Greater China and its surrounding countries.[27] Not surprisingly, then, the largest and most diversified offshore markets for the renminbi are, in fact, in Asia—Hong Kong, Singapore, and Taipei—whereas markets in other regions and in other emerging countries (for example, South Africa and Brazil) have developed at a much slower pace.[28] So far, the renminbi strategy has promoted currency regionalization—"Asianization" rather than internationalization.

PROBLEMS WITH THE SCHEME

The implementation of the renminbi strategy has had some undesirable consequences. For instance, since 2011, cases of arbitrage and speculation have increased, forcing the PBoC to absorb the inflows and accumulate even more dollars. Indeed, some enterprises from the mainland have turned their access to both onshore and offshore markets into an opportunity for arbitrage between the two, exploiting the differences in the exchange rates vis-à-vis the U.S. dollar. Since 2011, importers based in the mainland have been able to profit from the difference between the domestic exchange rate for the onshore nonconvertible renminbi (CNY) and the offshore fully convertible renminbi (CNH). Because the dollar was cheaper in the offshore market, firms could make a profit by buying dollars and selling renminbi in the offshore nondeliverable forward market and selling dollars and buying renminbi in the onshore market. Demand went up, supporting the use of the renminbi, creating a circle of demand and appreciation: more inflows led to more appreciation, and more appreciation attracted more inflows to profit from the "one-way bet" on the currency. The PBoC had to intervene to absorb dollars in order to manage the exchange rate and make renminbi available to meet demand, thus expanding its dollar reserves. (The weakening of the exchange rate in 2015 staunched such arbitrage activities.)

Differentials in the exchange rates between the CNY and the CNH tend to signal underlying market pressures on the currency. An onshore interest rate above that of its offshore counterpart indicates appreciation pressures on the CNY, whereas an onshore rate below that of its offshore counterpart indicates depreciation pressures. These differentials are also a consequence of inefficient capital controls that segment the onshore and offshore markets— for instance, a higher exchange rate in the onshore market indicates that capital inflows have not been stemmed effectively. The result is that capital flows in without offsetting changes in the current account.[29]

Although China has tried to control these "hot money" flows (short-term, speculative capital flows) into the mainland market, firms have found ways around the existing restrictions. The renminbi trade settlement scheme provides the main, and the legitimate, mechanism by which to transfer money between Hong Kong and the mainland: it supports these flows only if they are used to pay for goods—not if they are used for speculative purposes. But by overinvoicing, firms can sneak in money for speculation. For instance, a mainland company that sells goods to its Hong Kong subsidiaries can deliberately overcharge for its exports in order to bring more renminbi into the mainland than the trade transaction would require. One popular method is to inflate export invoices on goods that are difficult to value—such as electronic circuits—and then transform speculative cash into trade receipts and convert dollars into renminbi under the current account. Hence, a portion of this money is brought into mainland China for purely speculative purposes—that is, to profit from the differences in the exchange rates—but it is disguised as a payment for goods.[30] Although the former is illegal, the latter is legal.

The difference between China-reported exports to Hong Kong and Hong Kong–reported imports from the mainland—the so-called invoicing gap—provides an estimate of the disguised capital flows into the mainland. The invoicing gap peaked in the last quarter of 2012, a few months after the expansion of the renminbi trade settlement scheme, when the amount of renminbi used for import settlement was twelve times more than that used for export settlement. Even assuming that importers would be more easily persuaded than exporters to use the renminbi—for example, getting easier access to the Chinese market can be a significant incentive for many foreign firms—the gap is considerable and is explained by the strength of the Chinese currency until late 2014. The differences have narrowed considerably since then, and this narrowing has coincided with the weakening of the renminbi.[31]

Another drawback of the strategy as it has been implemented is Beijing's control of the liquidity in the offshore market. Although this is not a problem for Hong Kong, it is more of a constraint for London and other international financial centers outside China's jurisdiction that plan to be part of this market. The private sector may feel frustrated if it is unable to respond to and satisfy underlying demand for renminbi and renminbi-denominated assets—if and when demand picks up. There is therefore a potential conflict between China's strategy and what the private sector wants. The official statements from the UK government and the Bank of England hint at these concerns. As the Bank of England notes, "There might be scope for the official sector to play a catalysing role at the margin, but the key arbiter in determining if such a market develops will be whether the private sector can identify and satisfy any underlying demand for RMB denominated securities."[32]

BEYOND THE OFFSHORE MARKET: THE FREE MARKET ZONE

China has had to figure out ways around the shortcomings of its current strategy. As I discussed in chapter 6, China's renminbi strategy was originally designed to temporarily develop the international use of the Chinese currency during the transition to the full liberalization of capital movements. Thus, the offshore market was never intended to be a permanent solution.

In fact, back in 2010, China's monetary authorities considered the offshore market to be a temporary measure to provide the first steps toward the internationalization of the renminbi; in their view, the full liberalization of the capital account would eventually provide traction to the currency and make the offshore market (at least the policy-driven offshore market) unnecessary.

But it soon became clear, as I will discuss in details in the next chapter, that China was not ready to open its capital account. So, since the new leadership took over in March 2013, China has embarked on a new round of policy experimentation to liberalize capital movements under restricted conditions and thus to control money inflows and outflows. These policies go beyond the offshore market to include, for example, special economic zones. In the words of Sebastian Heilmann, these zones are the trademark of China's "experimentation under hierarchy."[33] They offer both local and central levels of government a way to test policies on the exporting and importing of manufacturing goods, land auctions, wholly foreign-owned companies, and labor-market liberalization, and they have helped the authorities to detect problems and make adjustments before turning these policies into broad-scale operational programs and extending them to the rest of the country.[34]

The first special economic zones were created in Guangdong, Fujian, and Hainan in the 1980s. By 2007, seventy-two cities had the status of "experimental point for comprehensive reform."[35] The free trade zone is a recently added type of special economic zone and is an experiment in financial opening. In 2012, a free trade zone was established in Qianhai (a district of Shenzhen) to serve as a financial hub that would push the internationalization of the renminbi. This initiatitive has not quite picked up, but it has, in fact, fully liberalized capital movements in China's domestic market in designated areas and within controlled conditions. The Shanghai free trade zone, established the following year, was designed to offer more channels to capital flows beyond the offshore market. These zones give the authorities the opportunity to test their new policies before extending them to other areas of the country, fine-tune the quotas on the basis of domestic financial conditions, and become more familiar with the management of capital movements before fully liberalizing China's capital account.

Through free trade zones and other measures, such as the Shanghai–Hong Kong Stock Connect, which links the stock exchanges of the two financial centers, China has found ways to expand the renminbi strategy—and China's financial opening—beyond the offshore market. And that, of course, was the idea all along—that steps like the trade settlement scheme and the offshore markets would help pave the way for the full liberalization of capital movements.

But this is no longer so certain. In the next chapter, I will consider the way forward for reforms as they are essential to China's full financial opening. I will then explore the debate among Chinese policy makers and scholars on whether the full liberalization of China's capital account is necessary to turn the renminbi into a full-fledged international currency.

9

MANAGING IS THE WORD

I N MAY 2012, I took part in a private dinner in Shanghai's financial district. Shanghai, authorities had recently announced, was to become China's international financial center by 2020. This investiture had sparked great excitement and a fierce debate. Which policies needed to be put in place in order to develop Shanghai's financial business? How could the best talent be attracted and nurtured—especially when the main competitor, Hong Kong, offered a particularly favorable tax regime? And, above all, how fast could the capital account be liberalized to facilitate the free circulation of capital from and to the overseas markets—a key requisite for an international financial center?

Although the central government in Beijing had not given the details of its development plan for Shanghai, many believed that a fully functioning financial center in mainland China needed a fully convertible currency and an open capital account. This was consistent with the plan for the development and reform of the financial industry that the People's Bank of China (PBoC) published in 2012 for the Twelfth Five-Year Plan (2011–2015).[1] The stated goal was to achieve "basic" convertibility of the capital account by 2015, with restrictions limited to short-term flows and the exchange rate regime fully flexible.

Therefore, 2020 became the implicit deadline for the renminbi to be a fully convertible international currency. In those days, many economists and policy makers in Shanghai had no doubt that the liberalization of China's capital account and the internationalization of the currency had to go hand in hand. For Shanghai economist Ya Fu, for instance, it was not possible to turn the renminbi into a full-fledged international currency without opening China's capital market and allowing the currency to become fully convertible under the capital account. A similar view was expressed by Arthur Kroeber, an analyst based in the United States; although he acknowledged the potential of the Chinese currency to see increased international use, he deemed it "extremely unlikely" that "the yuan will be anywhere close to achieving the status of a principal global reserve currency (like the US dollar or Euro)."[2] And Japanese scholar Takatoshi Ito stressed that China must "lift capital controls completely" for the renminbi "to become a genuine international currency."[3]

During that dinner in Shanghai, a former deputy governor of the PBoC made it clear that, along with opening the capital account, China needed to accelerate the reform of its banking and financial sector and bring it in line with international market practice. Letting money flow in and out of the domestic market was seen not only as a natural outcome of the policy of opening up but also as a way to force Chinese banks and financial organizations to reform in order to be able to compete in international financial markets. It was a case of sink or swim. China's accession to the World Trade Organization (WTO) and the notion that Zhu Rongji had used it to force reforms were brought up several times in the conversation. I continued to hear this parallel later in other discussions. As part of the WTO accession requirements, state-owned enterprises were transformed into publicly owned companies with shares tradable on the equity market, an example of how positive incentives can drive reforms.

Critics of this accelerated approach, on the other hand, argued that the opening of China's capital account needed to be gradual and sequenced. Their reasoning was that the financial sector was not ready and the reforms that would allow banks and other financial organizations to survive in the new environment would take years.[4]

In any case, both schools of thought were careful to stress the importance of the financial sector serving the real economy, and not vice versa.[5] Partly for historical reasons—the early reformers adopted financial reforms along with fundamental changes to the real economy—and partly as a reaction to recent financial crises, Chinese leaders have often stressed that finance should have no purpose other than to support investment and therefore economic growth. Thus, speculative finance, with short-term goals and complex instruments that risk distorting economic activity and creating instability, allegedly has no role in the development of China's financial sector.

Fast-forward to 2015, the year when China's capital account was expected to be fully open, and the debate had changed tone and priorities. According to Han Zheng, Shanghai Communist Party secretary and one of the twenty-five members of China's Communist Party Politburo: "Convertibility under the capital account does not equate to full convertibility under the capital account. These are different concepts."[6] This is no longer a case of sinking or swimming but of managed convertibility, as I discuss in the next section, or capital account liberalization "Chinese style." The monetary authorities can facilitate and make these movements easier while also monitoring inflows and outflows and ultimately intervening to curb undesired and excessive activity. In April 2015, PBoC Governor Zhou stated: "As suggested by the [International Monetary] Fund after the global financial crisis, countries may adopt temporary capital control measures when there are abnormal fluctuations in the international markets, or there are balance of payments problems."[7]

Unlike in the early days of China's renminbi strategy, allowing capital to freely move into and out of the Chinese market no longer seems to be part of the authorities' plans. They seem more cautious and more aware that China cannot achieve the full liberalization of the capital account without changing the exchange rate arrangements and switching from the current managed float to a fully floating exchange rate; otherwise, money inflows and outflows would force the PBoC to intervene even more massively to buy or sell dollars in the foreign exchanges to stabilize the exchange rate.

Capital outflows, which until recently the authorities mildly encouraged in order to release pressure on the exchange rate, are potentially more problematic than capital inflows—as the rapid depreciation of the renminbi in the second half of 2015 and early 2016 showed—because of China's huge household saving deposits, estimated at more than 40 trillion renminbi, or more than 75 percent of gross domestic product. If full liberalization was achieved, the impact of depositors moving a relatively small percentage of their saving overseas because they were able to find better returns in international markets would be significant. In addition, it could trigger more capital flight, which, in turn, could lead to a large devaluation—triggering further capital flight.

Yet it's clear that something must be done and that the costs of financial repression and exchange rate management outweigh the benefits.[8] Bank dominance, state intervention, and financial repression distort the allocation of financial resources and generate risks and imbalances.[9] Savings are mobilized and capital allocated to sectors and industries that the leadership has deemed essential to China's development—regardless of whether they are the most profitable. Savers are presented with limited investment options in the domestic stock and bond markets and are offered poor returns on bank deposits, whereas financial resources are allocated to projects with no profitability.

Not only do the existing distortions in China's banking and financial sector hamper the development of the renminbi as an international currency, but also they hinder the leadership's ambition to turn China into a harmonious, high-income society. As President Xi Jinping said at the Third Plenum of the Eighteenth Communist Party Congress in November 2013, when he unveiled an ambitious and far-reaching reform agenda to improve the country's economic performance during the next decade, "To boost the economy we must enhance the efficiency of the allocation of resources. . . . We should work harder to address the problem of market imperfection, too much government interference and lack of oversight."[10]

The Chinese leadership has concluded that the process of capital account liberalization needs to be gradual and carefully calibrated by policy (the recent episodes of high volatility, such as the "tapering tantrum" in 2013 and the turmoil in the stock market in the summer of 2015 and in early 2016, have made the Chinese authorities even more cautious), whereas the domestic banking and financial sector has to be reformed to become stronger, more diversified, and more resilient. The Twelfth Five-Year Plan highlights that China needs to "steadily proceed with the market-oriented interest rate reform, improve the managed floating exchange rate system to be based on demand and supply, reform the management of foreign exchange reserves, and gradually accomplish the convertibility of the RMB for capital account transactions."[11] This concept is reiterated in the Thirteenth Five-Year Plan.

The list of necessary reforms is long and detailed—the World Bank suggests, among others, to further liberalize the interest rate, deepen the capital market, strengthen the regulatory and legal framework, and build a financial safety net.[12] In this chapter, I will focus on the interest rates and the exchange rate—the two areas that are critical for the development of the renminbi as an international currency. Reforms are complex to implement, and financial repression is difficult to dismantle. Untangling the complicated web of vested interests that resist significant financial and monetary reforms—which includes powerful groups within the Chinese leadership itself as well as large state-owned companies—is challenging. And it is not clear how committed the authorities really are to dismantling a system that for many years has served them well and protected many of their interests. As economic and monetary considerations overlap with political concerns, the result is procrastination and "stickiness." The pace of reforms, as a result, has been very slow.

Just a few years ago, the dominant thinking, even among the Chinese authorities themselves, was that the country had to fully liberalize capital movements in order to turn the renminbi into a full-fledged international currency and to drive financial reforms at a faster pace and force them on various interest groups. The example of China joining the WTO is often cited in Beijing: the stakes were high enough to drive a series of reforms.

However, in the case of the banking and financial sector, forcing reforms through the liberalization of the capital account is illusory and risky. There are so many intertwined and overlapping interests between state commercial banks and other organizations—from state-owned enterprises to provincial governments—that it is difficult to implement a unified model of reforms from the top, as Governor Zhou had called for in a speech in 2010.[13]

Unlike the reforms in the years when China was preparing for WTO accession, financial reforms are unsuitable for a "one size fits all," top-down approach.

It has become clear therefore that domestic reforms must come before the opening of the capital account—thus, the timing of the latter depends on the pace of the former. And the so-called internationalization of the renminbi is wrapped up with both of these, so it is one of the elements of China's complex process of financial reforms—but not its main drive. Given this situation, understanding the web of reforms is the best way to understand the future of the renminbi as an international currency. And, because the reform of the domestic banking and financial sector will take a long time to fully implement, understanding the pace of these reforms gives an indication of the speed at which the renminbi will develop into a full-fledged international currency.

THE LONG MARCH OF BANKING AND FINANCE

Reforming the banking and financial system has always been an integral part of China's transition from plan to market, although it has happened in fits and starts, not in a linear way. The key theme of the whole program of economic reforms from Deng Xiaoping onward has been the creation of a market for capital, and this is not only in purely development terms—how the efficient allocation of capital could support economic growth—but also, and very importantly, in ideological terms. The debate about the ownership and the use of capital indeed touches on fundamental tensions in the Chinese system: "command vs market, central control vs efficiency, state vs private ownership, egalitarianism vs growth, and Party vs government control."[14]

Given the complexity of the whole reform process, policies that are easy to implement and that will bring concrete results in the short term—the so-called low-hanging fruit—have always been more attractive than policies that would be difficult to implement but more effective in the long run. The authorities have to pick their battles very carefully and are mindful to promote reforms that are more likely to deliver tangible results and thus win the political support to overhaul the system. As a former PBoC senior official told me in a private conversation, when the Chinese leaders, from Deng Xiaoping onward, and policy makers started to carry out market-oriented economic reforms, the focus was on policies that could be introduced and implemented in the short term and that would offer the best and quickest way to generate jobs and strong economic growth. Transforming China into a socialist market economy was bold, and bold action is not easy. "For those who are accustomed to the West, you think the market is nothing strange, but in 1992 to say 'market' here was a big risk," remarked Jiang Zemin in a conversation with Henry Kissinger.[15] As a result, it was critical to focus on making things happen and to respond to "concrete needs of the economy rather than to a master ideological blueprint."[16] This pragmatic approach to policy making is one common theme linking all the measures that have been introduced over more than three decades. Capital markets have developed in response to specific problems related to the allocation of capital: how to distribute profits, how to finance large infrastructure programs, and how to fine-tune monetary policy and control price increases.

However, this does not mean that individual policies are implemented in a haphazard, scattershot manner; rather, they follow the general vision and policy direction established by the leadership and expressed in the five-year plans—and, of course, the direction of institutional or policy reform, which is subject to change.[17] The decision at the Fifteenth Congress of the Chinese Communist Party in 1997 to lift many legal and economic barriers to private-sector growth and allow banks to lend to private businesses is an example of a substantial change of direction and a key policy shift toward private capital. A few years later, in 2004, the National Congress approved a constitutional amendment to protect private property rights, granting "private property" a legal status equal to that of "public property." This alignment of policies in a particular but shifting direction often means that reforms that have been brewing for years can get the green light and be implemented overnight. This is what happened, for example, in 1999, when during a visit to the United States Zhu Rongji announced China's bid to enter the WTO on terms that Chinese negotiators had previously resisted.

The change in the approach toward private property rights epitomizes the shift, in both policy and ideological terms, from complete reliance on state-owned and collective enterprises to a mixed economy, or "socialist market economy,"[18] in which private enterprises play a major role in promoting growth, innovation, and employment. This shift is evident, for instance, in the share of people employed in private firms—now approximately 80 percent of total employment, compared with 58 percent in 1998.[19] In line with the policy of further contraction in the state sector, the private sector has been leading the transformation of banks and finance providers, which are gradually being emancipated from the obligation to supply policy loans to the ailing state-owned enterprises. For instance, Shenzhen has developed as a financial center to respond to the need of small and medium-sized enterprises,[20] especially those that operate in the manufacturing and high-tech industries, and to provide more financial diversification.

However, these measures have not substantially changed the way capital is allocated—and thus have not corrected distortions and imbalances. Above all, they have not yet severed the deep links among China's political leadership, the state-owned enterprises, and the large banks, with the banks providing financial resources to the state-owner enterprises in order to address the government's policy goals (as was discussed in chapter 3). Thus, they have not been able to redress the peculiar mix of opening and continued repression, of the encouragement of private initiative and the continuing ability of the state to direct and allocate financial resources through the banking and financial system. In this sense, these financial and banking reforms are much more complex than shifting the real economy from plan to market.

Nonetheless, removing the key distortions that exist in the banking and financial sector and curbing credit-driven, poorly profitable investments and loss-making investments are essential to China's economic rebalancing—and, by implication, a critical step toward the development of the renminbi as a full-fledged international currency. The existing initiatives to reform the interest rate and improve the allocation of financial resources, as I explore further later in this chapter, are the most promising ways to achieve China's goals and to rebalance the economy in line with President Xi's objective. These are the reforms that the authorities are focusing on, albeit in a timid and cautious way.

REFORMING THE INTEREST RATES

As discussed in chapter 3, Chinese-style financial repression is both a cause and a consequence of interest rates that are being fixed by the monetary authorities to achieve policy objectives instead of being allowed to reflect the effective demand and supply of credit. This distorts the allocation of capital to state-owned enterprises and other entities that are politically connected but commercially unprofitable, making it more difficult for private firms to access financial resources. In addition, over the years, distorted capital allocation has favored investment over consumption and has resulted in an unbalanced growth model. Finally, savers (individuals and families, in particular) get poor returns for their money and are lured into making unregulated and more risky investments in shadow banking instruments, which promise higher returns.

Reforming the interest rate is therefore critical if China wants to improve the allocation of capital in the domestic market, to support the development of private enterprises, and to fairly remunerate savers—in other words, it is critical to the rebalancing of the Chinese economy. And it is an essential element in the transformation of the renminbi into an international currency. It is worth repeating here that a competitive, liquid, and well-diversified domestic banking and financial sector is necessary for the full liberalization of China's capital account.

The policy direction is clear: to move from a quantity-based system to a more price-based system (at the moment, there is a mixture of both). Price-based instruments use prices—notably, interest rates—to change the amount of money available in the financial system. Quantity-based instruments, on the other hand, focus on changing the amount of money available in the financial system. An example of these quantity-based measures is the reserve requirement—the amount of cash that banks must hold in their reserves. By increasing or reducing this requirement, the monetary authorities can control liquidity in ways that have expansionary or contractionary effects on the domestic economy. For instance, in April 2015, the PBoC cut the reserve requirement ratio by 100 basis points in order to create more liquidity and offset the impact of the exchange rate on exports—and therefore on growth.

Quantity-based instruments like this blur the transmission of monetary policy. In market economies, monetary policy works through the banking and financial system: changes in the interest rate are reflected in changes in the refinancing cost for commercial banks, which, in turn, transmit these changes to individuals and enterprises. Monetary policy decisions thus have an impact through the whole money chain, from the wholesale interbank market to retail deposits. But in China's mixed system of quantitative-based and price-based measures (and the need to give commercial banks access to funds at rates below the deposit rates to ensure that they are profitable) the transmission of monetary policy has been less fluid, making the interbank rate (such as, for example, the overnight or the seven-day repo rate)[21] less effective in guiding market interest rates and channeling wholesale funding to retail funding.

This distortion ultimately affects borrowing costs in the economy. The dominance of banks in China's financial system amplifies the problem and further constrains the transmission of interest rate changes to the wider economy—with negative effects on the disposable income of individuals and families.[22] The liberalization of rates on bank deposits would improve returns on savings, resulting in an increase in disposable income and thus in support for consumer demand. According to estimates, such liberalization could increase the income share of gross domestic product by 4–5 percent.[23]

The situation is currently up in the air—reforms are under way, but many elements of the old, quantity-based system still exist. For instance, the PBoC has removed all restrictions on money market and bond market rates in order to underpin interbank lending. There has also been movement in the reform of interest rates for bank loans and bank deposits, starting with the removal of all upper-end limits on lending rates (i.e., banks are allowed to set higher lending rates for high-risk borrowers) and the removal of all lower-end limits on deposit rates in 2004. However, the reform of lending rates took precedence over that of deposit rates and proceeded at a faster pace. The reasoning here is that a sudden change in the allocation of capital could dramatically disrupt the banking sector; the authorities therefore decided to protect banks' profit margins and gradually, rather than suddenly, expose them to more competition. In doing so, they were responding to and addressing the increasing concerns of, and resistance from, the banks. (A study published by the Swiss investment bank UBS at the beginning of this process found that a reduction in the deposit-loan spread of as little as 100 basis points would have wiped out all the profits of state-owned banks.[24]) As Jiang Jianqing, chairman of the Industrial and Commercial Bank of China, pointed out, "slower economic growth and interest-rate liberalization are among the factors that are curbing our profit growth."[25]

The most significant measures concerning the rates on bank deposits were announced in October 2015, when the PBoC said that it was going to scrap the ceiling on deposit rates. This followed several series of measures that began in June 2012, when the monetary authorities allowed banks to pay as much as 10 percent over the benchmark rate on deposits of various maturities. For example, if the benchmark rate on a one-year deposit was 3 percent, then banks could offer a maximum of 3.3 percent. A year later, in July 2013, the authorities pushed the reform of interest rates for bank loans further by allowing banks to set rates for loans below the PBoC benchmark rates. In May 2015, the State Council gave the banks more flexibility to offer better rates and raised the deposit rate ceiling to 1.5 times the benchmark level. In addition, it launched a new deposit insurance scheme covering deposits from businesses and individuals of up to 500,000 renminbi per bank. A fund run by the central bank backs this scheme so that increased competition among banks to offer higher rates does not put savers' money at risk—even if this creates a potential problem with "moral hazard." The deposit insurance is a step toward the final liberalization of the interest rates on bank deposits.

These are all important steps. The reform of China's interest rates is central to the upgrade of the country's financial sector and key to its opening to external competition. More importantly, this reform is critical in the transformation of interest rates into an effective instrument of monetary policy. For example, after rates are fully liberalized, the central bank can influence deposit and lending rates by guiding money market rates such as the SHIBOR. In order to fully control its monetary policy, as the central banks of the United States and the euro area do, the PBoC needs to release control of either the exchange rate or capital flows (chapter 4). But, as I discuss in the following sections, releasing control of one of the two—ideally, the exchange rate—is proving very hard for the Chinese monetary authorities.

REFORMING THE EXCHANGE RATE AND CHINA'S FEAR OF FLOATING

The reform of the exchange rate is another pillar of China's broader financial reform agenda. It has been a work in progress for years, moving cautiously through "a self-initiated, gradual and controllable process."[26] In chapter 4, I looked at the reforms that started in the early 1980s, when the old regime—a grossly overvalued exchange rate and rigid exchange controls that dated to the economic planning system initially adopted in the 1950s—was dismantled. Through a series of gradual steps between 1980 and 1995,[27] the exchange rate was substantially lowered and was pegged first to the dollar and later to a basket of currencies (among which the dollar dominates). Although this system of a capped and managed exchange rate served China's development well, it also cemented the status of the renminbi as a dwarf currency.

For the renminbi to become a full-fledged international currency, the exchange rate system needs to change. This is starting to happen, with the gradually increasing trading band that allows the renminbi's exchange rate to move above or below the PBoC's predetermined rate by a set percentage. This band has widened from 0.5 percent in 2010, to 1 percent in 2012, to 2 percent in 2014. The idea has been to overcome the ingrained market expectation of continuous currency appreciation—or, more recently, of continuous depreciation—and to create an expectation of two-way movement in the currency. By widening the trading band and intervening in the market, the PBoC aims to fend off pressures and let economic fundamentals, such as growth, inflation, and the country's external balance, influence the currency.[28] A further reform was introduced in August 2015, when the PBoC allowed thirty-five large banks to set the opening daily fix in the onshore foreign exchange market. In doing this, the PBoC gave up some control of the exchange rate and allowed it to be more market led while retaining the power to intervene as necessary.

By making the exchange rate more flexible and allowing the currency to depreciate as well as to appreciate, China's monetary authorities have also expanded the array of measures they can use to manage the exchange rate, to control liquidity and volatility, and to better respond to cyclical conditions in the economy. In theory, this wider band means that the central bank no longer needs to engineer significant market interventions in order to manage expectations—market players understand that the renminbi is no longer a one-way bet. In practice, however, China is now in the middle of the road with regard to exchange rate management—so why does this system remain problematic?

Part of the problem comes from conflicting objectives vis-à-vis a related set of policy measures—the liberalization of the capital account and the creation of offshore markets. It is difficult for the central bank to manage the exchange rate and keep it within the predetermined band when capital can easily flow in and out. Especially at times of rising market pressure, with more money flowing in or out, managing the exchange rate is a daunting task—and even more so if markets decide to test the determination (and the resources) of the monetary authorities to keep the exchange rate stable. China experienced these pressures in August 2015 and then again in January 2016, when the PBoC had to intervene and buy renminbi—and sell dollars—to keep the exchange rate aligned with the daily fix. And the existence of two exchange rates—one for renminbi in the onshore market (CNY) and one for renminbi in the offshore market (CNH)—creates the opportunity for exchange rate arbitrage and carry trades. If expectations are not aligned and one rate is stronger than the other, speculative activities generate considerable risks for financial stability. In January 2016, the spread between the CNY and the CNH was the widest since September 2011, due to market intervention in the onshore market; the CNY was trading at around 6.52 per dollar in the onshore market because of the PBoC intervention, whereas the CNH was trading at 6.65 per dollar in the offshore market.[29]

There are other problems that arise from opening the capital account without reforming the exchange rate. One is the increasing pressure to allow domestic interest rates to align with international levels, regardless of the conditions of the domestic economy, in order to avoid excessive inflows and outflows. Because the monetary absorption capacity of China's domestic capital market is lower than those of countries with more diversified capital markets, there is a significant risk of fast-rising inflationary pressure and asset price bubbles (such as, for example, in the real estate market).

Finally, the policy of managing the exchange rate is costly. As I discussed in chapter 5, it tends to result in a large accumulation of dollars in the foreign exchange reserves, with significant associated costs and risks, or in a depletion of dollars when interventions are necessary to prop up the exchange rate. Switching to a fully floating exchange rate would remove—or reduce—the need to intervene in exchange markets in order to keep the exchange rate aligned with the government's policy goals.

Given all these reasons why the policy of managing the exchange rate is suboptimal, why is there so much resistance to abandoning the managed float and switching to a fully floating exchange rate? First, the authorities are concerned about currency stability. A key international currency, as the renminbi aspires to be, is expected to be stable so that foreigners consider it a store of value and want to hold it. Second, they are worried that a fully floating exchange rate might make the renminbi too strong and thus decrease the competitiveness of Chinese exports. As a result, there is political pressure to contain the renminbi's potential for appreciation, especially as economic growth slows and the demand for Chinese exports softens.

These defensive arguments fail to account for the fact that the renminbi exchange rate seems to be close to its equilibrium level. As the International Monetary Fund (IMF) said in the 2015 Article IV Consultation on China that was published before the market turmoil of the second half of 2015, the renminbi is only "moderately undervalued."[30] This means that, if the renminbi became a fully floating currency, it would quickly reach its equilibrium level and would achieve two-way flexibility around this central parity, without the need for further intervention and foreign reserve accumulation. This is a necessary and sufficient condition in order to mitigate risks to financial stability.

The PBoC has struggled to control market pressures on the renminbi—the same forces that always end up battering emerging markets' currencies—and has intervened several times to settle the markets. In the meantime, however, the appreciation trend has reversed, and more money now flows in the opposite direction. In 2014, China's outbound foreign direct investment outstripped inbound investment for the first time. In December of the same year, foreign exchange purchases by domestic banks—a rough proxy for capital inflows—fell by 118 billion renminbi, the largest monthly decline on record, despite the biggest trade surplus on record. Since the beginning of 2015, capital outflows have been significant—in the whole 2015, approximately $676 billion left the country.[31]

In addition, like other emerging markets' economies, China has felt the impact of the stronger dollar since the expected change in the U.S. monetary policy started to crystallize in late 2014 (with a 0.25 rise in interest rates announced in December 2015). This has been compounded by the indirect effects of the fall in the euro, yen, and emerging markets' currencies over the same period. The global financial crisis had pushed international money toward emerging markets' economies—in particular, Brazil, Turkey, and India—increasing the value of their currencies. But expectations about the shift in U.S. monetary policy and then the actual increase in U.S. interest rates—coupled with quantitative easing by European and Japanese central banks—contributed to turn the tide.

Capital controls have partially insulated China from these movements. The steep depreciation of the renminbi through 2015 and the difficulties the monetary authorities had to keep the exchange rate stable are evidence of the problems that the complete removal of controls could trigger. The outflows could be much larger and the impact on the exchange rate much greater. Sterilized intervention, as I have discussed, is a way not only to manage the exchange rate but also to rein in excessive liquidity and harness large capital inflows that cannot be absorbed by the market. Absorbing or releasing liquidity in order to keep the currency stable within its fluctuation band is therefore used as a policy instrument that complements the gradual opening of the capital account.

As the renminbi becomes a "normal" currency and acquires more flexibility, the PBoC should be under less and less pressure to intervene in the foreign exchange market. Ideally, China should embrace a fully floating exchange rate or adopt a target zone—as has been done, for example, by India and South Africa—with a wide floating band (say, 10 percent above or below parity).

Therefore, instead of managing both the exchange rate and the opening of the capital account, the PBoC should manage only the latter. As Chinese companies and individuals gain more exposure to global financial markets through this managed opening, pressure from inflows and outflows should substantially stabilize, resulting in less structural appreciation and depreciation of the renminbi. Thus, although there are clear advantages to a fully floating exchange rate, the policy of managing the exchange rate is so closely interlinked with that of managing capital flows that the two must be considered in tandem. Discussing whether the Chinese authorities will liberalize the capital account—and if so, how—is therefore the best way to understand and predict how they will handle the management of the exchange rate.

MANAGED CONVERTIBILITY

We have considered reforms of the banking sector, interest rates, and the management of the exchange rate—all are crucial to the ultimate international success of the renminbi, and all are critical to the policies surrounding capital controls. But they are complex and take time, and China is not quite ready to undertake them. This point has been indirectly acknowledged by the Chinese leadership. In a speech at the IMF in April 2015, Governor Zhou clarified the policy direction, confirming a view that emerged about the time of the change of leadership at the end of 2012: the opening of China's banking and financial sector needs to be gradual, controlled, well sequenced, and well calibrated in order to contain and ideally avoid risks. Therefore, China will continue its financial liberalization, especially of the outflows, but without rushing and at a pace that is compatible with the country's development, economic policy goals, and financial stability.

In other words, the authorities will try to ensure that Chinese companies and individuals can diversify their portfolios by including nondomestic assets but without creating conflicts with policy goals or undermining the needs of the real economy. The drawback of managed convertibility is that it makes domestic financial reforms less urgent (but no less critical) as long as the monetary authorities retain some degree of control over the exchange rate.

In his 2015 speech to the IMF, Governor Zhou reiterated the importance of lifting controls on the medium- and long-term capital flows that support the real economy. According to the IMF, only five of forty items remain nonconvertible. In line with this assessment, the governor indicated four cases where China's monetary authorities will continue to retain control.[32] The first case, cross-border financial transactions that involve money laundering and terrorism, is broadly consistent with international practice. The second case involves managing the size of the external debt—again, a rather uncontroversial policy for emerging-market economies such as China that find it difficult to borrow in their own currency. In the third case, the authorities will manage short-term speculative capital flows when appropriate, and in the fourth, they will monitor balance-of-payments statistics in order to be able to adopt temporary capital control measures when there are abnormal fluctuations in the international markets—in line with the IMF's recent policy shift toward a "comprehensive, flexible and balanced approach for the management of capital flows" (in other words, the management of capital movements when these pose substantial risks to financial stability).[33]

Together, these measures amount to a policy of managed convertibility, which is sensible and reflects the change of approach toward capital movements after the global financial crisis. Even the IMF, which for years championed financial liberalization and stigmatized capital controls, now recognizes that unfettered capital movements are a source of instability and a trigger for financial crises.[34] For Chinese policy makers, this shift in thinking away from a push toward full liberalization fits well into China's gradualism in policy making and creates more time and space for reforms. Managed convertibility reflects a more accurate assessment of the possibilities for financial reforms, given that China's banks and the financial sector are not ready to let money move into and out of the country unrestrained. China's monetary authorities are attuned to the risks that volatile capital flows pose to financial stability, especially for countries that, like their own, manage the exchange rate. There is plenty of international evidence that countries with a managed exchange rate regime and a liberalized capital account are more vulnerable to crises, so maintaining control of capital movements (or managing convertibility) seems to be a wise choice.[35] Likewise, reforming interest rates and dismantling the link between state banks and state-owned enterprises must be timed in accordance with these overall policy goals, not tackled separately.

What does this policy shift mean for the renminbi? The authorities will continue to rely on the measures and schemes that so far have underpinned China's renminbi strategy (as discussed in chapter 6) in order to expand the currency's international use for trade and finance, and they will expand these schemes as a way of testing new directions. Back to Han Zheng, the Communist Party secretary of Shanghai, he carried on, in the interview with the *Financial Times*, explaining the recently established Shanghai free trade zone, "One of our key objectives is allowing qualified individuals within the free trade zone to open capital accounts in a gradual and orderly manner, on condition of good risk control."[36] Within the Shanghai free trade zone, for instance, investors—both Chinese and overseas—have much greater freedom to shift money into and out of the country and invest in financial assets such as stocks and bonds as well as physical assets such as real estate. The authorities use schemes like this to test ways to open China's domestic financial sector within controlled conditions.

For China's monetary authorities, the full liberalization of the capital account is no longer considered necessary in order to turn the renminbi into a full-fledged international currency. The country will continue to internationalize the renminbi in line with its own policy objectives and the strategy it has followed so far. This strategy, once deemed temporary, now looks much more durable. In recent years, in fact, the array of measures under this strategy has become broader in both scale and scope. Between 2010 and 2015, China's renminbi strategy focused on Hong Kong and the offshore market. Having Hong Kong as an experimental ground for test-ing renminbi-related policies and for relaxing portfolio flows into and out of the mainland removed significant pressure from Beijing and provided a safety valve for capital flows, especially outflows. Starting in 2014, however, new measures—such as the Shanghai free trade zone—have been added to the policy framework. It seems like the renminbi strategy—and China's financial opening—is now expanding beyond the offshore market.

10

THE AGE OF CHINESE MONEY

FORTY YEARS AGO, China was an enigma to most foreigners.[1] The renminbi was at the time "an untraded, inconvertible currency in most important respects,"[2] as members of the U.S. delegation wrote in their report to Congress at the end of their extensive visit, adding that "tightness of exchange controls would make any de facto trading in renminbi extremely difficult, if not impossible."[3] Even today, many Western policy makers and economists do not see the renminbi as a full-fledged international currency because of its restricted convertibility. As U.S. Treasury Secretary Jack Lew made clear: "If China wants the renminbi to increasingly be an international currency, a natural next step in the liberalization and reform of the Chinese economy, [it] will need to successfully complete difficult fundamental reforms, such as capital account liberalization, a more market-determined exchange rate, interest rate liberalization, as well as strengthening of financial regulation and supervision."[4]

Reforms of China's financial and banking system, as I have discussed throughout the book, hold the key to the next step in China's economic transformation into a significant player in international finance. The development of the renminbi as an international currency plays a critical role in this plan.

The Chinese leadership recognizes the importance of reforms. Common wisdom is that these reforms have to move in a careful sequence and at a gradual pace in order to create the background for the full liberaliza-tion of capital movement—in turn, a key element for the development of the renminbi. For other countries around the world, very liquid and open market-based financial sectors are a prerequisite for cementing a currency's international role.[5] If China chose this route, it would take many years for the renminbi to become a full-fledged international currency. However, the country's leadership is challenging this approach, implicitly arguing that the renminbi does not have to follow the path that other dominant interna-tional currencies—the pound and the dollar—have followed.

China's monetary authorities may have a point. Undoubtedly, the ren-minbi has made good progress and has significantly expanded its interna-tional use since the launch of the renminbi strategy in 2010. The inclusion of the renminbi in the Special Drawing Right (SDR) basket in December 2015 by the International Monetary Fund (IMF) was a turning point for the Chinese currency. But, although the IMF's decision solidifies the ren-minbi's status and recognizes its future potential, it also underscores the fact that the renminbi is very different from other currencies in the basket and that its development has been mainly regional.

What is the renminbi then? Is it a regional or an international currency? Is it convertible or nonconvertible? Fully usable or not? Does inclusion in the SDR basket mean that the people's money is ready for the "big show"? Will the Chinese currency replace the dollar as the dominant international currency—and, if so, when? And what will be the outcome for the international monetary system—and, more generally, for global economic governance?

WHICH CURRENCY IS THE RENMINBI?

There is a sense that the renminbi is here to stay and that it will eventu-ally become a key player in the world economy and international finance—as Christine Lagarde, the managing director of the IMF, put it: "it is not if, but when."[6] As I have argued, the renminbi is indeed an international currency in progress. But how close is it to qualifying as a full-fledged international currency? To answer this question, let's consider two dimensions: scope (whether the renminbi performs all three functions of international money—means of exchange, unit of account, and store of value) and domain (what the currency's geographical extension is).[7]

With regard to scope, the increase in the use of the renminbi to settle cross-border trade has been much more significant than the increase in the demand for renminbi-denominated assets. As I've said, renminbi are now used to settle more than 20 percent of China's trade, and the currency ranks fourth among the world's top payment currencies, with an approximately 2 percent share of global payments[8] (the dollar and the euro have 45 percent and 27 percent, respectively). So the renminbi scores well in terms of the first function of international money—means of exchange.

It is not clear, however, how much of the trade settled in renminbi is also priced in renminbi. Normally, trade settled in one currency is also priced/invoiced in the same currency—but it seems that the case of China is different. Figures are not easily available because data on trade invoicing are not routinely collected and, above all, not routinely disclosed. Anecdotal evidence suggests that the dollar is mostly used in invoicing China's trade, and in a research meeting in 2014, a People's Bank of China (PBoC) official said that only half of the trade settled in renminbi was invoiced in the same currency.[9] Assuming that this is the case, the renminbi scores poorly as a unit of account—the second function of money.

As for store of value, although the demand from non-Chinese for renminbi assets has considerably increased due to the second track of the renminbi strategy—in 2014, for instance, foreign investors' holdings of domestic Chinese bonds increased by 68 percent, compared to the previous year[10]—the market for renminbi-denominated assets remains limited. The managed convertibility of the capital account and the imposition of fiddly rules on inflows and outflows to put off speculators make it difficult for foreign investors to acquire relatively safe and liquid renminbi assets and even to open bank deposits. Bank deposits in renminbi held by nonresidents in the offshore centers (mainly Hong Kong) total 1.8 trillion renminbi—equal to approximately 1.5 percent of the onshore renminbi deposits. Offshore renminbi loans are tiny (about 188 billion renminbi), compared with the international banking liabilities denominated in U.S. dollars, euros, British pounds, and Japanese yen.[11] And although the renminbi offshore bond market has considerably expanded (especially between 2012 and 2014, when it grew approximately 30 percent on average), at 0.5 percent of the world total it is well behind the dollar-denominated market (40 percent of the total) and the euro-denominated market (41 percent)—and even the pound-denominated market (almost 10 percent) and the yen-denominated market (2 percent).

Finally, more than sixty central banks—including those from Chile, Nigeria, Malaysia, Thailand, Indonesia, Japan, and Korea—now hold renminbi in their foreign exchange reserves. The Chinese currency accounts for between 0.6 and 1 percent of global foreign exchange reserves held by central banks around the world.[12] This is a very positive achievement. Here, too, however, the numbers are tiny, compared, in particular, with the dollar and the euro, with total official reserve holdings of 62 percent and 23 percent, respectively.

We turn now to the second dimension—domain. As I've discussed throughout the book, the renminbi is used much more heavily in the Asia-Pacific region than in any other area of the world. Almost 90 percent of renminbi payments (in terms of value) take place within the region (and through the offshore centers), with Hong Kong holding the largest share at approximately 72 percent.[13] The use of the renminbi in the Asia-Pacific region has more than tripled over the past three years, outstripping the Japanese yen, the U.S. dollar, and the Hong Kong dollar. In July 2015, the renminbi was used for 33 percent of payments between China (including Hong Kong) and the rest of the region, up from 24 percent in July 2014.[14] The renminbi gained at the expense of the U.S. dollar, which was used in just 12 percent of payments in April 2015, down from approximately 22 percent in April 2012. (The yen and the Hong Kong dollar were also displaced but to a lesser degree.) Singapore, Taiwan, and South Korea now use the renminbi for most of their payments with China. In 2012, nineteen of the twenty-six countries in the region were "low users" of the currency, meaning the renminbi was used for less than 10 percent of their transactions with China; now, only nine low users remain.

Outside the Asia-Pacific region, the largest use of the renminbi is in the United Kingdom, with almost 5 percent of the total payments, and in the United States, with almost 3 percent. This is hardly surprising, given that these countries host the world's leading financial centers of London and New York. The difference between the two is that London is an offshore market for the renminbi (chapter 8), whereas New York is not. The use of the renminbi is growing in other countries in Europe—notably, Germany (which has significant trade with China) and France—but the share of payments in renminbi in these two countries remains marginal—just over 1 percent for France and 0.5 percent for Germany. European Union–China bilateral trade is likely to grow close to 1.5 times within the ten years to 660 billion euros, and this should increase the use of the renminbi to settle trade transactions (as much as 40 percent of the EU–China bilateral goods trade by 2024).[15]

Although these achievements show that China's renminbi strategy has worked, the first track of the strategy (the use of the renminbi for settling trade) has been more effective than the second track (the development of the renminbi as an investment asset that nonresidents are eager to hold). This is reflected in the renminbi's limited scope. As for its geographical extension, this is limited, too. More than five years after the launch of the renminbi strategy, the Chinese currency is fundamentally a regional currency rather than an international currency.

CHINA'S AMBITIONS

As I've argued throughout the book, currency is a proxy for a country's geopolitical power. "Great countries have great currencies." Thus, the internationalization of the renminbi has implications that go beyond the currency's "free usability"[16] in international trade and finance. The rise of the renminbi has become part of the public discussion in China despite the authorities' deliberate attempt not to bring too much attention to the renminbi strategy. Pride around the growth of the currency has as much to do with nationalism as it has with economics and finance.

In the narrative of the mainstream, popular media, it is a bit like the story of David against Goliath: the renminbi is the young kid fighting against the mighty giant, the dollar. The Chinese media have been hyping this story with the public since the launch of the cross-border trade settlement scheme, whereas the authorities have been playing the opposite role of taming expectations. In August 2010, for instance, the *People's Daily*, the official newspaper of China's Communist Party, anticipated "a bright future ahead of us." A few weeks later, an even more confident article was published in the *Financial Times*. Qu Hongbin, the chief China economist at HSBC, reckoned that the renminbi strategy could be the beginning of "a financial revolution of truly epic proportions." In his opinion, "if there is to be a rival to the dollar as the world's reserve currency in the twenty-first century, it must surely be the Chinese renminbi."[17] Around the same time, *China Daily*, one of the leading Chinese newspapers, in more measured tones expressed the same concept in an editorial: "Internationalizing the yuan is a natural progression resulting from the nation's unusually strong economic growth shown over the past decade."[18] This view was echoed by Liu Guangxi, the director of the Science and Technology Department under the State Administration of Foreign Exchange, who argued that it would not take long for the yuan to be internationalized, even if there was no timetable available.[19]

Expectations for the renminbi grew stronger between 2010 and 2014 as a result of currency appreciation. Not surprisingly, then, when the IMF crowned the renminbi as one of the elite currencies, the Chinese media were jubilant (even if by then the renminbi was weakening). "It's hard to overestimate the significance of the decision, a landmark recognition of China's increased role in the global economy and major progress in the evolution of the international financial system," wrote the *China Daily*.[20]

The official press and the public at large feel that with this inclusion the renminbi has been elevated to the same status as the dollar—and thus that China has been elevated to the same status as the United States, conveying the same influence in economic and financial affairs. "Without the inclusion of the yuan, the representativeness of the SDR and the legitimacy of the IMF would have been questioned," reiterated the *China Daily*.[21] For many Chinese, turning their currency into a peer of the dollar is a matter of national pride. Wu Jinglian, an economist at the China Academy of Social Sciences, expressed a common sentiment when he suggested that China "should try to increase the influence of renminbi."

Although Chinese leaders have been more tight-lipped, they, too, welcomed the IMF decision, albeit in a cautious way. The PBoC called it "an acknowledgment of China's economic development, reform and opening up" and further remarked that "China will continue to deepen and accelerate economic reforms and financial opening up, and contribute to promoting world economic growth, safeguarding financial stability and improving global economic governance."[22]

For the authorities, the inclusion of the renminbi in the SDR basket validates China's achievements through the years and is a formal recognition of the increased international demand for its currency. But they are also clear that the next five years are going to be critical for cementing and growing the renminbi's status as an international currency and for narrowing the gap with the currencies of the other "great nations." "The renminbi's importance had been set," noted PBoC Deputy Governor Yi Gang in 2015. "It will take on a greater role, especially in our neighbours and new silk road countries."[23]

With the IMF decision marking the end of the first five years of the renminbi strategy, it is appropriate to ask whether China will continue to use the two-pronged approach—trade settlement and the offshore market—to drive the international use of the renminbi. In other words, where does the Chinese leadership see the renminbi by 2020—and will the currency be able to meet these expectations?

Ambitions for the renminbi have considerably shifted with the transition to leadership of President Xi Jinping, and the steady growth of the renminbi as a key regional currency no longer seems to be a sufficient goal. As China has become more assertive and even more aggressive geopolitically, the objective now is for the renminbi to carve out a place for itself in the international monetary system.

The Chinese authorities see breaking the dominance of the dollar and offering more options to importers, exporters, investors, and savers as steps toward a more balanced and less volatile international monetary system.[24] The renminbi strategy, at least in the medium term, is motivated by economic pragmatism—the need to have a more diversified and therefore more liquid international monetary system in order to avoid dollar shortages. At the same time, it is driven by the ongoing process of reforming the Chinese economy. It is a way to prepare the ground for the use of the renminbi in the global market.

Replacing the dollar with the renminbi at the top of the currency pyramid[25] therefore does not seem to be a priority on China's agenda—which is sensible, given the dominance of the dollar standard. The authorities are also unwilling to release control of the exchange rate; maintaining the competiveness of China's exports seems to take priority, on the policy agenda, over achieving more flexibility in the exchange rate, with its related risk that the renminbi will become too strong. But a currency that aspires to a key international role needs to be strong and stable in order to perform the function of a store of value—regardless of the impact of the exchange rate on exports' competitiveness.

Some commentators—foreign but also domestic—reckon that the renminbi policies are the beginning of a long process that will eventually turn the Chinese currency into a rival for the dollar and even into a replacement for it. Arvind Subramanian, an American scholar, has even suggested that "the renminbi's potential eclipse of the dollar is no more than a decade away" and that the strength of the Chinese economy creates the conditions "for the imminent rise of its currency."[26] But this is reading too much into the Chinese authorities' plan.

THE RENMINBI AND THE DOLLAR

In March 2009, a few months into the global financial crisis, PBoC Governor Zhou Xiaochuan stirred up a lively debate both in China and internationally when he asked: "What kind of international reserve currency do we need to secure global financial stability and facilitate world economic growth . . . ?"[27] Without explicitly calling for an end to the dollar dominance in the international monetary system, he suggested moving to a "super-sovereign reserve currency" to eliminate "the inherent risks of credit-based sovereign currency" and make it possible "to manage global liquidity."[28] The sudden dearth of liquidity that followed the collapse of Lehman Brothers and almost brought international trade to a halt had made evident, the governor explained, the intrinsic fragility of the international monetary system and its inherent systemic risks. The country that issues the key reserve currency—Zhou was careful not to mention the United States in his speech—can sometimes be in a position where the goal of preserving the value of its currency conflicts with the goal of supporting the growth of the domestic economy. When faced with this dilemma, domestic priorities take precedence over other, more international considerations—and, as a consequence, there may be increasing costs and risks in using and holding that currency for international transactions and investments.[29]

Zhou was speaking from experience. For a trading nation like China, a shortage of dollars (the currency used to price and settle most international trade) can put orders on hold and create considerable delays throughout the whole supply chain. In addition, China is flush with dollars and dollar-denominated assets, making it particularly vulnerable to changes in the value of the greenback. Above all, as Zhou hinted in his speech, because of its exposure to the dollar, China is in the shadow of U.S. domestic policies.

In his speech, Zhou warned against having a dominant national currency like the dollar and proposed an international currency that would be "disconnected from economic conditions and sovereign interests of any single country"—an idea that gained some interest among scholars but was then dropped because of its almost impossible implementation.[30] Instead, the idea of shifting the international monetary system from a system dominated by the dollar to one dominated by multiple currencies began to gain traction. Many Chinese scholars[31] implicitly assume that the shift will happen by the time the renminbi is a full-fledged international currency.

The international monetary system is indeed changing, albeit slowly, as a result of changes in the world economic order, governance, and geopolitics. Having one dominant currency issued by the dominant economic and military power, as was the case in the second half of the twentieth century, may turn out to be the exception in economic and political history rather than the norm. Indeed, within the next ten to twenty years, both the renminbi and the dollar are due to become normal currencies. The renminbi's use internationally, in both trade and finance, will increase, as will its relative weight vis-à-vis other key currencies. The dollar, in turn, will see less relative weight—in regions like Asia, in particular, but also in Latin America and Africa, where China is expanding its commercial presence and its investments.

However, inertia and network externalities (as discussed in chapter 5) will play a significant role in slowing the erosion of dollar dominance. Only an economy as large as that of the incumbent stands a chance of developing a network large enough to challenge the leading currency's preeminence. True, China now has the critical mass—in terms of the size of its economy, exports, and now financial transactions—and the geopolitical influence to push its own policies and make an impact on the rest of the world. It has a strategy for the renminbi and a general policy direction. However, the renminbi has to go head to head against the dominant dollar. Will essential market infrastructure and a policy framework that encourages the use of the renminbi trigger strong enough demand from foreigners? And will foreigners be persuaded that China is a trustworthy partner—in terms of its leadership and policies?

Meanwhile, the dollar is facing challenges driven by anti-American sentiment and concerns about the use of fines, sanctions, and extraterritoriality imposed by the U.S. administration to push its own foreign policy agenda. Take, for instance, oil (although the example could be extended to other commodities: gold, silver, and aluminum as well as corn, wheat, soybeans, and cotton).[32] Oil prices are almost exclusively quoted in dollars,[33] and this has been the case since the first drilling in the United States in the middle of the nineteenth century. In February 1975, an oil agreement was negotiated and signed between the United States and Saudi Arabia to ensure that the Organization of the Petroleum Exporting Countries (OPEC) priced its oil exports in U.S. dollars. Similarly, oil-importing countries across the world are required to pay dollars for the oil imported from OPEC members. The benchmark oil contracts—light sweet crude traded on the New York Mercantile Exchange (NYMEX) and the Brent contract traded at Intercontinental Exchange (ICE) Futures Europe in London—are also quoted in dollars.

But, increasingly, oil-producing countries, especially those outside the U.S. area of influence, are threatening to price oil in other currencies as a retaliatory measure. In October 2000, for instance, the Iraqi government, then led by Saddam Hussein, demanded to settle its petroleum exports in euros under the Oil-for-Food Program managed by the United Nations.[34] And since 2005, Iran and Venezuela have been trying to switch to the euro, even though all other OPEC member countries still trade in dollars. In February 2006, Iran announced its plan to establish an Iranian Oil Bourse, with the goal of competing with the NYMEX and London's International Petroleum Exchange (IPE; now renamed ICE Futures). Later, in December 2007, Iran stopped accepting dollars for its oil and in February 2008 officially opened the oil bourse. In March 2008, the Venezuelan government opted to sign some oil contracts in euros rather than in dollars because of the decline in the value of dollar against the euro.[35] In January 2012, India held talks in Tehran to discuss alternative payment methods in the wake of the U.S. sanctions against Iranian oil exports. However, these threats have never looked credible because possible alternatives, like the euro and the yen, do not have enough influence in geopolitical terms, the former being a currency without a country and the latter being the currency of a country without an independent foreign and security policy.

Of course, U.S. sanctions and fines reach far beyond oil. In 2014, for example, a New York court fined French bank BNP Paribas $9 billion for violating sanctions and doing business in Sudan, Iran, and Cuba.[36] This has raised worries in the industry that foreign banks could be cut out of the dollar-payment system if they do not comply with U.S. guidelines and has stoked interest among sanctioned countries in promoting an alternative to the dollar. The use of the renminbi, and the new payment infrastructure that China is developing, is of particular interest to countries on which both the United States and the European Union have imposed sanctions—such as Russia, sanctioned in response to the Russian-led crisis in Ukraine. Russian companies are concerned about the risk of being locked out of the dollar market—and, to some extent, out of the euro market as well. They have been using the renminbi and other Asian currencies, and the chief executive of a Russian manufacturer that earns 70 percent of its export revenues in U.S. dollars has disclosed that "if something happens, we are ready to switch to other currencies, for example to the Chinese yuan or the Hong Kong dollar."[37] Information on exact volumes is very limited, but it seems that most of the renminbi trading on the Russian market is for contract settlements.[38]

State-owned oil and mining companies, such as Gazprom and Norilsk Nickel, have been making provisions to denominate long-term contracts in renminbi.[39] In 2015, Gazprom Neft, Russia's third-largest oil producer and the oil arm of the state-owned gas company Gazprom, began to settle all its exports to China in renminbi.[40] Russian banks—including JSC VTB Bank, Russian Agricultural Bank OAO, and Russian Standard Bank ZA—have so far raised a total of $482 million through issuances of renminbi-denominated bonds in the renminbi offshore market—mainly in Hong Kong.

All these activities, although interesting in geopolitical terms, have a marginal impact on international finance. For instance, the number of transactions in renminbi-ruble trading has been on the rise since early 2014, but the average monthly turnover is tiny, at approximately $300 million.[41] Even in sanctions-stricken Russia, companies are reluctant to switch to the renminbi because of its limited liquidity and higher transaction costs, especially because U.S.- and EU-imposed sanctions still allow payments in dollars and euros for oil and gas sales.

The renminbi provides some diversification on the margin and remains a remote and fundamentally weak threat to the United States (although that hasn't stopped the threat from being trumpeted in the American political debate, with some rather paranoid connotations: "Stop spend borrowed money! US dollar, here today . . . Yuan tomorrow," read a sign on a bank in Franklin, North Carolina).[42] So non-Americans still overwhelmingly prefer to hold dollars regardless of their opinions or concerns about the United States. During a discussion on the international monetary system that I held a few months ago with a group of senior civil servants in Hong Kong, one of them went on a long tirade against the dollar and, implicitly, against the dominance of the United States in Asia. "We hate the [U.S.] dollar," she concluded, as her colleagues nodded in approval. When I pointed out the fundamental problem with her argument—China's large holding of U.S.

dollars revealed a preference for the American money—she acknowledged that it was a case of love and hate and concluded: "We love the dollar, but we hate the United States."

In the end, the internationalization of the renminbi will increase its international use, and this will happen by reducing the relative weight of the dollar. But the ultimate role of the renminbi in the international monetary system will directly depend on how successful Beijing is in pushing forward financial and monetary reforms and in rebalancing its own economy. At the IMF–World Bank 2015 spring meetings in Washington, D.C., PBoC Governor Zhou promised that measures to improve the international use of the renminbi and "further increase capital account convertibility"[43] are in the pipeline. More channels will be opened to allow the flow of money to and from China's domestic market, and capital movements will be made easier. However, as the discussion in chapter 9 has shown, these flows will be managed—and "managed" here does not simply mean that regulations and prudential measures will be occasionally applied. China is not ready to fully open its capital account because of the existing shortfalls in its banking and financial system. Capital-account convertibility Chinese style means that the liquidity that supports the renminbi will continue to be controlled by the PBoC. In addition, the Chinese monetary authorities will continue to manage the exchange rate. Thus, they will continue to push the international use of the renminbi through the implementation of measures that will allow capital to flow into and out of the country even without the full liberalization of the capital account, as was predicted by the British and U.S. models.

As long as domestic policy concerns and vested interests—such as banks, provincial governments, state-owned enterprises, and exporters— continue to act as brakes on reforms—and, of course, assuming the continuation of managed convertibility, the development of the renminbi as a full-fledged international currency and a significant player in the international monetary system will remain constrained. How quickly the renminbi will morph into a full-fledged international currency and how influential it will become directly depend on the pace and depth of domestic financial reforms.

THE RENMINBI AND THE INTERNATIONAL
MONETARY SYSTEM

The renminbi differs from its peer currencies in other ways—it is, for instance, the only currency issued by a developing country that is included in the SDR basket. This challenges the notion that the main currencies can be issued only by advanced countries that are market economies and democracies. It also challenges China to adopt international standards of governance. Transparency, accountability, and separation of power—legislative, judiciary, and executive—are the elements of good governance that underpin confidence in a currency and thus its international use. Non-Chinese holders of the renminbi need to be sure that domestic policy objectives will not interfere with the value of the currency. Otherwise, they will question the rationale of holding a currency whose value and liquidity continue to be controlled by the government of an authoritarian state.

Thus, it is China's institutional shortfalls that limit the international use of the renminbi—as opposed to its convertibility, which can be continuously improved and even achieved under controlled conditions. Consider, for instance, the fact that the PBoC is not an independent central bank. It cannot set its final targets or its instruments without approval of the State Council. Its approach is to rule by consensus, and, therefore, it has to take into account the views of different stakeholders—such as, for example, exporting firms. This has resulted in excessive gradualism and sometimes in contradictory measures—for example, intervention in the foreign exchange market to keep the exchange rate stable in and after August 2015. As I have discussed throughout the book, the reform of the exchange rate remains patchy, sending out confusing messages and forcing the Chinese monetary authorities to resort to market intervention instead of following the path of the key international currencies, which have fully flexible, floating exchange rates. Market intervention undermines confidence in the renminbi, and, unlike the case of trade in goods, international finance requires a great deal of confidence and credibility to persuade savers and investors to part with their money.

As a result, Asia—where the renminbi has strong traction—is where it stands a chance to break the dominance of the dollar. The sheer size of China's trade and the PBoC's strategy of signing bilateral currency pacts with some of its major trading partners expanded the use of the renminbi as a settlement currency. In Asia, the renminbi can play a role largely similar to that of the euro in Europe and the dollar in the Americas. In this sense, Zhou is right to call for a new multicurrency monetary system in which the key international currencies are dominant in some regions but none is the monetary hegemon.

It will take some time for the renminbi to become a leading international currency in both trade and finance and a reserve currency. It will gain market share at the expense of the dollar, but this gain will be relative rather than absolute. In a study published in 2011, the IMF identified the renminbi as one of the three national-currency contenders that could challenge the dollar's status—the other two currencies are the euro and the Japanese yen.[44] It does look like the renminbi will be one of the key currencies in a multicurrency international monetary system, but it will not be the dominant one.[45] In other words, the end of the dollar's dominance will not mark the beginning of the renminbi's dominance.[46]

As I have discussed from chapter 6 onward, the renminbi is an international convertible currency insofar as the PBoC provides the necessary liquidity through designed channels—from the offshore centers to the free trade zones. China's central bank will continue to facilitate such movements, and volumes will increase. However, as discussed in chapter 9, these flows will be managed, and "managed" here does not simply mean that macro-prudential measures will be occasionally applied. China is not ready to fully open its capital account because of the existing shortfalls in its banking and financial system, so mechanisms and quotas to control inflows and outflows need to be kept in place. Capital-account convertibility Chinese style means that the liquidity that supports the renminbi will continue to be controlled by the PBoC—and the Chinese monetary authorities will continue to manage the exchange rate.

The trajectory of the renminbi as one of the key international currencies is clear—and the IMF decision has reinforced it. Then the pace and scope of this development ultimately depend on how deep and how fast the Chinese leadership is prepared to push the reforms. As I have discussed throughout the book, there are several (often opposite) views and interests, and the one prevailing puts gradualism and control ahead of fast reforms and opening up. Therefore, the situation is likely to stay more or less the same for years to come as the pool of easy-to-implement reforms—the low-hanging fruit that I described in chapter 9—dries up. The progress of the renminbi in the years ahead, as a result, is likely to be less rapid.

THE END OF THE STORY

The people's money as an international currency is a work in progress that is contributing to the transformation of the international monetary system to reflect the changing dynamics of the world economy in the last thirty years—of which China has been both a significant element and a catalyst. To shape the renminbi strategy, the country is looking at history, but it is also rewriting history. There is no road map it can refer to because its experience is fundamentally different from those of other countries that have gone through a similar process. China is a developing country and also a world power, but unlike Britain and the United States in the golden era of their currencies, it is not a superpower. It is still a middle power in terms of income per capita and definitely an immature power with regard to its financial sector. It is run by an authoritarian central power, and its economy is a hybrid of planning and market. And, unlike Britain and the United States at the time of the emergence of the pound and the dollar, it cannot rely on anchoring the value of the renminbi to a commodity like gold. In navigating its way forward, it is crossing the river by feeling the stones.

The world economic (and geopolitical) order is changing now, and China is a critical force for this development. At the same time, the country continues to harness the opportunities offered by a world economy that is much more integrated than was the case just thirty years ago, when the yen attempted its own internationalization. This timing may not be ideal, and the international economy may not provide the right context for the renminbi strategy. When the interest rates in the United States—and in other advanced economies—were near zero, China was subjected to the headwinds of inflows of hot money, which undermined the PBoC's monetary control and drove the country's domestic interest rates down too much. When the Federal Reserve monetary policy began to turn, China faced the opposite problem.

Even if the situation is far from ideal, China cannot wait a couple of decades to see its currency develop naturally; that is, it cannot wait until liquid and diversified financial markets are ready, capital flows are fully liberalized, and the renminbi is fully convertible. Ultimately, China is going through its transformation now. Therefore, managed convertibility and the renminbi strategy—beyond the offshore market—are going to be the norm in the foreseeable future.

Throughout this book, I have explored how China has managed its transformation from a poor and isolated country into the world's second-largest economy. I have argued that maintaining controls on capital movements and pegging the renminbi to the dollar suited China's growth model and pattern of development but also cemented the renminbi as a dwarf currency with little traction in international markets. China is now changing this.

The Chinese leadership's ambition is not to rival and eventually displace the dollar at the top of the international monetary system but rather to provide an alternative and let people choose. The alternative to the current dollar system is a multicurrency system that reflects the multipolarity of the global economic order—no longer with the United States as the economic super-power. The key question, for which there is no answer yet, is whether this system will be truly complementary or whether different standards—for instance, incompatible payment systems—will result in a fundamental fragmentation. China has developed its economy and engineered its transformation within the dollar system. On many occasions, it has signaled its willingness to go along with the existing, but reformed, multilateral financial institutions such as the IMF and the World Bank.

At the same time, China has been active in promoting regional multilateral organizations such as the Asian Infrastructure Investment Bank (AIIB). In Asia, the renminbi has already started to break the dominance of the dollar, and initiatives such as the AIIB, the New Development Bank, and the plan to build road and maritime links between Asia and Europe can ensure the renminbi's regional dominance. In addition to the economic argument that demand for infrastructure investment in Asia is large enough to accommodate another development bank in the region, there is an important geopolitical dimension. The new bank may be seen as a counterweight to the influence of the Asian Development Bank (ADB). The ADB's main shareholders are the United States and Japan. China holds limited influence.

We are at an interesting juncture for the governance of the world economy. In 2015, China showed its willingness to shape international economic governance, with the launch of AIIB, and was welcomed in, with the inclusion of the renminbi in the IMF's SDR basket. The country's leadership is eager to work toward a new model of governance that no longer emanates from Washington, D.C., and the Bretton Woods institutions. Will China succeed in steering efforts toward building "an innovative, invigorated, interconnected and inclusive world economy," as President Xi Jinping announced in December 2015 during the inaugural speech of his country's 2016 Group of 20 (G20) presidency? In other words, will the United States and Europe—notably, Britain, Germany, and France—be willing to reform a governance framework that goes back to the years after World War II and make space for the so-called emerging powers?

There are two roads to the age of Chinese money. One road may lead to fragmented governance, conflicting trade and investment standards, and two blocs—the dollar bloc and the renminbi bloc—facing off against each other. The other may lead to a world that is more open, more integrated, and more peaceful. It is not clear which road the world will travel, but either way, the renminbi is here to stay.

NOTES

INTRODUCTION

1. Figure for April 2016. PBoC figures available on Reuters Datastream.

1. MONEY IS THE GAME CHANGER

1. Barry Eichengreen, *Globalizing Capital: A History of the International Monetary System* (Princeton, N.J.: Princeton University Press, 1998), 1.

2. Benn Steil and Robert E. Litan, *Financial Statecraft: The Role of Financial Markets in American Foreign Policy* (New Haven, Conn.: Yale University Press, 2006), 3.

3. The survey on which the foreign exchange data are based is conducted only every three years, and the turnover levels are measured only for the month of April of the reference year. See Bank for International Settlements, *Triennial Central Bank Survey: Foreign Exchange Turnover in April 2013: Preliminary Global Results* (Basel: Bank for International Settlements, September 2013). The global foreign exchange market turnover was $5.3 trillion per day in April 2013. The 2016 Triennial Survey is due to be published in December 2016.

4. Oxford Economics Datastream data series.

5. Adjusted net national income per capita at constant 2005 U.S. dollars. Oxford Economics Datastream data series.

6. Figures for 2012, "World DataBank: World Development Indicators," World Bank, http://data.worldbank.org/country/ghana.

7. Thomas Piketty, *Capital in the Twenty-First Century* (Cambridge, Mass.: Harvard University Press, 2014), 435.

8. "The World's Billionaires 2016," *Forbes*, March, 1st 2016, http://www.forbes.com /billionaires/list/#version:static.

9. Sovereign wealth funds lack a universally accepted definition, with the result that these funds are often confused with sovereign pension funds and official foreign exchange reserves. Clay Lowery, acting under secretary for international affairs at the U.S. Treasury, defined a sovereign wealth fund as "a government investment vehicle which is funded by foreign exchange assets, and which manages these assets separately from official reserves." Robert Kimmitt, "Public Footprints in Private Markets: Sovereign Wealth Funds and the World Economy," *Foreign Affairs* 87 (2008): 119–130.

10. Nathaniel Popper, *Digital Gold* (New York: HarperCollins, 2015).

11. In the economic literature, the concepts of confidence and trust are treated as synonyms. Here I prefer to keep them separate, as they underlie the two features of money: value (confidence) and liquidity (trust).

12. George S. Tavlas and Yuzuru Ozeki, *The Internationalization of Currencies: An Appraisal of the Japanese Yen*, IMF Occasional Paper 90 (Washington, D.C.: International Monetary Fund, 1992).

13. IMF, Currency Composition of Official Foreign Exchange Reserves (COFER), http://data.imf.org/?sk=E6A5F467-C14B-4AA8-9F6D-5A09EC4E62A4&ss =1408243036575.

14. "Swiss National Bank Acts to Weaken Strong Franc," BBC Business News, September 6, 2011, http://www.bbc.co.uk/news/business-14801324.

15. "Swiss Stun Markets and Scrap Franc Ceiling," *Financial Times*, January 15, 2015, http://www.ft.com/cms/s/0/3b4f6c14-9c9a-11e4-971b-00144feabdc0 .html#slideo.

16. The SDR is an international reserve currency that the IMF created in 1969. It is neither a currency of nor a claim on the IMF; rather, it is a claim on the freely usable currencies of the IMF members. These currencies can be obtained through voluntary exchanges between IMF members. Alternatively, the IMF can designate IMF members with strong external positions to purchase SDRs from members with weak external positions.

17. "IMF Executive Board Completes the 2015 Review of SDR Valuation," Press Release 15/543, International Monetary Fund, December 1, 2015, http://www.imf .org/external/np/sec/pr/2015/pr15543.htm.

18. IMF, Currency Composition of Official Foreign Exchange Reserves (COFER), http://data.imf.org/?sk=E6A5F467-C14B-4AA8-9F6D-5A09EC4E62A4&ss =1408243036575.

19. Eichengreen, *Globalizing Capital*.

20. Armand van Domael, *Bretton Woods: Birth of a Monetary System* (London: Macmillan, 1978): 200–202, quoted in Harold James, "Cosmos, Chaos: Finance, Power and Conflict," *International Affairs* 90, no. 1 (2014): 47.

21. On the Bretton Woods conference and the Bretton Woods system, see Harold James, *International Monetary Cooperation Since Bretton Woods* (Oxford: Oxford University Press, 1996), and Benn Steil, *The Battle of Bretton Woods: John Maynard Keynes, Harry Dexter White, and the Making of a New World Order* (Princeton, N.J.: Princeton University Press, 2013).

22. This, however, is not a necessary condition, and no theory argues that a current-account deficit is needed. A key currency can be provided even with a current-account surplus, through intermediation on the capital account, as the United States did for many years after World War II.

23. Benjamin Cohen, "Bretton Woods System," in *Routledge Encyclopedia of International Political Economy*, ed. R. J. Barry Jones (London: Routledge, 2001), 95–102.

24. Bank for International Settlements, *Locational Banking Statistics—External Position of Banks in Individual Reporting Countries* (Basel: Bank for International Settlements, December 2012).

25. Bank for International Settlements, *Locational Banking Statistics—External Position of Banks in Individual Reporting Countries* (Basel: Bank for International Settlements, December 2015); "Table 1.1.5, Gross Domestic Product," National Data, Bureau of Economic Analysis, U.S. Department of Commerce, November 24, 2015, http://www.bea.gov/itable/.

26. By the end of 2005, the Fed had raised the level of the target federal funds by 175 basis points in order to cool off market activity.

27. Alan Greenspan, "Federal Reserve Board's Semiannual Monetary Policy Report to the Congress" (testimony before the Committee on Financial Services, U.S. House of Representatives, February 17, 2005).

28. Ben Shalom Bernanke, "The Global Saving Glut and the U.S. Current Account Deficit" (Sandridge Lecture, Virginia Association of Economists, Richmond, March 10, 2005).

29. Alan Greenspan, *The Age of Turbulence: Adventures in a New World* (New York: Penguin, 2008).

30. It was William McChesney Martin, chairman of the Federal Reserve Board from 1951 to 1970, who coined the phrase "taking away the punch bowl" to describe the role of a central banker: "I'm the fellow who takes away the punch bowl just when the party is getting good." Quoted in Lou Schneider, "Trade Winds: Credit Controls Policy Unchanged," *Greensboro Record*, October 25, 1955.

31. Michiyo Nakamoto and David Wighton, "Citigroup Chief Stays Bullish on Buy-Outs," *Financial Times*, July 9, 2007, http://www.ft.com/cms/s/0/80e2987a-2e50-11dc-821c-0000779fd2ac.html.

32. Jonathan Wheatley and Peter Garnham, "Brazil in a 'Currency War' Alert," *Financial Times*, September 27, 2010, http://www.ft.com/cms/s/0/33ff9624-ca48-11df-a860-00144feab49a.html.

33. Robin Harding, John Aglionby, Delphine Strauss, Victor Mallet, and Amy Kazmin, "India's Raghuram Rajan Hits Out at Unco-ordinated Global Policy," *Financial Times,* January 30, 2014.

34. IMF Committee on Balance of Payments Statistics, *Annual Report 2006* (Washington, D.C.: International Monetary Fund, October 3, 2006).

35. As the United States has been importing more than it has been exporting since the early 1980s, current-account deficits have been a constant feature, with the notable exception of a surplus in 1991.

36. IMF Committee on Balance of Payments Statistics, *Annual Report 2006* (Washington, D.C.: International Monetary Fund, January 2012). After reaching a peak of $420 billion, or 9.3 percent of GDP, in 2008, China's surplus has dropped: in 2013, it was approximately $183 billion. Despite this drop, China's capacity to generate a current-account surplus remains in excess of $2 billion every month—an increase of more than 300 percent since the 1980s.

37. Ben Shalom Bernanke, "Global Economic Integration: What's New and What's Not?" (speech, Federal Reserve Bank of Kansas City's Thirtieth Annual Economic Symposium, Jackson Hole, Wyoming, August 25, 2006).

38. Olivier Blanchard and Gian Maria Milesi-Ferretti, *(Why) Should Current Account Balances Be Reduced?* IMF Staff Discussion Note 11/03 (Washington, D.C.: International Monetary Fund, March 1, 2011).

39. Max Corden, "Global Imbalances and the Paradox of Thrift," *Oxford Review of Economic Policy* 28, no. 3 (2012): 431–444.

40. Ronald I. McKinnon, *The Unloved Dollar Standard* (Oxford: Oxford University Press, 2013), 17–29.

2. CHINA'S EXTRAORDINARY BUT STILL UNFINISHED TRANSFORMATION

1. Angus Maddison, *The World Economy*, vol. 2, *Historical Statistics* (Paris: OECD Publishing, 2007).

2. In those years, China depended heavily on machinery and equipment imported from the Soviet Union. Nicholas R. Lardy, *China in the World Economy* (Washington, D.C.: Peterson Institute for International Economics, 1994), 1.

3. Maddison, *The World Economy*.

4. Lardy, *China in the World Economy*, 1.

5. According to a statement issued by the North China People's Government: "To meet the needs of national economic construction, we have reached a consensus with the government of Shandong province, the Shaanxi-Gansu-Ningxia Border Area, and the Shanxi-Suiyuan Border Area to adopt a unified currency for circulation in north China, northeast China and northwest China." Chen Yulu,

Chinese Currency and the Global Economy: The Rise of the Renminbi (New York: McGraw-Hill, 2014), 21.

6. *China: A Reassessment of the Economy: A Compendium of Papers Submitted to the Joint Economic Committee, Congress of the United States* (Washington, D.C.: U.S. Government Printing Office, July 10, 1975), 41.

7. "The Death of Gradualism," *Economist*, March 8, 1997.

8. IMF, "World Economic Outlook April 2016," http://www.imf.org/external /pubs/ft/weo/2016/01/pdf/text.pdf. It is worth repeating that at the beginning of this transformation in the late 1970s China's share of world GDP was just over 2 percent.

9. *Selected Works of Deng Xiaoping*, vol. 3, *1982–1992* (Beijing: Foreign Languages Press, 1994), 370, quoted in Henry Kissinger, *On China* (London: Allen Lane, 2011), 445.

10. World Trade Organization, China country profile, http://stat.wto.org /CountryProfile/WSDBCountryPFView.aspx?Language=E&Country=CN (accessed May, 16 2016).

11. Ibid.

12. "Practice of a planned economy is not equivalent to socialism because there is planning under capitalism too; practice of a market economy is not equivalent to capitalism because there are markets under socialism too."

13. Nicholas R. Lardy, *Foreign Trade and Economic Reform in China, 1978–1990* (Cambridge: Cambridge University Press, 1993), 11–12.

14. Edward S. Steinfeld, *Playing Our Game: Why China's Rise Doesn't Threaten the West* (Oxford, England: Oxford University Press, 2010), 29.

15. Ibid.

16. "Statistics Database," World Trade Organization, accessed May 16, 2016, http:// stat.wto.org/Home/WSDBHome.aspx.

17. Ibid. During 1927–1929, at the peak of its precommunist performance, China's trade was 2 percent of world trade; see Lardy, *China in the World Economy*, 1.

18. "China's integration into the world economy is today having a bigger global impact than other emerging economies, or than Japan did during its period of rapid growth from the mid-1950s onwards." "From T-Shirts to T-Bonds," *Economist*, July 28, 2005, http://www.economist.com/node/4221685.

19. David D. Hale, *China's New Dream: How Will Australia and the World Cope with the Re-emergence of China as a Great Power* (Barton: Australian Strategic Policy Institute, February 2014), 3.

20. Ibid.

21. Ibid., 9.

22. OICA 2015 Production Statistics, http://www.oica.net/category/production -statistics/ (accessed on May, 16 2016).

23. Matteo Ferrazzi and Andrea Goldstein, "The Automotive Industry," in *The World's Industrial Transformation* (London: Chatham House, July 2013), 15.

24. In November 2013, China refused to reach an agreement on trade in information technology products and to expand the 1996 Information Technology Agreement, which currently covers $4 trillion in annual trade, to include 200 new products, ranging from flat-screen televisions to next-generation semiconductors.

25. Hale, *China's New Dream*, 8.

26. U.S. Energy Information Administration, *Short Term Energy Outlook* (Washington, D.C.: U.S. Government Printing Office, November 2015), table 3A.

27. Hale, *China's New Dream*, 8. The rapid growth in steel output has turned China from a coal exporter into a coal importer.

28. World Bank, *World Development Indicators 2011* (Washington, D.C.: World Bank, 2011).

29. *Selected Works of Deng Xiaoping*, 3:361, quoted in Kissinger, *On China*, 442–443.

30. For instance, in 1985, China borrowed approximately $1.1 billion from the World Bank and almost $500 million through bilateral borrowing. In the same year, it received almost $2 billion worth of foreign direct investment. Contracted inward foreign direct investment totaled over $6 billion. State Statistical Bureau, *Chinese Statistical Abstract 1993*, cited in Lardy, *China in the World Economy*, 63.

31. Peter Nolan, *Is China Buying the World?* (Cambridge, England: Polity Press, 2012), 85.

32. Figures for 2014. United Nations Conference on Trade and Development (UNCTAD), *Global Investment Trends Monitor*, No. 18 (Geneva: UNCTAD, January 29, 2015).

33. Nolan, *Is China Buying the World?*, 93. They account for around two-thirds of the overall value added in high-tech industries.

34. Figures for 2012. Valentina Romei and Rob Minto, "Chart of the Week: Who Makes China's Exports—Local Companies or Foreign?," *Beyondbrics* (blog), *Financial Times*, September 10, 2012, http://blogs.ft.com/beyond-brics/2012/09/10/chart-of-the-week-who-is-making-chinas-exports/.

35. Hale, "China's New Dream," 8. More precisely, the percentages of total auto sales from Chinese joint ventures were Volkswagen, 28.8 percent; General Motors, 28.9 percent; Nissan, 20.9 percent; Hyundai, 19.5 percent; Kia, 17.7 percent; Honda, 17.1 percent; Peugeot, 14.8 percent; Mazda, 13.8 percent; Ford, 8.4 percent; BMW, 8.0 percent; and Toyota, 7.6 percent.

36. Kissinger, *On China*, 358.

37. This, however, was not Deng's first visit to the United States. He had been there in 1974 as part of a Chinese delegation to a special session of the UN General Assembly. Kissinger, *On China*, 322.

38. However, according to Henry Kissinger, Deng never learned French and did not understand English: "languages are hard." Kissinger, *On China*, 324.

39. "Sino-U.S. Relations: Facts and Figures—Historic Figures in Sino-U.S. Relations: Deng Xiaoping," accessed November 9, 2015, http://www.china.org.cn/world/china_us_facts_2011/2011-07/11/content_22967238.htm.

40. Xi Jinping, "Study, Disseminate and Implement the Guiding Principles of the 18th CPC National Congress," in *The Governance of China* (Beijing: Foreign Languages Press, 2014), 6–22.

41. David Shambaugh, *China Goes Global* (Oxford, England: Oxford University Press, 2013), 177.

42. Jiang Zemin, "Text of Political Report by Jiang Zemin at the 15th National Congress of the Communist Party of China," September 12, 1997.

43. Shambaugh, *China Goes Global*, 5.

44. Alessia Amighini, Roberta Rabellotti, and Marco Sanfilippo, "Do Chinese State-Owned and Private Enterprises Differ in Their Internationalization Strategies?," *China Economic Review* 27 (2013): 312–335; Alessia Amighini, Roberta Rabellotti, and Marco Sanfilippo, "China's Outward FDI: An Industry-Level Analysis of Host-Country Determinants," *Frontiers of Economics in China* 8 (2013): 309–336.

45. Julie Jiang and Chen Ding, *Update on Overseas Investments by China's National Oil Companies: Achievements and Challenges Since 2011*, Partner Country Series (Paris: International Energy Agency, 2014), http://www.iea.org/publications /freepublications/publication/partner-country-series—-update-on-overseas -investments-by-chinas-national-oil-companies.html.

46. Earlier, in 2005, the Chinese National Offshore Oil Corporation had attempted, but failed, to acquire the American company Unocal for $18.5 billion in cash.

47. Jiang, "Text of Political Report." http://www.bjreview.com.cn/document/txt /2011-03/25/content_363499.htm.

48. "Ford Motor Company/2008 Annual Report," 18, Ford Motor Company, http://ophelia.sdsu.edu:8080/ford/12-30-2012/doc/2008_annual_report.pdf; "Ford Motor Company/2009 Annual Report," 24, Ford Motor Company, http://ophelia.sdsu.edu:8080/ford/12-30-2012/doc/2009_annual_report.pdf.

49. In addition, empirical research suggests that state-owned enterprises are more likely to invest abroad, compared to private companies, when the renminbi appreciates, given that the government grants them easier access to capital and foreign reserves.

50. Jonathan Kaiman, "China Agrees to Invest $20bn in Venezuela to Help Offset Effects of Oil Price Slump," *Guardian*, January 8, 2015, http://www.theguardian .com/world/2015/jan/08/china-venezuela-20bn-loans-financing-nicolas -maduro-beijing.

51. At current prices and current exchange rates. "Foreign Direct Investment: Inward and Outward Flows and Stock, Annual, 1980–2014," United Nations Conference on Trade and Development Statistics (UNCTADstat), http://unctadstat.unctad .org/wds/ReportFolders/reportFolders.aspx?sCS_ChosenLang=en.

52. Ibid.

53. "Chinese Investment Into Europe Hits Record High in 2014," Baker & McKenzie, last modified February 11, 2015, http://www.bakermckenzie.com/news /Chinese-investment-into-Europe-hits-record-high-in-2014-02-11-2015/.

54. News Analysis: The global impact of China's 13th Five-Year Plan, Xinhua News, March 10, 2016, http://news.xinhuanet.com/english/2016-03/10/c_135175652.htm.

55. United National Conference on Trade and Development, *World Investment Report 2015: Reforming International Investment Governance* (Geneva: United Nations, 2015), 39, http://unctad.org/en/PublicationsLibrary/wir2015_en.pdf.

56. David Brown and Christopher Chan, "PwC M&A 2015 Review and 2016 Outlook," Pricewaterhouse Coopers Hong Kong, January 26, 2016, http://www.pwchk.com/webmedia/doc/635893311472912475_ma_press_briefing _jan2016.pdf.

57. Chinese National Offshore Oil Corporation's aborted bid, in 2005, to acquire U.S. oil company Unocal exemplifies the difficulties that surround acquisitions by Chinese enterprises. Nolan, *Is China Buying the World?*, 98–99.

58. Richard McGregor, "The World Should Be Braced for China's Expansion," *Financial Times*, December 22, 2004, http://www.ft.com/cms/s/0/5b387e88-53be -11d9-b6e4-00000e2511c8.html.

59. These days Lenovo is a conglomerate that includes the original firm, Lenovo China, headquartered in Beijing, and Lenovo US, headquartered in Morris-ville, North Carolina. Lenovo China is the business unit and runs manufactur-ing, R&D, software development, and business services. It is a wholly owned foreign-invested enterprise, being 100 percent owned by Hong Kong Lenovo, a legal foreign entity.

60. Nolan, *Is China Buying the World?*, 98–99.

61. Thomas Buckley and Thomas Mulier, "AB InBev, SABMiller Reach Agreement on Acquisition," Bloomberg Business, October 13, 2015, http://www.bloomberg .com/news/articles/2015-10-13/ab-inbev-agrees-to-buy-sabmiller-for-104 -billion-in-record-deal.

62. Patrick Jenkins, "Indebted Chinese Banks Sidestep 'Too Big to Fail' Capital Buffers," *Financial Times*, February 17, 2015, http://www.ft.com/cms/s/0 /0d1649e4-b5ea-11e4-a577-00144feab7de.html.

63. The concept of a "strategic" company is often stretched to include enterprises without obvious national interests.

64. Nolan, *Is China Buying the World?*, 108–109.

65. Kevin P. Gallagher and Margaret Myers, "China–Latin America Finance Database," Inter-American Dialogue, accessed November 13, 2015, https:// www.thedialogue.org/map_list.

66. Toh Han Shih, "China to Provide Africa with US$1 Trillion Financing," *South China Morning Post*, November 18, 2013, http://www.scmp.com/business /banking-finance/article/1358902/china-provide-africa-us1tr-financing, cited in Yun Sun, "China's Aid to Africa: Monster or Messiah?," Brookings, February 2014, http://www.brookings.edu/research/opinions/2014/02/07-china-aid -to-africa-sun.

3. A FINANCIALLY REPRESSED ECONOMY

1. Quoted in Gabriel Wildau, "China Shadow Bank Collapse Exposes Grey-Market Lending Risk," *Financial Times*, December 4, 2014, http://www.ft.com/cms/s/0/82ac1f0e-7ac0-11e4-8646-00144feabdco.html.

2. World Bank and Development Research Center of the State Council, People's Republic of China, "China: Structural Reforms for a Modern, Harmonious, Creative Society," in *China 2030: Building a Modern, Harmonious, and Creative Society* (Washington, D.C.: World Bank, 2013), 115.

3. Carmen M. Reinhart, Jacob F. Kierkegaard, and M. Belen Sbrancia, "Financial Repression Redux," *Finance and Development* 48, no. 1 (June 2011), http://www.imf.org/external/pubs/ft/fandd/2011/06/Reinhart.htm.

4. Ibid. This article draws attention to the fact that some macro-prudential regulations can result in financial repression.

5. Michael Pettis has calculated that—with lending rates between 4 to 7 percentage points below adjusted GDP growth rates and with household deposits (including farm deposits) equal to anywhere from 80 to 100 percent of GDP, or approximately 122 trillion renminbi—the total transfer from households to state-owned enterprises, infrastructure investors, and other favored institutions amounts to anywhere from 3 to 8 percent of GDP annually. Michael Pettis, *The Great Rebalancing: Trade, Conflict, and the Perilous Road Ahead for the World Economy* (Princeton, N.J.: Princeton University Press, 2014), 85.

6. Nicholas R. Lardy, *Markets Over Mao* (Washington, D.C.: Peterson Institute for International Economics, 2014), 131.

7. "World Development Indicators: Domestic Credit Provided by Financial Sector (% of GDP)," World Bank, accessed May 18, 2016, http://databank.worldbank.org/data/.

8. Ibid.

9. Pettis, *The Great Rebalancing*, 86.

10. Lardy, *Markets Over Mao*, 11.

11. Nicholas R. Lardy, *China's Unfinished Economic Revolution* (Washington, D.C.: Brookings Institution Press, 1998), 23.

12. Peter Nolan, *Is China Buying the World?* (Cambridge, England: Polity Press, 2012), 56–58.

13. World Bank and Development Research Center of the State Council, *China 2030*, 104–109.

14. Michael Firth, Chen Lin, Ping Liu, and Sonia M. L. Wong, "Inside the Black Box: Bank Credit Allocation in China's Private Sector," *Journal of Banking and Finance* 33 (2009): 1145.

15. Edward Steinfeld, *Playing Our Game: Why China's Rise Doesn't Threaten the West* (Oxford, England: Oxford University Press, 2010), 32–33.

16. The list of national champions is longer and includes China Mobile, China Unicom, and China Telecom in the telecommunication industry; Sinopec, China National Petroleum Corporation, China National Offshore Oil Corporation, and Sinochem in the oil and chemical sector; Aviation Industry of China in the aerospace industry; and China North and China South in military and related industries. For a more exhaustive list, see Nolan, *Is China Buying the World?*, 59–60.

17. Ibid., 60.

18. State-Owned Assets Supervision and Administration firms include the three national oil companies—China National Petroleum Corporation, Sinopec, and China National Offshore Oil Corporation; the large state telecommunication companies—China Guodian Corporation and China Huadian Corporation; China's largest state-owned coal producer, Shenhua Group; the major state power distribution companies—State Grid Corporation and China Southern Power Grid Company; and the major state airlines—Air China, China Southern, and China Eastern. Lardy, *Markets Over Mao*, 51.

19. Steven P. Feldman, *Trouble in the Middle: American-Chinese Business Relations, Culture, Conflict and Ethics* (New York: Routledge, 2013), 122. Of the 183 officials on the State Council above the vice-ministerial level (from nineteen ministries and commissions), 56, or 30.6 percent, have experience working in state-owned enterprises. Sheng Hong and Zhao Nong, *China's State-Owned Enterprises: Nature, Performance and Reform*, vol. 1 of Series on Chinese Economic Research (London: World Scientific Publishing, 2013), xxiii.

20. It controlled almost four-fifths of all deposits in banks and credit cooperatives and was the source of 93 percent of all loans by financial institutions. Lardy, *China's Unfinished Economic Revolution*, 61.

21. Ibid.

22. Ibid., 64–65. These four banks had been created or recreated—in the case of the Agriculture Bank, which had been abolished in 1965—at the end of the 1970s. For instance, the Bank of China was separated from the PBoC, and in 1980, a payment agency under the Ministry of Finance was converted into the Construction Bank.

23. Joint Economic Committee Congress of the United States, 1975, (Washington, D.C.: U.S. Government Printing Office, 1976), 658–659.

24. Ibid., 531.

25. Yasheng Huang, *Capitalism with Chinese Characteristics: Entrepreneurship and the State* (Cambridge: Cambridge University Press, 2008), 143.

26. Agricultural Bank of China, "Nongcun Geti Gongshangye Daikuan Shixing Banfa [Provisional regulations on loans to rural individual industrial and commercial businesses]," in *1984 Nian Nongcun Jingrong Guizhang Zhidu Xuanbian* [Selection of rural financial regulations in 1984], ed. General Office of the

Agricultural Bank of China (Tianjin: Zhongguo jingrong chubanshe, 1986), cited in Huang, *Capitalism with Chinese Characteristics*, 145–146.

27. China Banking Society, *Almanac of China's Finance and Banking 1996* (Beijing: China Financial Publishing House, 1996), 428, cited in Lardy, *Markets Over Mao*, 103.

28. Lardy, *China's Unfinished Economic Revolution*, 71–72.

29. China Banking Society, *Almanac of China's Finance and Banking 1995* (Beijing: China Financial Publishing House, 1995), 578, cited in Lardy, *Markets Over Mao*, 103.

30. The overall banking system includes credit cooperatives.

31. China Banking Society, *Almanac of China's Finance and Banking 2012* (Beijing: China Financial Publishing House, 2012), 419, 423–427; and Audrey Redler, "International Comparison of Banking Sectors," European Banking Federation, March 18, 2014, www.ebf-fbe.eu. Cited in Lardy, *Markets Over Mao*, 32. The figures are for 2011 and are the latest from the China Banking Society.

32. State-owned commercial banks, in particular, have gone through a large public recapitalization, have cleaned up their balance sheets by removing nonperforming loans, and have reduced the number of branches and employees. The four largest state-owned commercial banks went through public listing, with shares sold to strategic foreign partners. Governance in the whole sector was improved with, among other measures, the creation of a bank supervisor. On the whole, Chinese banks have become more open, more competitive, and more market oriented despite continuing to face a number of challenges. Morris Goldstein and Nicholas R. Lardy, *The Future of China's Exchange Rate Policy* (Washington, D.C.: Peterson Institute for International Economics, July 2009), 45–46.

33. Firth et al., "Inside the Black Box," 1146.

34. Lardy, *Markets Over Mao*, 104.

35. At the end of 1995, approximately 83 percent of outstanding bank loans were to state-owned enterprises and local governments. Lardy, *China's Unfinished Economic Revolution*, 83.

36. Firth et al., "Inside the Black Box," 1146.

37. See ibid., 1144–1155.

38. "BIS Statistics Explorer: Debt Securities Issues and Amounts Outstanding," Bank for International Settlements, accessed December 1, 2015, http://stats.bis .org/statx/toc/LBS.html.

39. The figure is for government bonds outstanding in 2013.

40. People's Bank of China, "China Monetary Policy Report Quarter Two, 2015," August 7 2015, http://www.pbc.gov.cn/english/130727/130879/2941536/3011604 /index.html.

41. "Household Savings," Organization for Economic Cooperation and Development, accessed December 1, 2015, doi:10.1787/cfc6f499-en.

42. Marcos Chamon and Eswar Prasad, "Determinants of Household Saving in China" (working paper, International Monetary Fund, Washington, D.C., 2005), http://www.researchgate.net/publication/228728598.

43. Lardy, *China's Unfinished Economic Revolution*, 60.

44. Reuters Datastream, accessed on May 18, 2016.

45. Figure to the end of July 2015. Lucy Hornby, "China tightens grip on internet financing platform," *Financial Times*, July 19, 2015, http://www.ft.com/cms/s/0/6b6a6ac4-2dcd-11e5-8873-775ba7c2ea3d.html.

46. Xiao Gang, "Regulating Shadow Banking," *China Daily*, October 12, 2012, http://www.chinadaily.com.cn/opinion/2012-10/12/content_15812305.htm.

47. IMF, People's Republic of China 2014 Article IV Consultation—Staff Report; Press Release; and Statement by the Executive Director for the People's Republic of China. IMF Country Report, No 14/235, https://www.imf.org/external/pubs/ft/scr/2014/cr14235.pdf.

48. I thank the staff in the IMF China office for providing the estimate on wealth management products.

49. Chris Flood. "China tightens money market regulation," *Financial Times*, January, 31 2016, http://www.ft.com/cms/s/0/66f85d72-b949-11e5-bf7e-8a339b6f2164.html.

50. Richard Dobbs, Susan Lund, Jonathan Woetzel, and Mina Mutafchieva, *Debt and (Not Much) Deleveraging* (London: McKinsey, February 2015).

51. Ruchir Sharma, "China Has Its Own Debt Bomb," *Wall Street Journal*, February 25, 2013, http://www.wsj.com/articles/SB10001424127887324338604578325962705788582.

4. CHINA: A TRADING NATION WITHOUT AN INTERNATIONAL CURRENCY

1. For both residents and nonresidents. More specifically, an international currency can be used for private purposes, such as currency substitution and trade and financial transaction invoicing and denomination. It can also be used for public purposes, such as official reserves, a vehicle currency for foreign exchange intervention, and an anchor currency for pegging. Peter B. Kenen, *The Role of the Dollar as an International Currency*, Occasional Paper 13 (New York: Group of Thirty, 1983); Menzie Chinn and Jeffrey Frankel, "Will the Euro Eventually Surpass the Dollar as Leading International Reserve Currency?" (Working Paper 11510, National Bureau of Economic Research, Cambridge, MA, 2005).

2. Indeed, Mundell wrote in 1993 that "great nations have great currencies." Robert Mundell, "EMU and the International Monetary System: A Transatlantic Perspective" (Working Paper 13, Austrian National Bank, Vienna, 1993).

3. Benjamin Cohen, *The Future of Sterling as an International Currency* (London: Macmillan, 1971), 62.

4.   Catherine R. Schenk, *The Decline of Sterling: Managing the Retreat of an International Currency, 1945–1992* (Cambridge: Cambridge University Press, 2010).

5.   Nicholas R. Lardy, *Foreign Trade and Economic Reform in China 1978–1990* (Cambridge: Cambridge University Press, 1992), 19–20. There was a complete separation between domestic and world market prices that had been introduced by the mid-1950s.

6.   World Bank, *China: Long-Term Issues and Options* (Baltimore, Md.: John Hopkins University Press, 1985), 97, quoted in Lardy, *Foreign Trade*, 20.

7.   Lardy, *Foreign Trade,* 20. This was the case especially in the 1950s and 1960s.

8.   Deng Xiaoping lamented that exchange rate trade on the black market "disrupts the smooth implementation of economic reforms." Graham Earnshaw, "China's Currency Blackmarket Blossoms," Reuters, August 18, 1984–1996, http://www.earnshaw.com/other-writings/chinas-currency-blackmarket-blossoms.

9.   Lardy, *Foreign Trade,* 120.

10. Ibid., 113.

11. William H. Overholt, *The Rise of China: How Economic Reform Is Creating a New Super Power* (New York: Norton, 1993), 162.

12. Ronald I. McKinnon and Kenichi Ohno, *Dollar and Yen: Resolving Economic Conflict Between the United States and Japan* (Cambridge, Mass.: MIT Press, 1997), 183, 188, 199.

13. Richard McGregor, Edward Alden, Andrew Balls, and John Burton, "China Ends Renminbi's Decade-Old Peg to Dollar," *Financial Times,* July 22, 2005, http://www.ft.com/cms/s/0/f56082a0-f9d9-11d9-b092-00000e2511c8.html.

14. This figure was for 2006. "Report to Congress on International Economic and Exchange Rate Policies," 29, U.S. Treasury Department, June 2007, https://www.treasury.gov/resource-center/international/exchange-rate-policies/Documents/2007_FXReport.pdf.

15. Ibid., 32–33.

16. "China Launches Currency Shake-Up," BBC News, July 22, 2005, http://news.bbc.co.uk/1/hi/business/4703477.stm.

17. Yongding Yu, "Rebalancing the Chinese Economy," *Oxford Review of Economic Policy* 28, no. 3 (2012): 552, doi:10.1093/oxrep/grs025.

18. Claude Barfield, "Congress and Chinese Currency Legislation," VoxEU, April 16, 2010, http://www.voxeu.org/article/congress-and-chinese-currency-legislation.

19. And the Chinese were equally eager to avoid it. See Paul Blustein, *A Flop and a Debacle: Inside the IMF's Global Rebalancing Acts,* Paper 4 (Waterloo, Ontario: Centre for International Governance Innovation, June 2012), 11–13, 22.

20. Ibid., 8.

21. "Further Propelling the Currency Reform and Strengthening the Flexibility of the Renminbi Exchange Rate," People's Bank of China, June 19, 2010, http://www.pbc.gov.cn/publish/zhengcehuobisi/641/2010/20100621164121167284376/20100621164121167284376.html.

22. This comment was from Zhang Tao, director general of the International Department of the People's Bank of China. See Ding Qingfen and Wang Xing, "Official: Currency Reform 'Our Own Affair,'" *China Daily*, June 28, 2010, http://www.chinadaily.com.cn/china/2010g20canada/2010-06/28/content_10025959.htm.

23. Robin Harding and Josh Noble, "US Warns China After RMB Depreciation," *Financial Times*, April 8, 2014, http://www.ft.com/cms/s/0/3355dc74-bed7-11e3-a1bf-00144feabdc0.html.

24. "Report to Congress on International Economic and Exchange Rate Policies," 4, Office of International Affairs, U.S. Treasury Department, October 15, 2014, https://www.treasury.gov/resource-center/international/exchange-rate-policies/Documents/2014-10-15%20FXR.pdf.

25. "RMB Exchange Rate Has a Solid Foundation to Remain Stable Against a Basket of Currencies," People's Bank of China, December 14, 2015, http://www.pbc.gov.cn/english/130721/2989190/index.html.

26. Alice Y. Ouyang, Ramkishen S. Rajan, and Thomas D. Willett, "China as a Reserve Sink: The Evidence from Offset and Sterilization Coefficients," *Journal of International Money and Finance* 29, no. 5 (September 2010): 951–972, doi:10.1016/j.jimonfin.2009.12.006; John Greenwood, "The Costs and Implications of PBC Sterilization," *Cato Journal* 28, no. 2 (Spring–Summer 2008): 205–217, http://object.cato.org/sites/cato.org/files/serials/files/cato-journal/2008/5/cj28n2-4.pdf. For the recent change in reserve requirement ratio see Bloomberg News, "China Cuts Banks' Reserve Requirement Ratio," February 29, 2016, http://www.bloomberg.com/news/articles/2016-02-29/china-cuts-reserve-ratio-in-latest-step-to-support-growth.

27. Haihong Gao and Yongding Yu, "Internationalisation of the Renminbi" (paper presented at the BoK–BIS Seminar on Currency Internationalization in Seoul, South Korea, March 19–20, 2009), http://www.bis.org/repofficepubl/arpresearch200903.05.pdf. This study uses data for the capital account at the end of 2007.

28. Xiaolian Hu, "Convertibility of RMB-Denominated Capital Accounts: Process and Experience," in *China's Emerging Financial Markets: Challenges and Global Impact*, ed. Min Zhu, Cai Jinqing, and Martha Avery (Singapore: Wiley, 2009), 449–458.

29. Chen Yulu notes that the best order is as follows: "capital inflows first and capital outflows next; direct investment first and portfolio investment next; portfolio investment first and bank credit next; long-term investment first and short-term investment next; institutions first and individuals next; debt securities first and equities and derivatives next; offering markets first and trading markets next; transactions backed by a true deal first and transactions not backed by a true deal next." Chen Yulu, *Chinese Currency and the Global Economy* (Chicago: McGraw-Hill, 2014), 123.

30. The authorities plan to establish a QDII program (for qualified domestic individual investors) to allow Chinese residents (and not only institutional investors) to invest in overseas capital markets.

31. Gao and Yu, "Internationalisation of the Renminbi," 8–9.

32. I am grateful to Haihong Gao for this update based on her yet unpublished research.

33. "IMFC Statement by Zhou Xiaochuan, Governor, People's Bank of China" (Thirty-First Meeting of the International Monetary and Financial Committee, International Monetary Fund, Washington, D.C., April 18, 2015), 5, https://www.imf.org/External/spring/2015/imfc/statement/eng/chn.pdf.

5. LIVING WITH A DWARF CURRENCY

1. National Bureau of Statistics of China, "9-1 Price Indices" and "4-11 Average Wage of Employed Persons in Urban Units and Related Indices," in *China Statistical Yearbook 2015* (Beijing: China Statistics Press, 2015), http://www.stats.gov.cn/tjsj/ndsj/2015/indexeh.htm.

2. Imbalances on the international balance sheet are common in Asia: see, in particular, Ronald McKinnon and Gunther Schnabl, "The East Asian Dollar Standard, Fear of Floating, and Original Sin," *Review of Development Economics* 8, no. 3 (2004): 331–360.

3. Figures at the end of 2013, Andrew Sheng and Ng Chow Soon, eds, *Shadow Banking in China. An Opportunity for Financial Reform*, Wiley-Fung Global Institute, 2016, table 3.16. In 2011, China's net international investment position was $1.7 trillion, with $4.7 trillion in assets and $2.9 trillion in liabilities. See Yongding Yu, "The 'Asset Crisis' of Emerging Economies," Project Syndicate, September 30, 2011, http://www.project-syndicate.org/commentary/the—asset-crisis—of-emerging-economies.

4. Patrick McGuire and Goetz von Peter, "The US Dollar Shortage in Global Banking," *BIS Quarterly Review*, March 2009, 47–63, http://www.bis.org/publ/qtrpdf/r_qt0903f.pdf.

5. Zhou Xiaochuan, "Reforming the International Monetary System" (speech), People's Bank of China, March 23, 2009, http://www.pbc.gov.cn/english/130724/2842945/index.html.

6. Ronald McKinnon and Gunther Schnabl, "China's Exchange Rate and Financial Repression: The Conflicted Emergence of the RMB as an International Currency," *China & World Economy* 22, no. 3 (May/June 2014): 13, doi:10.1111/j.1749-124X.2014.12066.x.

7. Ibid., 15.

8. Barry Eichengreen and Ricardo Hausmann, "Exchange Rates and Financial Fragility," in *New Challenges for Monetary Policy*, Symposium 1999 (Kansas City,

Mo.: Federal Reserve Bank of Kansas City, 1999): 330–331, https://www
.kansascityfed.org/publicat/sympos/1999/s99eich.pdf.

9. Jonathan Kaiman, "China Agrees to Invest $20bn in Venezuela to Help Offset Effects of Oil Price Slump," *Guardian*, January 8, 2015, http://www.theguardian .com/world/2015/jan/08/china-venezuela-20bn-loans-financing-nicolas-maduro -beijing.

10. David Cook and James Yetman, "Expanding Central Bank Balance Sheets in Emerging Asia: A Compendium of Risks and Some Evidence," in *Are Central Bank Balance Sheets in Asia Too Large?*, Paper 66 (Basel: Bank for International Settlements, October 2012): 30–75.

11. Russia is another country where the monetary authorities have been using market interventions as a way to control capital flows and maintain stability. For example, in December 2012, Russia's large trade surplus and strong capital inflows forced the central bank to buy $476 billion. This has considerably expanded Russia's official reserves, which are some of the largest in the world. It was not an isolated episode. Some years earlier, in 2008, the Central Bank of Russia spent one-third of the $600 billion it held as official reserves, the world's third-largest reserves at that time, to contain the depreciation of the ruble.

12. In September 2015, China agreed with the International Monetary Fund to partially disclose the composition of its foreign exchange reserves. In a few years, China will report its holdings. Ian Talley and Lingling Wei, "China Begins Disclosing Reserves to IMF," *Wall Street Journal*, September 30, 2015, http:// www.wsj.com/articles/china-begins-disclosing-reserves-to-imf-1443624985.

13. Cook and Yetman, "Expanding Central Bank Balance Sheets," 30–75.

14. James Mackintosh, "Deep Pockets Support China's Forex Politics," *Financial Times*, September 27, 2010, http://www.ft.com/cms/s/0/19f52ea0-ca7b-11df-a860 -00144feab49a.html.

15. "U.S. International Transactions Accounts Data 2012," U.S. Bureau of Economic Analysis, December 2012, http://www.bea.gov/international/index.htm.

16. Calculation based on 2010 poverty headcounts at $1.90 a day (2011 purchasing power parity). The World Bank moved its poverty threshold to $1.90 a day on October 1, 2015, but data for poverty headcounts in China are available only up to 2010. "World DataBank: World Development Indicators," World Bank, accessed November 24, 2015, http://databank.worldbank.org/data/.

17. Michael Mackenzie, "China Sells US Treasury Debt Amid Strong Haven Demand," *Financial Times*, October 18, 2011, http://www.ft.com/cms/s/0 /b1d54b0e-f98e-11e0-bf8f-00144feab49a.html#axzz2QdBUo8Iv.

18. In 2014, China's gross domestic product (GDP) at the current dollar exchange rate was approximately $10.4 trillion, putting it in second place after the United States, which stood at $17.4 trillion. However, with purchasing power parity,

China had a GDP of $18 trillion. "World DataBank: World Development Indicators," World Bank, accessed November 24, 2015, http://databank.world bank.org/data/.

19. But it was used to settle only 2.4 percent of imports in 1980, an insignificant figure. "Relative Economic Size and Relative Use of Currencies," Ministry of Finance Japan, accessed on November 24, 2015, http://www.mof.go.jp/english /about_mof/councils/customs_foreign_exchange/e1b064c2.htm.

20. More precisely, 38 percent of exports and 22 percent of imports are settled using the yen. Takatoshi Ito, Satoshi Koibuchi, Kiyotaka Sato, and Junko Shimizu, "Why Has the Yen Failed to Become a Dominant Invoicing Currency in Asia? A Firm-Level Analysis of Japanese Exporters' Invoicing Behavior" (Working Paper 16231, National Bureau of Economic Research, Cambridge, Mass., July 2010), 7, doi:10.3386/w16231.

6. CREATING AN INTERNATIONAL CURRENCY

1. Jonathan Wheatley, "Brazil and China Eye Plan to Axe Dollar," *Financial Times*, May 18, 2009, http://www.ft.com/cms/s/0/996b1af8-43ce-11de-a9be -00144feabdc0.html.

2. "UPDATE 1-BIS-China, Brazil Working on Trade FX Deal-Cenbanks," Reuters, June 28, 2009, http://www.reuters.com/article/2009/06/28/bis-trade -idUSLS14673020090628.

3. BBC News, "China and Brazil Sign $30bn Currency Swap Agreement," March 27, 2013 http://www.bbc.co.uk/news/business-21949615.

4. Mitsuhiro Fukao, "Capital Account Liberalisation: The Japanese Experience and Implications for China," in *China's Capital Account Liberalisation: International Perspective*, Paper 15 (Basel: Bank for International Settlements, April 2003), 47, http://www.bis.org/publ/bppdf/bispap15h.pdf.

5. Ministry of Finance Japan, "Chronology of the internationalization of the Yen," http://www.mof.go.jp/english/about_mof/councils/customs_foreign_exchange /e1b064c1.htm.

6. Specific approaches and measures for promoting the internationalization of the yen are outlined in "Current Status and Prospects for Financial Liberal- ization and the Internationalization of the Yen," a document that sets out the policy framework for the promotion of the international use of the Japanese currency.

7. Masahiro Kawai, "Renminbi (RMB) Internationalization: Japan and China" (seminar presentation at Renminbi Internationalization: Japan and the People's Republic of China, Beijing, May 21, 2012), http://www.adbi.org/conf-seminar papers/2012/05/29/5072.renminbi.internationalization.japan.prc/.

8. In 1990, the aggregate economy of the European Union was second to that of the United States. Then called the European Community, it was less economically integrated than it is today, and it did not have a currency union and a single currency. It was also much smaller, with only twelve member states. Today they are twenty-eight.

9. OECD, *OECD Economic Outlook*, vol. 2014/2 (Paris: OECD Publishing, 2014 [revised 2015]), doi:10.1787/eco_outlook-v2014-2-en.

10. IMF COFER. See also Paola Subacchi, "Expanding Beyond Borders: The Yen and the Yuan" (Working Paper 450, Asian Development Bank Institute, Tokyo, December 2013), 16, https://openaccess.adb.org/bitstream/handle/11540/1203/2013.12.03 .wp450.expanding.beyond.borders.yen.yuan.pdf?sequence=1.

11. IMF, *World Economic Outlook* April 2016, http://www.imf.org/external/pubs /ft/weo/2016/01/pdf/text.pdf.

12. Robert Mundell, "The Case for a Managed International Gold Standard," in *The International Monetary System: Choices for the Future*, ed. Michael Connolly (New York: Praeger, 1983), 1–19; Alexander Swoboda, "Financial Integration and International Monetary Arrangements," in *The Evolution of the International Monetary System*," ed. Yoshio Suzuki, Jun'ichi Miyake, and Mitsuaki Okabe (Tokyo: University of Tokyo Press, 1990); George S. Tavlas and Yuzuru Ozeki, *The Internationalization of Currencies: An Appraisal of the Japanese Yen*, Occasional Paper 90 (Washington, D.C.: International Monetary Fund, 1992).

13. The figure is for 1992.

14. C. Randall Henning, *Currency and Politics in the United States, Germany, and Japan* (Washington, D.C.: Institute for International Economics, 1994); William W. Grimes, "Internationalization of the Yen and the New Politics of Monetary Insulation," in *Monetary Orders: Ambiguous Economics, Ubiquitous Politics*, ed. Jonathan Kirshner (Ithaca, N.Y.: Cornell University Press, 2003).

15. Paola Subacchi, "Expanding Beyond Borders: The Yen and the Yuan" (Working Paper 450, Asian Development Bank Institute, Tokyo, December 2013), 16, https://openaccess.adb.org/bitstream/handle/11540/1203/2013.12.03.wp450. expanding.beyond.borders.yen.yuan.pdf?sequence=1.

16. Yong Wang, "Seeking a Balanced Approach on the Global Economic Rebalancing: China's Answers to International Policy Cooperation," *Oxford Review of Economic Policy* 28, no. 3 (2012): 569–586; Bin Xia and Dennis Chen, 从'广场协议'看日元升值的教训及启示 [Implications from the yen's appreciation and lessons from Plaza Accord] (内蒙古金融研究 [Inner Mongolia Financial Research], 2010); J. Yin, 日元国际化模式的教训及启示 [Lessons from the internationalization of the Japanese yen] (求知 [Seeking Knowledge], 2012); J. Wei, 日本的教训: 日元升值与泡沫经济 [Lessons from Japan: On yen's appreciation and its bubble economy] (西安金融 [Xi'an Finance], 2006), http://d.wanfangdata.com.cn/periodical_xajr200601001.aspx.

17. In summer 1995, both the Federal Reserve and the Bank of Japan—Japan's central bank—intervened jointly several times to sell dollars in order to dampen the yen.

18. Y. Yu and J. Wei, "定人民，我怎: 与学家 中国 率政策" [How should we stabilize the RMB: To discuss the PRC's monetary policies with economists], 金融 [Financial Times], September 5, 2003; X. Zhao, "燕生: 全球化与通膨胀" [Interview with Zhang Yansheng: Globalization and Inflation], 中国金融 [Journal of China Finance, no. 12] (2008); Z. Yu, "率制度改革必主" [Reforms of foreign exchange rate must safeguard currency sovereignty], 旗文稿 [Red Flag Working Paper 11] (2010); Wei, 日本的教训 [Lessons from Japan].

19. Yunwei Fu and Minmin Jin, "New Analysis: Cross-Border RMB Trade Settlement Marks Key Step for Yuan to Become World Currency," CRIENGLISH, July 7, 2009, http://english.cri.cn/6909/2009/07/07/2041s499305.htm.

20. The forum was held under the Chatham House Rule: "When a meeting, or part thereof, is held under the Chatham House Rule, participants are free to use the information received, but neither the identity nor the affiliation of the speaker(s), nor that of any other participant, may be revealed." Accessed November 24, 2015, https://www.chathamhouse.org/about/chatham-house-rule.

21. "Speech by Governor Zhou at Hong Kong Session of Boao Forum," People's Bank of China, April 29, 2014, http://webcache.googleusercontent.com/search?q=cache:4bWzVkSaApYJ:www.pbc.gov.cn/english/130721/2806467/index.html&hl=en&gl=uk&strip=1&vwsrc=0.

22. Paola Subacchi, *One Currency, Two Systems: China's Renminbi Strategy* (London: Chatham House, October 2010), https://www.chathamhouse.org/publications/papers/view/109498.

23. Quoted in Howard Chao and Sean Tai, "The Coming Age of the Renminbi," *Deal Magazine*, November 2, 2009, last updated December 16, 2009, http://www.mondaq.com/x/91212/M+A+Private%20equity/The+Coming+Age+Of+The+Renminbi.

24. Haihong Gao and Yongding Yu, "Internationalization of the Renminbi" (paper presented at BoK-BIS Seminar in Seoul, South Korea, March 19–20, 2009). Neighboring countries included Hong Kong SAR, Macau SAR, and the members of ASEAN: Brunei, Cambodia, Indonesia, Laos, Malaysia, Burma/Myanmar, Philippines, Singapore, Thailand, and Vietnam.

25. Overseas participating banks, onshore settlement banks, and domestic agent banks have to be approved by both the Hong Kong Monetary Authority and the PBoC to be eligible to conduct renminbi cross-border trade settlements.

26. In those days, the Hong Kong dollar, rather than the renminbi, was the preferred currency in much of the southern province of Guangdong. William H. Overholt, *The Rise of China: How Economic Reform Is Creating a New Superpower* (New York: W. W. Norton, 1993), 165.

27. Mark L. Clifford and Dexter Roberts, "Commentary: Should China Revalue? Soon, It May Have No Choice," *Bloomberg Magazine*, August 3, 2003, http://www .bloomberg.com/bw/stories/2003-08-03/commentary-should-china-revalue -soon-it-may-have-no-choice.

28. As there was total segregation between the official foreign exchange market on the mainland and the "informal" unregulated markets in neighboring countries —notably, Hong Kong—exchange rates in the latter diverged from the official mainland rates, giving ample opportunity for arbitrage.

29. Chinese report, private communication.

30. Arvind Subramanian, *Preserving the Open Global Economic System: A Strategic Blueprint for China and the United States*, Policy Brief 13–16 (Washington, D.C.: Peterson Institute for International Economics, June 2013), 5, http://piie.com /publications/pb/pb13-16.pdf.

31. In July 2009, 365 enterprises were approved as mainland designated enterprises under the pilot scheme and thus were allowed to use renminbi for international trade settlement. Enterprises in the five mainland pilot cities could become designated enterprises upon recommendation from their respective provincial governments and approval by the central authorities. No specific eligibility requirements were set for enterprises outside the mainland that chose to participate in the pilot scheme. Hong Kong Monetary Authority, "Renminbi Trade Settlement Pilot Scheme," *Hong Kong Monetary Authority Quarterly Bulletin*, September 2009, http://www.hkma.gov.hk/media/eng/publication-and-research/quarterly -bulletin/qb200909/fa2_print.pdf.

32. "HSBC to Become Involved in Cross-Border RMB Settlement's First Foreign Trip," Xinhua News Agency, July 6, 2009, http://money.163.com/09/0706/14 /5DI0QHET0025335L.html.

33. "The Pilot RMB Trade Settlement Scheme and RMB Internationalisation," HKTDC Research, May 29, 2015, http://economists-pick-research.hktdc.com /business-news/article/Economic-Forum/The-Pilot-RMB-Trade-Settlement -Scheme-and-RMB-Internationalisation/ef/en/1/1X000000/1X05VOBP.htm.

34. Ho Wah Foon, "Betting on China," *Infinite Horizons* (HSBC Bank Malaysia Berhad) 4 (November 2009): 4, https://www.hsbc.com.my/1/PA_ES_Content _Mgmt/content/website/commercial/news_events/bizmag-infinite_horizons /magazine_pdfs/infinite_horizons_vol4_nov2009.pdf.

35. "RMB Preferred for Sino-Vietnamese Border Trade Settlement," Sohu News, September 3, 2009, http://business.sohu.com/20090903/n266423192.shtml.

36. "China-ASEAN FTA to Accelerate RMB Regionalization," Xinhua News Agency, October 23, 2009, http://news.xinhuanet.com/english/2009-10/23/content _12308041.htm.

37. Edward Russell, "HSBC Launches RMB Current Accounts in Hong Kong," *FinanceAsia*, May 30, 2010, http://www.financeasia.com/News/170641,hsbc -launches-rmb-current-accounts-in-hong-kong.aspx.

38. Private communication.
39. Beijing, Tianjin, Inner Mongolia, Liaoning, Shanghai, Jiangsu, Zhejiang, Fujian, Shandong, Hubei, Guangdong, Guangxi, Hainan, Chongqing, Xichuan, Yunnan, Jilin, Heilongjiang, Xizang (Tibet), and Xinjiang.
40. Here mainland China indicates the area under the direct jurisdiction of the People's Republic of China.
41. Trade enterprises need to be authorized by both the PBoC and the HKMA in their respective jurisdictions. Once a renminbi-based cross-border transaction has been agreed upon, commercial banks incorporated inside mainland China and abroad implement the settlement.
42. Hans Genberg, "Currency Internationalisation: Analytical and Policy Issues" (Working Paper 31, Hong Kong Institute for Monetary Research, October 31, 2009), 6, doi:10.2139/ssrn.1628004.
43. "China RMB Trade Settlement Reshape Global Forex," Success Business Fund, October 31, 2012, http://bizfundedge.com/economic/china-rmb-trade-settlement-reshape-global-forex/.
44. Dong He and Robert Neil McCauley, "Offshore Markets for the Domestic Currency: Monetary and Financial Stability Issues" (Working Paper 320, Bank for International Settlements, Basel, September 2010), http://www.bis.org/publ/work320.pdf.
45. Ibid.

7. BUILDING A MARKET FOR THE RENMINBI

1. I owe this observation to John Nugée.
2. Dong He and Robert McCauley, "Eurodollar Banking and Currency Internationalisation," *BIS Quarterly Review*, June 2012, 35–36.
3. For the definition of official liquidity and private liquidity as the two components of aggregate liquidity, see Dietrich Domanski, Ingo Fender, and Patrick McGuire, "Assessing Global Liquidity," *BIS Quarterly Review*, December 2011, 59–62. Aggregate liquidity depends on "the interaction of funding and market liquidity" and is driven by the actions of the public sector (including monetary authorities) as well as financial institutions and private investors. Ibid., 58.
4. Over the years, the eurodollar market has shifted from being a pure offshore market to intermediating funds, mainly between borrowers and lenders outside the United States. It acts to a lesser extent as a conduit between borrowers and lenders within the United States but hardly at all as a conduit between borrowers in the United States and lenders abroad. He and McCauley, "Eurodollar Banking," 42.
5. At the end of January 2015, up 35 percent from 1.63 trillion renminbi in January 2014. Deutsche Bank, *Harnessing the RMB Opportunity: A Brief*

Guide to China's Global Currency (Hong Kong: Deutsche Bank, May 2015), 6, https://www.db.com/en/media/Harnessing-the-RMB-opportunity—A-brief -guide-to-China-s-global-currency.pdf.

6. New rules promulgated in January 2011 should increase China's foreign direct investment toward Hong Kong. They allowed enterprises in mainland China to conduct and settle overseas direct investment in renminbi, and banks in Hong Kong can provide renminbi funds to facilitate such transactions. Hong Kong Monetary Authority, *Hong Kong: The Global Offshore Renminbi Business Hub* (Hong Kong: Hong Kong Monetary Authority, January 2016), http://www .hkma.gov.hk/eng/key-functions/international-financial-centre/renminbi -business-hong-kong.shtml.

7. Institute of International Finance (figures are published by the Institute of International Finance and are available only to members: https://www.iif.com /publication/capital-flows/tracking-china-s-capital-flows-iif-framework). See also Shawn Donnan, "Capital Flight from China Worse than Thought," *Financial Times,* January 20, 2016.

8. Dong He, "International Use of the Renminbi: Developments and Prospects" (speech at Columbia-Tsinghua Conference on Exchange Rates and the New International Monetary System, Beijing, June 28, 2011), 25, http://www.hkimr .org/uploads/news/54/news_0_65_dhe-presentation-28-june-2011.pdf.

9. Paola Subacchi, Helena Huang, Alberta Molajoni, and Richard Varghese, *Shifting Capital: The Rise of Financial Centres in Greater China* (London: Chatham House, May 2012); Haihong Gao and Yongding Yu, "Internationalization of the Renminbi" (paper presented at BoK-BIS Seminar, Seoul, South Korea, March 19–20, 2009).

10. On currency swaps see also Julia Leung, *Facing the Flood: How Asia Is Coping with Volatile Capital Flows* (London: Chatham House, November 2014).

11. Ma Rentao and Zhou Yongkun, "Currency Swap: Effective Method of Partici- pating in International Financial Rescue and Enforcing RMB Internationalization," *China Finance* 4, no. 658 (2009).

12. There are no official documents that explicitly refer to the importance of the swap agreements, but it is widely acknowledged that they are an essential element of China's renminbi strategy. They are signed "for the purpose of promoting bilateral financial cooperation, facilitating bilateral trade and investment, and maintaining regional financial stability." "Establishment of a Bilateral Local Currency Swap Agreement Between the People's Bank of China and the State Bank of Pakistan," People's Bank of China, December 28, 2011, http://www.pbc .gov.cn/english/130721/2856547/index.html. The State Council decides on the arrangements, selection, and volume of each bilateral agreement.

13. Figures at the end of July 2015. People's Bank of China, *RMB Internationaliza- tion Report* (Beijing: China Financial Publishing House, 2015), 32.

14. The Chiang Mai Initiative—a multilateral currency swap arrangement among the ten members of ASEAN, China, Japan, and South Korea—was launched in 2010 to provide a financial safety net to countries facing a liquidity crisis. It currently has $240 billion, up from the $120 billion originally committed in 2010.

15. Figures at the end of July 2015. People's Bank of China, *RMB Internationalization Report*, 41–42.

16. "People's Bank of China and Hong Kong Monetary Authority Renew Currency Swap Agreement," Hong Kong Monetary Authority, November 22, 2011, http://www.hkma.gov.hk/eng/key-information/press-releases/2011/20111122-3 .shtml.

17. "Renminbi Liquidity Facility to Renminbi Business Participating Authorized Institutions" (press release), Hong Kong Monetary Authority, June 14, 2014, http://www.hkma.gov.hk/eng/key-information/press-releases/2012/20120614-4 .shtml.

18. Robert Cookson, "Hong Kong to Offer Renminbi Loans to Banks," *Financial Times*, June 14, 2012, http://www.ft.com/cms/s/2/7e62666e-b601-11e1-a511-00144 feabdco.html.

19. "CDB Chairman: BRICS Will Sign Agreements to Formalize Local Currency Invoicing and Lending," CBD News, March 28, 2012, http://www.cdb.com.cn /english/NewsInfo.asp?NewsId=4046; Henny Sender and Joe Leahy, "China Offers Other Brics Renminbi Loans," *Financial Times*, March 7, 2012, http:// www.ft.com/cms/s/0/3e46ac04-67fd-11e1-978e-00144feabdco.html.

20. The HVPS is the backbone of the mainland's China National Advanced Payment System and is a real-time gross settlement system that is primarily used for high-value renminbi transfers. International Monetary Fund, *People's Republic of China: Detailed Assessment Report: CPSS Core Principles for Systemically Important Payment Systems*, IMF Country Report No.12/81 (Washington, D.C.: International Monetary Fund, April 2012): 4, 19. In January 2012, the PBoC decided to upgrade the China National Advanced Payment System to better facilitate the renminbi cross-border trade settlement scheme. Lingling Wei, "China Is Easing Yuan-Pay System," *Wall Street Journal*, January 5, 2012, http://www.wsj.com /articles/SB10001424052970203513604577139981921915046.

21. The RTGS system is a fund-transfer system in which the interbank transfer of high-value amounts of money or securities takes place in real time and on a gross basis (i.e., the settlement of funds occurs on a transaction-by-transaction basis without netting debits against credits). Bank for International Settlements, *Real-Time Gross Settlement Systems: Report Prepared by the Committee on Payment and Settlement Systems of the Central Banks of the Group of Ten Countries* (Basel: Bank for International Settlements, 1997), http://www.bis.org/cpmi/publ /d22.pdf.

22. Hong Kong Interbank Clearing Limited, Participants of Hong Kong Clearing System, April 26, 2016, http://www.hkicl.com.hk/clientbrowse.do?docID=7199 &lang=en.

23. Currently, the limits are no more than the equivalent of 6,000 renminbi per person per transaction if the exchange is made in cash and no more than the equivalent of 20,000 renminbi per person per day if the exchange is made through a deposit account—the same limits that were established in 2005; see "Hong Kong: The Global Offshore Renminbi Business Hub," Hong Kong Monetary Authority, January 2016, 22, Q4, http://www.hkma.gov.hk/media/eng/doc/key -functions/monetary-stability/rmb-business-in-hong-kong/hkma-rmb-booklet .pdf. Also see "HKMA Scraps 20,000 Yuan Daily Conversion Cap in Landmark Reform," *South China Morning Post*, November 13, 2014, http://www.scmp. com/business/economy/article/1638077/hkma-says-yuan-exchange-cap-lifted -november-17-when-stock-connect; and Norman T. L. Chan, "Removal of RMB Conversion Limit for Hong Kong Residents" (speech), Hong Kong Monetary Authority, November 12, 2014, http://www.hkma.gov.hk/eng/key-information /speech-speakers/ntlchan/20141112-1.shtml.

24. Here the daily remittance limit is 50,000 renminbi per person. The unused portion of such outward remittance can be remitted back to renminbi accounts in Hong Kong under the same name.

25. Also included are renminbi-denominated bonds, insurance policies, and other investment products on the Hong Kong market.

26. "Standard Chartered Says Has Completed Yuan Clearing for Sweden's IKEA Via CIPS," Reuters Hong Kong, October 7, 2015, http://www.reuters.com /article/2015/10/08/china-economy-cips-yuan-idUSL3N1280KK20151008.

27. "Bank of China Launches Renminbi Bonds in Hong Kong," BOC News, Bank of China, September 12, 2007, http://www.bankofchina.com/en/bocinfo /bi1/200810/t20081027_8054.html?keywords=hong+kong+3+billion+rmb+bond +offering.

28. Steve Chan, "Debt Market Industry in Hong Kong," HKTDC Research, September 15, 2014, http://hong-kong-economy-research.hktdc.com/business -news/article/Hong-Kong-Industry-Profiles/Debt-Market-Industry-in -Hong-Kong/hkip/en/1/1X000000/1X003UPT.htm.

29. Patrick McGee, "Panda bonds triumph over dim sum debt after turmoil," *Financial Times*, November 30, 2015, http://www.ft.com/cms/s/2/511cb962-7f15-11e5-98fb -5a6d4728f74e.html?siteedition=uk#slideo.

30. International Monetary Fund, *People's Republic of China—Hong Kong Special Administrative Region: 2012 Article IV Consultation Discussions*, Country Report 13/11 (Washington, D.C.: International Monetary Fund, January 2013), 15, https://www.imf.org/external/pubs/ft/scr/2013/cr1311.pdf.

31. "Properly Adjust Liquidity and Maintain the Stability of Money Market," People's Bank of China, June 26, 2013, http://www.pbc.gov.cn/english/130721/2895330

/index.html; "Communiqué of the Third Plenary Session of the 18th Central Committee of the Communist Party of China," January 15, 2014, http://www .china.org.cn/china/third_plenary_session/2014-01/15/content_31203056.htm.

32. "Administrative Rules on Settlement of RMB-Denominated Foreign Direct Investment, PBC Document No. 23 [2011]," People's Bank of China, October 13, 2011, http://www.pbc.gov.cn/english/130733/2862916/index.html.

33. "Hong Kong Says in Talks with Beijing to Raise RQFII Quota," Reuters Hong Kong, June 9, 2015, http://www.reuters.com/article/2015/06/09/china-rqfii-id USL3N0YV2QN20150609.

34. People's Bank of China, RMB Internationalization Report, 32.

35. As of May 7, 2015, 571 Chinese stocks were covered by the program. "Shanghai–Hong Kong Stock Connect," Citibank, accessed December 8, 2015, https://www .citibank.com.hk/english/investment/shanghai-hongkong-stock-connect.htm.

36. Josh Noble, "Demand for China's Stock Connect Slumps," *Financial Times*, November 19, 2014, http://www.ft.com/cms/s/0/e138d20e-6fc8-11e4-90af-00144 feabdco.html. Also see Bourse Consult, *London RMB Business Volumes 2014*, City of London Renminbi Series (London: City of London Corporation, June 2015), https://www.cityoflondon.gov.uk/business/economic-research-and -information/research-publications/Documents/Research-2015/London -RMB-business-volumes-2014.pdf.

37. Josh Noble and Gabriel Wildau, "Hong Kong–Shanghai Exchange Deal Sees Money Head North," *Financial Times*, November 17, 2015, http://webcache .googleusercontent.com/search?q=cache:JQvANkOWjkAJ:www.ft.com /cms/s/0/fd78b37a-6e07-11e4-bf80-00144feabdco.html+&cd=9&hl=en&ct =clnk&gl=uk.

38. The Chinese authorities are currently assessing the possibility of expanding the program to the Shenzhen Stock Exchange as well as to stock exchanges in other financial centers in Asia and Europe.

39. Shanghai-Hong Kong Stock Connect, Monthly Statistics, http://www.hkex .com.hk/eng/csm/chinaConnect.asp?LangCode=en. People's Bank of China, *RMB Internationalization Report*, 50.

40. Ibid.

41. Cf. Z/Yen Group, *Global Financial Centres Index 8* (London: Long Finance, October 2010), http://www.zyen.com/GFCI/GFCI%208.pdf.

42. The expression "one country, two systems" was first used by Deng Xiaoping in 1984. Deng Xiaoping, "One Country, Two Systems," in *Selected Works of Deng Xiaoping*, vol. 3, *1982–1992* (Beijing: Foreign Languages Press, 1994), 46.

43. William H. Overholt, *The Rise of China: How Economic Reform Is Creating a New Superpower* (New York: W. W. Norton, 1993), 197, 203.

44. On the risks to monetary and financial stability in the home economy posed by the development of offshore markets and the policy options to manage such risks, drawn from the euromarket experience, see Dong He and Robert

N. Mccauley, "Offshore Markets for the Domestic Currency: Monetary and Financial Stability Issues" (Working Paper 320, Bank for International Settlements, Basel, September 2010).

45. "The 2009–10 Policy Address: Breaking New Ground Together," 3, 5, Hong Kong Government, accessed December 8, 2015, http://www.policyaddress.gov .hk/09-10/eng/docs/policy.pdf.

46. "SWIFT RMB Tracker: A Stellar Performance in 2011 Positions London as Next RMB Offshore Centre," 1, SWIFT, January 2012, https://www.swift.com /assets/swift_com/documents/products_services/SWIFT_RMB_Tracker _January2012.pdf.

47. SWIFT is a network that enables financial institutions worldwide to exchange information about financial transactions in a secure environment.

48. The U.S. dollar remains in the top position, and the Hong Kong dollar follows close behind the renminbi.

49. HKMA, *Monthly Statistical Bulletin*, May 2016, No. 261, http://www.hkma .gov.hk/eng/market-data-and-statistics/monthly-statistical-bulletin/table .shtml#section3.

50. Jesús Seade, Ping Lin, Yue Ma, Xiandong Wei, and Yifan Zhang, "Hong Kong as an International Centre for China and the World" (draft, Department of Economics, Lingnan University, Hong Kong, July 7, 2010).

8. THE RENMINBI MOVES AROUND

1. Ben Yue, "Cross-Border Trade in Yunnan Shows the Road Ahead," *China Daily*, July 5, 2013, http://www.chinadailyasia.com/business/2013-07/05/content _15077137.html.

2. "IMF's Executive Board Completes Review of SDR Basket, Includes RMB Renminbi," Press Release No. 15/540, November 30, 2015, https://www.imf.org /external/np/sec/pr/2015/pr15540.htm.

3. "Yuan Rising: Singapore's RMB Usage Climbs by 4 Percent in 2014," *Singapore Business Review*, July 9, 2014, http://sbr.com.sg/financial-services /news/yuan-rising-singapore%E2%80%99s-rmb-usage-climbs-4-in -2014#sthash.GH8TlkEO.dpuf.

4. However, having mainland China as its largest trade partner—by far—is also a weakness for Taipei.

5. The memoranda were signed in November 2009. "Taipei, Beijing Sign Financial MOUs," *Taiwan Today*, November 17, 2009, http://taiwantoday.tw/ct.asp?xI tem=78329&ctNode=452&mp=9. Also see Shuching Chou, Shin-Hung Lin, Hui-Lan Yang, and Yi-Ting Shen, "The Market Reactions to the Cross -Border Banking-Evidence of Taiwan Banks in China," *International Journal of Business and Social Science* 4, no. 10 (August 2013): 217; and Wendy Zeldin,

"China; Taiwan: Financial MOUs Signed," Global Legal Monitor, Library of Congress, November 19, 2009, http://www.loc.gov/law/foreign-news/article /china-taiwan-financial-mous-signed/.

6. Paola Subacchi and Helena Huang, "Taipei in the Renminbi Offshore Market: Another Piece in the Jigsaw," Chatham House Briefing Paper, London, Chatham House, June 2013.

7. In the first six months of 2012, renminbi-settled trade accounted for less than 1 percent of the total value of bilateral trade between Japan and China. Ben McLannahan, "Sluggish Start for Yen/Renminbi Market," *Financial Times*, November 29, 2012, http://on.ft.com/TnWjyt.

8. "Guidance: Doing Business in China: China Trade and Export Guide," UK Trade and Investment, updated December 21, 2015, https://www.gov.uk /government/publications/exporting-to-china/exporting-to-china.

9. Bourse Consult, *London: A Centre for Renminbi Business*, City of London Renminbi Series (London: City of London Corporation, April 2012), https://www.cityoflondon.gov.uk/business/support-promotion-and-advice /promoting-the-city-internationally/china/Documents/London_A_Centre _for_RMB_business_2013.pdf.

10. Bourse Consult, *London RMB Business Volumes 2014*, City of London Renminbi Series (London: City of London Corporation, June 2015), http://www .cityoflondon.gov.uk/business/economic-research-and-information/research -publications/Documents/Research-2015/London-RMB-business-volumes -2014.pdf.

11. Catherine R. Schenk, "The Origins of the Eurodollar Market in London: 1955–1963," *Explorations in Economic History* 35, no. 2 (April 1998): 221–238.

12. Bourse Consult, *London RMB Business Volumes 2014*, City of London Renminbi Series (London: City of London Corporation, June 2015), 23, https:// www.cityoflondon.gov.uk/business/economic-research-and-information /research-publications/Documents/Research-2015/London-RMB-business -volumes-2014.pdf. The 2011 figure for renminbi deposits in London was misreported as 109 billion renminbi in an April 2012 report on the size of London's renminbi business. Such miscalculation was reflected in the significant apparent drop in London's renminbi deposits (to 10.2 billion at the end of June 2012) in a January 2013 report.

13. Stefan Wagstyl, "HSBC Raises $300m in Renminbi Bond Issue," *Financial Times*, April 18, 2012, http://www.ft.com/cms/s/0/067703e4-8974-11e1-85b6 -00144feab49a.html.

14. HM Treasury and The Right Honorable George Osborne MP, "Britain Issues Western World's First Sovereign RMB Bond, Largest Ever RMB Bond by Non-Chinese Issuer," October 14, 2014, https://www.gov.uk/government/news /britain-issues-western-worlds-first-sovereign-rmb-bond-largest-ever-rmb -bond-by-non-chinese-issuer.

15. London Stock Exchange, "Renminbi Bonds on London Stock Exchange," May 2016, http://www.londonstockexchange.com/specialist-issuers/debts-bonds /renminbi/rmb-presentation.pdf.

16. HM Treasury and The Right Honorable George Osborne MP, "Speech by the Chancellor of the Exchequer, Rt Hon George Osborne MP, at the City of London RMB Launch Event," April 18, 2012, https://www.gov.uk/government /speeches/speech-by-the-chancellor-of-the-exchequer-rt-hon-george-osborne -mp-at-the-city-of-london-rmb-launch-event.

17. "HSBC Launching London's First Offshore Yuan Bond" (press release), People's Bank of China, April 19, 2012, http://www.pbc.gov.cn/english/130721/2860119 /index.html.

18. Weihao Cao and Gabriel Wildau, "Daimler AG to Launch First-Ever Bond Sale in China by Foreign Non-financial Company—Sources," Reuters, January 22, 2014, http://www.reuters.com/article/china-bond-daimler-idUSL3 N0KW1NY20140122.

19. These figures refer to the third quarter of 2015.

20. Thomson Reuters Datastream (2014). However, the pace at which China's trade settled in renminbi was expanding has already slowed, having reached a record high of 662 billion renminbi in March 2014.

21. "RMB strengthens its position as the second most used currency for documentary credit transactions," SWIFT, January 26, 2015, https://www.swift.com /insights/press-releases/rmb-strengthens-its-position-as-the-second-most -used-currency-for-documentary-credit-transactions.

22. Figure for January 2015. "RMB Now 2nd Most Used Currency in Trade Finance, Overtaking the Euro," SWIFT, December 3, 2013, http://www.swift.com/about _swift/shownews?param_dcr=news.data/en/swift_com/2013/PR_RMB_nov.xml.

23. Arvind Subramanian and Martin Kessler, "The Renminbi Bloc Is Here: Asia Down, Rest of the World to Go?" (Working Paper 12–19, Peterson Institute for International Economics, Washington, D.C., August 2013), https://www.piie .com/publications/wp/wp12-19.pdf.

24. National Bureau of Statistics of China, "11-6 Value of Imports and Exports by Country (Region) of Origin/Destination," in *China Statistical Yearbook 2014* (Beijing: China Statistics Press, 2014).

25. The discrepancy in the trade balance is primarily due to the types of products that each country produces. The majority of Vietnam's exports are either raw materials or low-value-added manufactured goods, such as coal, crude oil, rubber, seafood, and footwear. In comparison, the top products China exports to Vietnam are value-added manufactured goods, such as machinery, pharmaceuticals, and petroleum.

26. China Ministry of Commerce, "Brief Statistics on China's Non-Financial Direct Investment Overseas in January-February 2016," http://english.mofcom.gov.cn /article/statistic/foreigntradecooperation/201604/20160401297794.shtml. China Ministry of Commerce, "Investment and Cooperation Statistics along 'One Belt

and One Road' Countries from Jan to Feb in 2016," http://english.mofcom.gov .cn/article/statistic/foreigntradecooperation/201604/20160401297830.shtml.

27. Jesús Seade, Ping Lin, Yue Ma, Xiandong Wei, and Yifan Zhang, "Hong Kong as an International Centre for China and the World" (draft, Department of Economics, Lingnan University, Hong Kong, July 7, 2010).

28. "RMB Internationalisation: Perspectives on the Future of RMB Clearing" (white paper), 6, SWIFT, accessed December 9, 2015, http://www.swift.com/resources /documents/SWIFT_White_paper_RMB_internationalisation_EN.pdf.

29. Yongding Yu, "How Far Can Renminbi Internationalization Go?" (Working Paper 461, Asian Development Bank Institute, Tokyo, February 2014).

30. Gabriel Wildau, "Renminbi Fights Back as PBoC Intervention Subsides," *Financial Times*, August 19, 2014, http://www.ft.com/cms/s/0/e27b87c4-2775 -11e4-be5a-00144feabdc0.html.

31. On this topic, see Yongding Yu, "Revisiting the Internationalization of the Yuan" (Working Paper 366, Asian Development Bank Institute, Tokyo, July 2012).

32. Chris Salmon, "Three Principles for Successful Financial Sector Reform" (speech, City Week 2012: The International Financial Services Forum, London, February 7, 2012), 7, http://www.bankofengland.co.uk/publications/Documents /speeches/2012/speech545.pdf.

33. Sebastian Heilmann, "Policy Experimentation in China's Economic Rise," *Studies in Comparative International Development* 43, no. 1 (March 2008): 23, quoted in Daniel A. Bell, *The China Model: Political Meritocracy and the Limits of Democracy* (Princeton, N.J.: Princeton University Press, 2015), 183. Bell stresses how a repertoire of policy experiments helped Deng Xiaoping reframe the main mission of the Chinese Communist Party from achieving communism to achieving rapid economic growth.

34. Bell, *The China Model*, 183–184.

35. Heilmann, "Policy Experimentation," 8–9, quoted in Bell, *The China Model*, 184.

9. MANAGING IS THE WORD

1. Sheng Songcheng, "来源： 中国证券报·中证网 " [China is now at the stage to further open up capital account] (staff paper, People's Bank of China, Beijing, February 2012), http://news.gxtv.cn/201202/news_7343571.html.

2. Arthur Kroeber, "The Chinese Yuan Grows Up—Slowly" (policy paper, New America Foundation, Washington, D.C., March 18, 2011), 2.

3. Takatoshi Ito, *The Internationalization of the Renminbi* (New York: Council on Foreign Relations, 2011), 11.

4. See for example, Yongding Yu, "Revisiting the Internationalization of the Yuan," ADBI Working Paper Series, No. 366, July 2012.

5. This is a point that Chinese policy makers—for example, Hu Xiaolian, deputy governor of the PBoC—repeatedly stress. Hu Xiaolian, "Hu Xiaolian: Successful Experiences of Further Reforming the RMB Exchange Rate Regime," BIS Review 105/2010, Bank for International Settlements, July 30, 2010, www.bis .org/review/r100812d.pdf; Hu Xiaolian, "RMB Internationalization and the Globalization of China's Financial Sector" (speech, Lujazhui Forum 2012: Reforming Global Financial Governance for Real Economic Growth, Shanghai, June 28–30, 2012), 127, http://en.sjr.sh.gov.cn/coverage/lujiazui/pdf/2012-forum .pdf.

6. Gabriel Wildau, "Authorities Are Taking a Cautious Approach to Shanghai Test Ground," *Financial Times*, November 4, 2014.

7. "IMFC Statement by ZHOU Xiaochuan, Governor, People's Bank of China" (Thirty-First Meeting of the International Monetary and Financial Committee, International Monetary Fund, Washington, D.C., April 18, 2015), https://www .imf.org/External/spring/2015/imfc/statement/eng/chn.pdf.

8. World Bank and Development Research Center of the State Council, People's Republic of China, "China: Structural Reforms for a Modern, Harmonious, Creative Society," in *China 2030: Building a Modern, Harmonious, and Creative Society* (Washington, D.C.: World Bank, 2013), 115–117.

9. For example, price controls distort the allocation of resources, whereas regulatory barriers impede the entry of private firms in a number of domains—notably, the services sector, where state firms retain near complete control.

10. Xi Jinping, "Explanatory Notes to the 'Decision of the Central Committee of the Communist Party of China on Some Major Issues Concerning Comprehensively Continuing the Reform,'" in *The Governance of China* (Beijing: Foreign Languages Press, 2014), 84. In November 2014, Keqiang Li, China's premier, announced a ten-point plan for financial reform.

11. Quoted in Chen Yulu, *Chinese Currency and the Global Economy* (Chicago: McGraw-Hill, 2014), 124.

12. More precisely, it suggested (1) fully commercializing and rationalizing the financial system; (2) further liberalizing interest rates; (3) deepening the capital market; (4) upgrading financial infrastructure and the legal framework; (5) strengthening the regulation and supervision framework; (6) building a financial safety net and developing crisis management; and (7) recasting the rights and responsibilities of government. World Bank and Development Research Center of the State Council, "China: Structural Reforms," 118–125.

13. Zhou Xiaochuan, "Speech at the Annual Forum of Chinese Economists," December 1, 2010, cited in Yang Jiang, "The Limits of China's Monetary Diplomacy," in *The Great Wall of Money*, ed. Eric Helleiner and Jonathan Kirshner (Ithaca, N.Y.: Cornell University Press, 2014), 160.

14. William H. Overholt, *The Rise of China: How Economic Reform Is Creating a New Superpower* (New York: W. W. Norton, 1993), 149.

15. Henry Kissinger, *On China* (London: Allen Lane, 2011), 485.

16. Overholt, *The Rise of China*, 150. "For example, they let institutions like the bond market develop organically—and somewhat chaotically—then stepped in to regulate them when they felt they understood the needs of the economy and the options for regulation."

17. Yasheng Huang, *Capitalism with Chinese Characteristics. Entrepreneurship and the State*, Cambridge: Cambridge University Press, 2008:145.

18. The shift in terminology from *market socialism* to *socialist market economy* happened in late 1992 at the Fourteenth Congress of the Chinese Communist Party. Edward S. Steinfeld, *Playing Our Game* (Oxford, England: Oxford University Press, 2010), 57.

19. Small and medium-sized enterprises are evidence of "the government's compromise between ideological correctness and economic pragmatism." Michael Firth, Chen Lin, Ping Liu, and Sonia M. L. Wong, "Inside the Black Box: Bank Credit Allocation in China's Private Sector," *Journal of Banking and Finance* 33 (2009): 1145.

20. Paola Subacchi, Helena Huang, Alberta Molajoni, and Richard Varghese, Shifting Capital: The Rise of Financial Centres in Greater China (London: Chatham House, May 2012).

21. In China, banks actively borrow and lend among themselves through collateralized repo transactions. The seven-day repo and three-month SHIBOR rates, which are responsive to changes in liquidity and credit conditions in the money market, have become more widely used benchmarks to gauge interbank liquidity.

22. Wensheng Peng, Hongyi Chen, and Weiwei Fan, "Interest Rate Structure and Monetary Policy Implementation in China," *China Economic Issues* (Hong Kong Monetary Authority), no. 1/06 (June 2006): 1–13; Li-gang Liu and Wenlang Zhang, "A New Keynesian Model for Analyzing Monetary Policy in Mainland China" (Working Paper 18, Hong Kong Monetary Authority, 2007).

23. David Hale, *China's New Dream: How Will Australia and the World Cope with the Re-emergence of China as a Great Power?* (Barton: Australian Strategic Policy Institute, February 2014), 24, www.aspi.org.au/publications/chinas-new-dream-how-will-australia-and-the-world-cope-with-the-re-emergence-of-china-as-a-great-power/SR64_China-_Hale.pdf.

24. Jonathan Anderson, "The Sword Hanging Over China's Banks," UBS Investment Research, Asian Focus, December 15, 2006, quoted in Morris Goldstein and Nicholas R. Lardy, *The Future of China's Exchange Rate Policy* (Washington, D.C.: Peterson Institute for International Economics, 2009), 49.

25. Lingling Wei, "China to Begin Deposit Insurance in May," *Wall Street Journal*, May 31, 2015, http://www.wsj.com/articles/china-to-begin-deposit-insurance-from-may-1427794649.

26. Hu, "Hu Xiaolian: Successful Experiences," 5–6.

27. Between 1980 and 1995, the renminbi was devalued by about 70 percent in real effective terms. Goldstein and Lardy, *The Future*, 24.

28. In the weeks following the authorities' intervention, the renminbi weakened by almost 1.5 percent against the dollar—and took a couple of deep dives in July 2014.

29. "Spread Between Onshore, Offshore Yuan Widest Since September 2011," Reuters, January 5, 2016, http://www.reuters.com/article/us-china-yuan -idUSKBN0UJ0PG20160105.

30. IMF, "People's Republic of China 2015 Article IV Consultation," IMF Country Report No 15/234, August 2015, https://www.imf.org/external/pubs/ft/scr/2015 /cr15234.pdf.

31. Report published by the Institute of International Finance but not publicly available. See Shawn Donnan, "Capital Flight from China Worse Than Thought," *Financial Times*, January 20, 2016

32. "IMFC Statement by Zhou Xiaochuan, Governor, People's Bank of China" (Thirty-First Meeting of the International Monetary and Financial Committee, International Monetary Fund, Washington, D.C., April 18, 2015), 5, https://www .imf.org/External/spring/2015/imfc/statement/eng/chn.pdf.

33. "The Liberalization and Management of Capital Flows: An Institutional View," International Monetary Fund, November, 14, 2012, http://www.imf.org/external /np/pp/eng/2012/111412.pdf.

34. Ibid.

35. Eswar Prasad, Thomas Rumbaugh, and Qing Wang, "Putting the Cart Before the Horse?: Capital Account Liberalization and Exchange Rate Flexibility in China" (Policy Discussion Paper 05/1, International Monetary Fund, Washington, D.C., January 2005), https://www.imf.org/external/pubs/ft/pdp/2005 /pdp01.pdf; Hongyi Chen, Lars Jonung, and Olaf Unteroberdoerster, "Lessons for China from Financial Liberalization in Scandinavia" (Economic Paper 383, European Commission, Brussels, August 2009), http://ec.europa.eu /economy_finance/publications/publication15805_en.pdf.

36. Lifen Zhang, "China to Ease Cross-Border Capital Path," *Financial Times*, November 16, 2014, www.ft.com/cms/s/0/d66a9ce2-6d78-11e4-bf80-00144feabdco .html#axzz3y2rxKotg.

10. THE AGE OF CHINESE MONEY

1. *China: A Reassessment of the Economy: A Compendium of Papers Submitted to the Joint Economic Committee, Congress of the United States* (Washington, D.C.: U.S. Government Printing Office, July 10, 1975), iii.

2. Ibid., 659. The report indicated that, "while the RMB can be held by Westerners and can be converted (under certain conditions) into foreign currency, the RMB account is held within China and cannot be traded except between the foreign entity and the Bank of China."

3. Ibid. The report also noted that China was unique among other countries with a centralized, planned economy because it used the renminbi in international trade and allowed "Western entities" to hold renminbi accounts in correspondent banks.

4. Jack Lew, "Remarks on the International Economic Architecture and the Importance of Aiming High" (speech, Asia Society Northern California, San Francisco, March 31, 2015).

5. On this point, see also Eric Helleiner and Anton Malking, "Sectoral Interests and Global Money: Renminbi, Dollars, and the Domestic Foundations of International Currency Policy" *Open Economies Review* 21:1 February, 2012, p. 41.

6. Speech at Fudan University in March 2015. "IMF's Lagarde says inclusion of China's yuan in SDR basket question of when," Reuters, March 20, 2015, http://uk.reuters.com/article/uk-china-imf-idUKKBN0MG0YJ20150320.

7. Benjamin J. Cohen, *The Geography of Money*, Ithaca: NY, Cornell University Press, 1998.

8. By contrast about 95 percent of U.S. exports and 85 percent of U.S. imports are invoiced in dollars. Linda S. Goldberg and Cédric Tille, "Vehicle Currency Use in International Trade," Federal Reserve Bank of New York Staff Reports, Staff Report no. 200 January 2005, p. 19. However, the majority of products using the dollar for reference pricing are traded via organized exchanges outside the U.S. market.

9. SWIFT RMB Tracker, April 2016, https://www.swift.com/our-solutions /compliance-and-shared-services/business-intelligence/renminbi/rmb-tracker /document-centre#topic-tabs-menu.

10. James Kynge, "Renminbi Tops Currency Usage Table for China's Trade with Asia," *Financial Times*, May 27, 2015.

11. According to Standard Chartered, at the end of September 2014, international banking liabilities in dollars were $12 trillion, those in euros were the equivalent of $7.6 trillion, those in pounds were the equivalent of $1.4 trillion, those in yen were the equivalent of $703 billion, and those in renminbi were the equivalent of $30 billion. Standard Chartered research, Special Report, "Renminbi Internationalisation—The Pace Quickens," June 10, 2015.

12. Ibid.

13. Figures as per April 2016. SWIFT Insight, "UK Jumps Ahead of Singapore as the Second Largest Offshore RMB Clearing Centre," 28 April 2016, https://www .swift.com/insights/press-releases/uk-jumps-ahead-of-singapore-as-the-second -largest-offshore-rmb-clearing-centre.

14. SWIFT Insight, "South Korea and Taiwan use the RMB for the majority of payments with China and Hong Kong," September 1, 2015, https://www.swift .com/insights/press-releases/south-korea-and-taiwan-use-the-rmb-for-the -majority-of-payments-with-china-and-hong-kong.

15. Syetarn Hansakul and Hannah Levinger, "China-EU relations: Gearing up for growth," Deutsche Bank Research, July 1, 2014, p. 1, p. 10, https://www.db.com /specials/en/docs/China-EU-relations.pdf.

16. Free usability is the criterion that the IMF set in 2010 for the review of the SDR basket. IMF, "Review of the Special Drawing Right (SDR) Currency Basket," April 6, 2016, https://www.imf.org/external/np/exr/facts/sdrcb.htm.

17. Qu Hongbin, "Renminbi Will Be World's Reserve Currency," *Financial Times*, November 10, 2010.

18. Editorial: "Timely Move," *China Daily*, June 24, 2010, http://www.chinadaily.com.cn/opinion/2010-06/24/content_10011970.htm.

19. "Internationalization of RMB Foreseeable: Expert," *China Daily*, December 8, 2010, http://www.chinadaily.com.cn/bizchina/2010-12/08/content_11669825.htm.

20. "Yuan and SDR: A Welcome Change for China and World," *China Daily*, December 1, 2015, http://europe.chinadaily.com.cn/business/2015-12/01/content_22596512.htm.

21. Ibid.

22. "PBC Welcomes IMF Executive Board's Decision to Include the RMB Into the SDR Currency Basket" (communiqué), People's Bank of China, December 1, 2015, http://www.pbc.gov.cn/english/130721/2983967/index.html.

23. Quoted in Lucy Hornby, Tom Mitchell, and Jennifer Hughes, "China Pledges No More Renminbi 'Sudden Changes' After IMF Decision on Currency," *Financial Times*, December 2, 2015. New Silk Road countries are those on the new Silk Road across Eurasia.

24. Many officials have expressed this view to me. However, there is no official document that spells out this strategy.

25. Benjamin J. Cohen, *The Geography of Money* (Ithaca, N.Y.: Cornell University Press, 1998); Benjamin J. Cohen, *The Future of Money* (Princeton, N.J.: Princeton University Press, 2004).

26. Arvind Subramanian, "Renminbi Reign: The Countdown Begins," Business Standard, September 16, 2011, http://www.business-standard.com/article/opinion/arvind-subramanian-renminbi-reign-the-countdown-begins-111091600084_1.html; Arvind Subramanian, *Eclipse: Living in the Shadow of China's Economic Dominance* (Washington, D.C.: Peterson Institute for International Economics, 2011).

27. Zhou Xiaochuan, "Reform [sic] the International Monetary System" essay posted on the PBoC website on March 23, 2009, http://www.pbc.gov.cn/english/130724/2842945/index.html.

28. Ibid.

29. Ibid.

30. Ibid.; "Report of the Commission of Experts of the President of the United Nations General Assembly on Reforms of the International Monetary and Financial System," United Nations, September 21, 2009, http://www.un.org/ga/econcrisissummit/docs/FinalReport_CoE.pdf. For a discussion on using SDRs as supranational currency, see Paola Subacchi and John Driffill, eds., *Beyond the Dollar* (London: Chatham House, March 2010).

31. See, for example, Chen Yulu, *Chinese Currency and Global Economy* (Chicago: McGraw-Hill, 2014), 125–149.

32. All these commodities are priced in dollars. Only the prices for cocoa, rubber, copper, lead, and tin are denominated in other currencies. According to the list of commodities price series published by the UNCTAD, http://unctadstat .unctad.org/wds/ReportFolders/reportFolders.aspx, three-month cocoa futures are priced in SDRs; rubber is priced FOB Singapore in Singapore dollars; the London Metal Exchange official cash settlement prices for copper and lead are expressed in pounds, and the ex-smelter price for tin in the Kuala Lumpur market is expressed in Malaysian dollars.

33. In a few countries, such as India, Japan, and China, domestic contracts, both spot and futures, are settled in the domestic currency. See Elitza Mileva and Nikolaus Siegfried, *Oil Market Structure, Network Effects and the Choice of Currency for Oil Invoicing*, Occasional Paper 77 (Frankfurt: European Central Bank, December 2007).

34. "U.N. to Let Iraq Sell Oil for Euros, Not Dollars," CNN, October 30, 2000. Archived article available at http://pegab.weebly.com/blog/un-to-let-iraq-sell -oil-for-euros-not-dollars.

35. Agnes Lovasz and Daniel Kruger, "Venezuela, Oil Producers Buy Euro as Dollar, Oil Fall," Bloomberg, December 18, 2006.

36. "U.S. Imposes Record Fine on BNP in Sanctions Warning to Banks," Reuters, July 1, 2014, http://www.reuters.com/article/us-bnp-paribas-settlement -idUSKBN0F52HA20140701.

37. Jack Farchy and Kathrin Hille, "Russian Companies Prepare to Pay for Trade in Renminbi," *Financial Times*, June 8, 2014.

38. Evgenia Pismennaya, "Moscow's 'Mr Yuan' Builds China Link as Putin Tilts East," Bloomberg, September 24, 2014, http://www.bloomberg.com/news /articles/2014-09-23/moscow-s-mr-yuan-builds-china-link-as-putin-tilts-east.

39. Farchy and Hille, "Russian Companies Prepare to Pay for Trade in Renminbi."

40. Jack Farchy, "Gazprom Neft Sells Oil to China in Renminbi Rather Than Dollars", *Financial Times*, June 1, 2015.

41. Chiara Albanese, "Russia Shuns Dollar as Putin Strengthens Ties with China," *Wall Street Journal*, November 14, 2014, http://www.wsj.com/articles /russia-shuns-dollar-as-putin-strengthens-ties-with-china-1415972720.

42. As quoted in Benjamin J. Cohen, "The Yuan Tomorrow? Evaluating China's Currency Internationalization Strategy," *New Political Economy* 17, no. 3 (2011): 361–371.

43. "IMFC Statement by Zhou Xiaochuan, Governor, People's Bank of China" (Thirty-First Meeting of the International Monetary and Financial Committee, International Monetary Fund, Washington, D.C., April 18, 2015), 5, https://www .imf.org/External/spring/2015/imfc/statement/eng/chn.pdf.

44. Strategy, Policy and Review Department, IMF, 2011.

45. Cohen, "The Yuan Tomorrow?"

46. On this point, see also Kirshner, "Regional Hegemony," 236–237.

INDEX

DATE DUE

02/5/2019			
3/5/2019			
			PRINTED IN U.S.A.